POLITICS AND LITERATURE

POLITICS AND LITERATURE
AT THE TURN OF THE MILLENNIUM

MICHAEL KEREN

© 2015 Michael Keren

University of Calgary Press
2500 University Drive NW
Calgary, Alberta
Canada T2N 1N4
www.uofcpress.com

This book is available as an ebook. The publisher should be contacted for any use which falls outside the terms of that licence.

LIBRARY AND ARCHIVES CANADA CATALOGUING IN PUBLICATION

Keren, Michael, author
          Politics and literature at the turn of the millennium
/ Michael Keren.

Includes bibliographical references and index.
Issued in print and electronic formats.
ISBN 978-1-55238-799-3 (paperback).–ISBN 978-1-55238-801-3 (pdf).
–ISBN 978-1-55238-802-0 (epub).–ISBN 978-1-55238-803-7 (mobi)

          1. Fiction–21st century–History and criticism. 2. Politics in literature. 3. Politics and literature. 4. Authors–Political and social views. I. Title.

PN51.K47 2015   809'.93358   C2015-903014-5
                                            C2015-903015-3

The University of Calgary Press acknowledges the support of the Government of Alberta through the Alberta Media Fund for our publications. We acknowledge the financial support of the Government of Canada through the Canada Book Fund for our publishing activities. We acknowledge the financial support of the Canada Council for the Arts for our publishing program.

      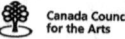

Cover images: # 2505055 (colourbox.com)
Cover design, page design, and typesetting by Melina Cusano

TABLE OF CONTENTS

Acknowledgments	vii
1. Politics and Literature	1
2. The "Original Position" in José Saramago's *Blindness*	25
3. Absurdity and Revolt in Cormac McCarthy's *The Road*	47
4. The Bystander's Tale: Gil Courtemanche's *A Sunday at the Pool in Kigali*	69
5. Fiction and the Study of Slums: Anosh Irani's *The Cripple and His Talismans*	89
6. Narrative and Memory in Haruki Murakami's *Kafka on the Shore*, Günter Grass's *Crabwalk* and André Brink's *The Rights of Desire*	101
7. The Politics of Victimhood in John Le Carré's *Absolute Friends*	125
8. The Quest for Identity in Sayed Kashua's *Let It Be Morning*	141
9. Political Escapism in Contemporary Israel: David Grossman's *To the End of the Land*	163
10. Body and Mind in Margaret Atwood's *Oryx and Crake*	185
11. A Canadian Alternative to the Clash of Civilizations: Yann Martel's *Life of Pi*	207
Notes	227
Bibliography	243
Index	249

ACKNOWLEDGMENTS

This study was conducted at the University of Calgary, where I was granted a Canada Research Chair in the departments of Political Science and Communication, Media and Film. I am grateful to the CRC Program and to my colleagues at the university for their support and inspiration over the years, especially Maria Bakardjieva, David Bercuson, Barry Cooper, Roger Gibbins, Richard Hawkins, Rob Huebert, Karim-Aly Kassam, Rainer Knopff, David Mitchell, Ted Morton, Pablo Policzer, Stephen Randall, Kathleen Scherf, and David Taras. I greatly benefited from my conversations on various aspects of this study with Cassandra Atherton of Deakin University, Glenda Abramson of the University of Oxford, Yvon Grenier of St. Francis Xavier University, Michael Kochin of Tel-Aviv University, Neil Mclaughlin of McMaster University, and all participants in the annual Harvard conferences on public intellectuals. I received much inspiration from my graduate students, especially Julia Brotea, Naor Cohen, Janis Goldie, and Gillian Steward. I am indebted to my research assistants Andrea Matishak, Cassandra Dam, and Nycole Wetmore for their effective and conscientious help on this book.

Politics and Literature at the Turn of the Millennium is a sequel to my 2003 book *The Citizen's Voice: Politics and Literature in the 20th Century*, also published by the University of Calgary Press. I would like to thank the wonderful staff at the U of C Press, including director Brian Scrivener, former interim director John Wright, designer Melina Cusano, operations manager Michelle Lipp, editorial secretary Karen Buttner, and editors John King and Peter Enman.

Finally, I acknowledge the publishers who gave me permission to include in this book the following material:

Michael Keren, "The Original Position in José Saramago's Blindness," *Review of Politics* 69, no. 3 (Summer 2007): 447–63. Copyright 2007 University of Notre Dame. Reprinted with the permission of Cambridge University Press.

Michael Keren, "Absurdity and Revolt in Cormac McCarthy's 'The Road'," *Phaenex: Journal of Existential and Phenomenological Theory and Culture* 7 (Spring/Summer 2012): 221–43. ISSN: 1911-1576.

Michael Keren, "The Bystander's Tale: Gil Courtemanche's *A Sunday at the Pool in Kigali* and the Rwandan Genocide," *Studies in Canadian Literature* 34, no. 2 (2010): 22–39.

Michael Keren, "Fiction and the Study of Slums: Anosh Irani's *The Cripple and His Talismans*," *Journal of Poverty* 12, no. 2 (2008): 251–61, reprinted by permission of Taylor & Francis (http://www.tandfonline.com).

Michael Keren, "Shared Narratives and the Politics of Memory: Toward Reconciliation," in *Life and Narrative: The Risks and Responsibilities of Storying Experience*, ed. Brian Schiff, Sylvie Patron, and Elizabeth McKim (Oxford University Press, 2015 [in press]).

Michael Keren, "The Quest for Identity in Sayed Kashua's Let It Be Morning," *Israel Studies* 19, no. 1 (Spring 2014): 126–44. Indiana University Press.

Michael Keren, "Political Escapism in Contemporary Israel: Lessons from David Grossman's *To the End of the Land*." *Journal of Modern Jewish Studies* 14 no. 2 (2015): 246–60, reprinted by permission of Taylor & Francis (http://www.tandfonline.com).

Michael Keren, "A Canadian Alternative to the 'Clash of Civilizations." *International Journal of Canadian Studies* 37 (2008): 41–55. Copyright 2008 International Council for Canadian Studies, DOI: 10.7202/040794ar, reprinted with permission from University of Toronto Press (www.utpjournals.com).

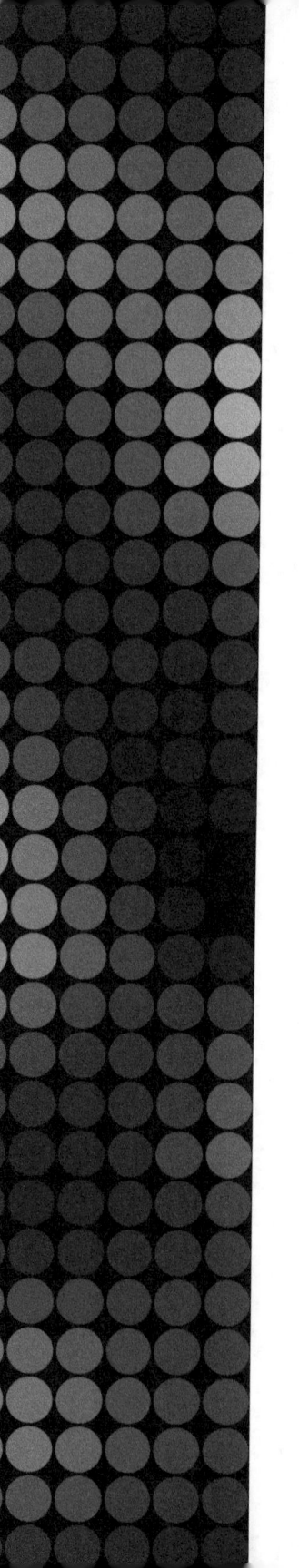

POLITICS AND LITERATURE

As a graduate student in the United States in the 1970s, I was exposed to the power of the social sciences. The search for solid social theories, the emphasis on rigorous methodology for empirical research, and political activism on campus and beyond, combined to create a fascinating learning environment. Systems theory, structural functionalism, modernization theory, computer simulations, social indicators, cost-benefit analysis, quantitative content analysis, simulations, stochastic models, and other conceptual and methodological devices were part of a new intellectual endeavour conducted for a good cause: to help the campaign against hunger, poverty, disease, crime, discrimination, and other social ills. Following the Great Society initiative, social programs were designed, replacing the grand ideologies of the inter-war era with piecemeal social engineering. Social scientists devoted to progress based on empirical research rather than on mobilization of the masses were seen as an asset for government. And although the alignment of "politics and the professors"[1] was not expected to be easy, the massive recruitment of university graduates by the Kennedy and Johnson administrations, and the introduction of academic methods such as operations research, game theory, and PPBS (Planning, Programming, and Budgeting System) into major government departments, signalled the victory of sociology over ideology.

In 1960 Daniel Bell declared that among Western intellectuals the old passions were spent. The title of his volume of essays *The End of Ideology* became a landmark for a generation of baby boomers arriving on Western campuses in the mid-1960s who could easily identify with the claim that "the new generation, with no meaningful memory of... old debates, and no secure tradition to build upon, finds itself seeking new purposes within a framework of political society that has rejected, intellectually speaking, the old apocalyptic and chiliastic visions."[2] As Bell observed, the devastation brought about by Communism and Fascism led to a refusal by that new generation to formulate social issues in simplified ideological terms, but this had not diminished its incumbents' emotional energies and quest for utopia, their need for "some vision of their potential, some manner of fusing passion with intelligence."[3] Much of that passion was devoted in those years to political protest against the Vietnam War, but – fused with the new theories and methods of the social sciences – it also inspired social research and action on the limits to growth, environmental protection, the population explosion, urban decay, the welfare state, women rights, global inequality, and other issues.

Among the seminal works read by social science students in those years by David Riesman, Talcott Parsons, Edward Shils, Gabriel Almond, Robert Dahl, David Easton, Herbert Simon, Harold Lasswell, Anatol Rapoport, Kenneth Bolding, Herman Kahn, B.F. Skinner, Paul Lazarsfeld, Anthony Downs, and others, three books stood out for me: John Kenneth Galbraith's *The New Industrial State*, Amitai Etzioni's *The Active Society* and Karl Deutsch's *The Nerves of Government*. These books, written in the 1960s, came very close to fulfilling the need identified by Bell for a passionate intelligence. Dismissing former ideological notions, including both uncontrolled socialism and wild capitalism, the three scholars – an economist, a sociologist, and a political scientist – pointed the way and set the conditions for social progress based on human knowledge and creativity.

Galbraith introduced the concept of the "technostructure," the stratum of middle range managers in organizations who are increasingly taking charge of corporate and government decision making in the technological society due to the growing demand for their professionalism. This concept provided a fresh alternative to economic, social, and political theories which, since the Enlightenment, had placed the individual at centre stage. Galbraith claimed that power in the business enterprise and in society had passed to organizations rather than to individual entrepreneurs. Modern economic theory, he wrote, "can only be understood as an effort, wholly successful, to synthesize by organization a group personality far superior for its purposes to a natural person and with the added advantage of immortality."[4] Galbraith highlighted the role of professional knowledge in the workings of organizations and showed the need to move from the traditional reliance on the market to planning and coordination between the business corporation and its ally – the state. He emphasized the growing importance of the educational–scientific estate in the modern industrial state in which the modern scholar of science, mathematics, information systems, and communications theory is ever more in demand. Galbraith expected the social sciences to lower, as a result of that demand, their "overtones of revolution."[5]

Etzioni also reserved an important role for social scientists in his model of the "active society" – a self-directing society that is not subdued to technological and political determinants and is not led by power elites manipulating faceless masses but rather transforms itself toward a new phase by a conscious and active approach to its environment. The conscious and active orientation requires knowledge of society in general and verified knowledge in particular. "As an intellectual process overlaying normative commitments," he wrote in 1968, "as a critical evaluator of existing social combinations, as an explorer of alternative combinations and their transformations, the social sciences are able to clarify basic commitments and to make them more realistic and, thus, more sustained."[6] Etzioni claimed that one need not believe in the omnipotence of science or advocate social engineering to see that the social sciences have a growing part to play in societal activation and transformation. To him, the integration of the social sciences in the political process was "predetermined."[7] As critics have noted, Etzioni remained ambivalent about the role of young radicals he met on American campuses in the 1960s were to play in the active society,[8] but it should be noted that his model included not only experts, of the kind composing Galbraith's technostructure, but also "unattached intellectuals"[9] who resided in bohemian quarters, autonomous policy-research centres, and universities and were more concerned with evaluative interpretations than with reality testing.

Influenced by Norbert Wiener's science of cybernetics, the science of communication and control in organizations, Karl Deutsch proposed a theory of politics, the study of power relations in human systems, which emphasized these systems' "learning capacity."[10] He operationalized that capacity by the range of internally available re-combinations of knowledge, manpower, and facilities that may allow political organizations such as political parties and states to steer their way in a changing environment by cumulating and acting upon feedback, including goal-changing feedback. By stressing the learning capabilities of political organizations, Deutsch put less emphasis on power, which, in his theory, no longer stood at the centre of politics. The essence of politics had now become "the dependable coordination of human effort and expectations for the attainment of the goals of society."[11] Deutsch did not ignore Machiavelli's view of politics as the use of power, force, and deception. He realized that to behave in politics in a way that is morally good, and yet pragmatically successful, is considered impossible in an atomic age in which the Augustinian perception of politics as evil is taking hold again. He was also aware of the potential of power to disrupt the learning capacity of political organizations by dissipating the material and human resources required for their continuation. But he expected the powerful to be increasingly concerned with the mobilization of the resources needed to steer political systems. As he wrote in the concluding words of his 1963 book, "government and politics will long remain indispensable instruments for accelerated social learning, by which mankind in its various subdivisions, still organized in states, can adapt more quickly to the dangerous but hopeful tasks of growing up."[12]

The three books were exciting because they diverged from traditional views of social relations in terms of market competition, group conflict, and power manipulation, emphasizing instead the learning function of society. The corporation, the social unit, and the polity were modelled as open systems whose chance to flourish depends less on the wheeling and dealing by entrepreneurs, competing social groups, and politicians than on the knowledge units informing the system about its environment. The cybernetic model of society, concerned with the social system's open exchange with its environment, was appealing because it promised solutions to social problems on the basis of fresh knowledge rather than old politics and corresponded to the preference of many for apolitical redesigns of society. It also became a useful teaching device, as students were easily attracted to prescriptions for knowledge-based decision making in which they were to have a significant role after graduation. The cybernetic model allowed researchers to explain variance among systems; the success of the West in the Cold War was seen as the outgrowth of the West's open, active, self-steering economies, societies, and polities as against the closed system of the Soviet Union. Studies focused on the conditions allowing systems to adapt to the contingencies of the outer world and to the role of information processing units in the adaptation. Organizational experts worked on the goal-seeking behaviour of organizations, political development scholars studied the symbolization of environmental factors in developing societies, and researchers in international relations studied the mutual modification of images through processes of international communications.[13]

But the cybernetic model worked only as long as the observed economic, social, and political phenomena could be conceptualized as elements of more or less working systems. It failed to cope with severe breakdowns of systems and with historical events, like the Rwandan genocide of 1994, whose primordial nature defied understanding in terms of the international system, the national system, and even the tribal system in Central Africa. The optimism of the 1960s about the ability of humans to overcome the destruction caused by two world wars and reconstruct social systems with a tendency to survive and a capacity to flourish in a changing environment began to wind down as the twentieth century came to an end. Human behaviour all over the globe did not always correspond to theoretical templates in which outputs were related to inputs, action was seen as goal-oriented, and systems were believed to seek goal-changing feedback. No theory could account for self-destructive acts in which the system's survival was the last thing on anybody's mind. The more urbanization took place, the less megacities like Lagos, Dhaka, Cairo, Mumbai, Mexico City, and Los Angeles seemed bound to urban planning, and the more foreign aid projects were designed, the less capable these projects seemed of combatting poverty and misery. Modernization did not prevent sickness, violence, and corruption, and technological development was often associated with human misery, cultural decay, and economic inequality. The truism that humans have reached the moon but are unable to clean the slums on earth became a commonplace.

At the turn of the century, the social sciences still flourished, but many began to seek alternative sources of knowledge to explain social reality. The problems facing the world at the turn of the millennium seemed too complex, contingent, and unpredictable to be comprehended and solved by the theories, typologies, and data-gathering devices available to researchers. Predictions based on quantitative and qualitative analyses of economic, social, and political trends turned out too frequently to be wrong. Political observers failed to predict the revolutions in Europe in 1989–90 in which the Communist regimes in Eastern Europe collapsed and the Cold War ended. Theories on the new world order proposed in the aftermath of these revolutions, such as Francis Fukuyama's *The End of History*, took hold for a while but were soon shown to be the product of wishful thinking, which diminished the confidence that reliable intellectual tools were at hand to comprehend world trends. Systems theory, which provided satisfactory explanations of national policies in functioning states and of international relations during the Cold War, had little to say about the increasing number of failed states in the early twenty-first century, or about the international order after the Cold War. The mysticism surrounding the Y2K discourse over the use of two digits rather than four to represent the year in computers, which, it was feared, would disrupt, at midnight (!) between December 31, 1999 and January 1, 2000 the world's power stations, financial institutions and other systems, and make planes fall off the sky, was only a symptom of a growing distrust of the advanced technological society and the theories guiding it. The attacks on the World Trade Center and the Pentagon the following year challenged the solidness and sturdiness of some of the world's mightiest systems, which aggravated that distrust.

Scholars seeking understanding of society without turning to rigid positivism on one hand and mysticism on the other searched for new forms of inquiry, which resulted in greater attention given in the social sciences to literature, the visual arts, film, and other aesthetic representations. As a political scientist, I turned more and more to novels. In lectures on public administration I found Franz Kafka's depiction of the contingencies of bureaucracy to be of no less explanatory power than Max Weber's legal-rational ideal-type of the bureaucratic structure; in learning about totalitarianism, I became more convinced by George Orwell's portrayal of the party elite in totalitarian states as composed of common thugs than by Karl Friedrich's description of that elite as a unique phenomenon related to the modern state's control of the means of communication; and in discussions on the 1989–90 revolutions, I found no better explanation for the collapse of the Communist regimes in Eastern Europe than Milan Kundera's insights in *The Joke*, in which he exposed the absurdity of these regimes.

Such novels were useful in updating notions conveyed year after year in introductory political science courses. Social contract theory, for example, the product of European thinkers of the seventeenth and eighteenth centuries who based the political obligation of citizens to the state on popular consent, could not be easily taught in the early twenty-first century without some attention to the forces diminishing the consent, an idea forcefully expressed in William Golding's *Lord of the Flies*. The question of the individual's responsibility to society, which became much harder to conceive in mass societies in which individuals feel helpless vis-à-vis their surroundings, was enriched by reference to Albert Camus's *The Stranger*, whose protagonist is given full responsibility over the circumstances in spite of his lack of control over them. And the theory of pluralist democracy, according to which civic activity and political articulation lead to more or less representative governments, required adjustment in the television age in which media figures replaced civic and political actors, as shown in Jerzy Kosinsky's *Being There*.

Although the use of fiction has traditionally been dismissed by political scientists – a tradition going back to Plato – it had quite an appeal for students. At the turn of the century, world travel became easier, which allowed many Western students to visit foreign lands. Canadian, American, European, and Australian backpackers travelled across the globe, where they were often exposed to new forms of social relations, and different relations between humans and nature. Upon their return to the classroom, they looked for new ways to comprehend social reality, which required a reconsideration of the usefulness of former intellectual guides like Weber's *The Protestant Ethic and the Spirit of Capitalism* or Lenin's *What Is to be Done?* It was students returning from their travels who introduced me, for example, to Yann Martel's *Life of Pi*, a tale about the coexistence between a sixteen-year-old boy and a Bengali tiger on a life boat in the Pacific Ocean, as an alternative to the realism prevailing in the fields of strategic studies and international relations. And it was the need to reach out to inquisitive young people that made me include in course outlines on political theory José Saramago's *Blindness*, a novel questioning the ability of societies under stress to maintain political order.

Novels like *Life of Pi* and *Blindness* are not necessarily more helpful in learning about the political world than scholarly essays, but they provide fresh perspectives about reality by allowing us to temporarily transcend it. Fiction is mostly an escape from reality, but it is also a way to imagine hidden dimensions that may not reveal themselves in a straightforward empirical investigation, such as behavioural scenarios that have not been materialized, and may never do so, but whose consideration gives meaning to existing practices and allows value judgments about them. Utopian tales, for example, construct an imaginary political order and hence provide insights into the existing order and a standard for its evaluation.[14] By doing so, these tales not only complement empirical investigations but save them from stagnation. As Yann Martel puts it, "If we, citizens, do not support our artists, we sacrifice our imagination on the altar of crude reality and we end up believing in nothing and having worthless dreams."[15] It may seem paradoxical to consider the crude realist as having worthless dreams and the artist composing imaginary tales as contributing to the comprehension of reality, but this should not deter us from searching for answers to the complexities of the world in novels.

Martha Nussbaum argues that many people who think of literature as illuminating about the workings of the personal life and the private imagination believe that it is idle and unhelpful when the larger concerns of classes and nations are at issue. In their understanding of the political arena, she writes, they search for something "more reliably scientific, more detached, more sternly rational."[16] But the distinction between the personal and the political has largely been blurred today; few people can lead their lives in separation from political matters, such as the threat of terror, that constrain and direct it. As Paul Dolan states, a large segment of modern consciousness is embodied in political structures, which in turn shape and are shaped by that consciousness. Therefore, he claims, "politics cannot be understood only as the political scientist, the historian, the economist, the sociologist, the psychologist, or even the philosopher understand it. The novel provides its special kind of knowledge because it deals with the conscious and unconscious experience of politics as a human, moral, psychological and aesthetic phenomenon."[17]

The novel not only provides a special kind of knowledge but also a sense of moderation over the knowledge we hold on to, often with great zeal. As Milan Kundera writes, "Outside the novel, we're in the realm of affirmation: everyone is sure of his statements: the politician, the philosopher, the concierge. Within the universe of the novel, however, no one affirms: it is the realm of play and of hypotheses. In the novel, then, reflection is essentially inquiring, hypothetical."[18] And while politicians, philosophers, and concierges – especially those guarding the gates of knowledge – may prefer the affirmative over the hypothetical, some have realized the advantages of the novel.

> Just go off and be alone with it. Let it do with you what it will. You'll see; it will release you from yourself a little, loosen your attachment to those clever ideas of yours, so that when you turn back to them again at last, as you will, they will seem to you less securely attractive or just, and your own attachment to them will perhaps seem to you less virtuous.[19]

Such advocacy could not be expected to end the tendency to make affirmative statements, but an aesthetic approach marked by modesty about the empirical observation of reality began to take hold among mainstream political scientists at the turn of the millennium. For example, in his presidential address to the International Studies Association in 2003, Steven Smith criticized the discipline's retreat into what he called a methodological and epistemological bunker in which a narrow research agenda supportive of US power and US interests is followed in the name of a legitimate social science, narrowly defined. The discipline, he said, defined its core concerns in such a way as to exclude the most marked forms of violence in world politics. In the wake of the 9/11 attacks, however, a different notion of understanding and representation was needed. Using the example of René Magritte's paintings, in which a faithful reproduction of objects is presented only to undermine their commonly accepted meanings, Smith called for the discipline to abandon the assumption that the social world is open to simple observation. International relations scholars, he claimed, should engage in judgments and interpretations of reality, recognizing that it can never be directly accessed. Truth should be treated not as a property of the world waiting to be discovered but as a matter for negotiation and interpretation.[20]

The aesthetic turn in political science largely stemmed from the difficulty in coming up with theories based solely on behaviouralism (the application of scientific-positivistic methods to the study of political behaviour) about such issues as violence, terrorism, poverty, cruelty, and torture.[21] In an article titled "Why Political Scientists Want to Study Literature," Catherine Zuckert noted the prominence of behaviouralism among political scientists in the 1960s. In an effort to make the study of politics scientific, she writes, researchers sought quantifiable data and did studies that could be replicated. This, however, turned out to be insufficient:

> Unfortunately for the behaviouralists, the major political events of that decade, including the civil rights movement and the war in Vietnam, could not be studied solely in quantitative or positivistic terms. The events were singular, and the issues they raised obviously included questions of principle or value. There was a post-behavioral reaction, if not revolution. As a result, the discipline became more democratic in its internal organization and more pluralistic in its definition of subject matter.[22]

This greater pluralism allowed political philosophers, for example, to turn to fiction when moral theorizing seemed too narrowly focused on "rules and general principles."[23] As Horton and Baumeister write, "It is in developing a richer, more nuanced and realistic understanding of political deliberation that imaginative literature may have an especially valuable role to play. Novels and plays, for example, seem much better at exhibiting the complexities of political experience and the open-textured and necessarily incomplete character of real political arguments."[24]

What is it in novels and other aesthetic forms – poems, plays, films, photographs, paintings, and the like – that make them useful in the study of contemporary politics? In a seminal article in *Millennium*, Roland Bleiker provides a preliminary answer. Bleiker contrasts aesthetic with mimetic forms of representation. The latter, he writes, seek to represent politics as realistically and authentically as possible, aiming to capture world politics as-it-really-is. An aesthetic approach, by contrast, assumes that there is always a gap between a form of representation and what is represented therewith. It recognizes that the inevitable difference between the represented and its representation is the very location of politics.

> Issues of global war and Third World poverty are far too serious and urgent to be left to only one form of inquiry, especially if this mode of thought suppresses important faculties and fails to understand and engage the crucial problem of representation. We need to employ the full register of human perception and intelligence to understand the phenomena of world politics and to address the dilemmas that emanate from them. One of the key challenges, thus, consists of legitimising a greater variety of approaches and insights to world politics. Aesthetics is an important and necessary addition to our interpretative repertoire. It helps us understand why the emergence, meaning and significance of a political event can be appreciated only once we scrutinise the representational practices that have constituted the very nature of this event.[25]

Bleiker considers aesthetic approaches to politics necessary because, as he argues, political reality does not exist in an a priori way; it comes into being only through the process of representation. The political event does not determine from what perspective it is seen and thus its observation cannot be reduced to the event itself. Aesthetic approaches engage the gap that inevitably opens up between a form of representation and the object it seeks to represent. These approaches do not see this gap as a threat to knowledge and political stability but accept its inevitability. In that article and in subsequent works in which he responded to critics advocating the primacy of mimesis, Bleiker acknowledges the human tendency to associate the represented with the real. "The belief in resemblance and recognition," he writes, "is part of our desire to order the world."[26] He warns, however, of taking this tendency too far by disguising the subjective origins of a representation, treating it as if it were reality. He calls for a more fundamental reorientation of thought and action: "a shift away from harmonious common sense imposed by a few dominant faculties toward a model of thought that enables productive flows across a variety of discordant faculties."[27]

Those who adhere to dominant approaches such as realism in the study of international relations and behaviouralism in the study of domestic politics have not necessarily ignored the gap between political objects and their representation. Everyone recognizes, of course, that Picasso's painting *Guernica* is not a realistic depiction of war but rather an abstract representation of its cruelty. The aesthetic approach, however, asks for more than such recognition; it locates politics within the above gap and calls for a political science that explores it. This is a diversion from the previous emphasis on scientific methods intended to reveal "the way things 'really' happen."[28] In an article which largely set the "behaviouralist mood" in political science, Robert Dahl defined behaviouralism as an attempt to make the empirical component of the discipline more scientific. He singled out voting studies as providing the ground for hope that "if political scientists could only master the tools employed in the other social sciences – survey methods and statistical analysis, for example – they might be able to go beyond plausible generalities and proceed to test hypotheses about how people in fact do behave in making political choices."[29]

Dahl believed that studies of American elections have significantly altered and deepened the understanding of "what in some ways is the most distinctive action for a citizen of a democracy – deciding how to vote, or indeed whether to vote at all, in a competitive national election."[30] He mentioned several important findings of these studies: "that 'independent' voters tend to be less interested, involved, or informed than partisan voters; . . . that socio-economic 'class' whether objectively or subjectively defined is not a factor of constant weight in American presidential elections but a variable subject to great swings; and that only a microscopic proportion of American voters can be said to bring any ideological perspectives, even loosely defined, to bear on their decisions."[31]

What we have here is a legitimate representation of the American voter as an individual making choices, which brings up questions about the degree to which these choices are constrained by class affiliation, whether they are based on ideology, or how informed they are. It must be remembered, however, that this representation is no more real or mimetic than, say, George Caleb Bingham's oil painting "The County Election," in which the 1850 election in Saline County, Missouri, is depicted as an event involving a great deal of chance, as reflected in a figure tossing a coin or two children playing a game of knife throwing. This is not to say that positivistic political science is less valuable than art history or that chance is a more solid building block of voting theory than choice but rather that conceptual theories can be supplemented and sometimes altered by artistic works exposing the representational nature of notions, such as that of the voter as chooser, which are mistaken for reality. However satisfying our data and theories on voting behaviour, it is sometimes quite useful to consider alternative representations such as José Saramago's imaginary tale *Seeing*, in which a whole electorate does not arrive at the polls on election day and, when it finally does, casts a blank ballot, thus raising the possibility that democratic elections may not only be designed for citizens to choose leaders but also for leaders to maintain power. Another example of an aesthetic piece sparking fresh thoughts on voting behaviour is Richard Mock's linocut print of 2000 "Voting in America," showing the American voter to be bruised, battered, and subjected to extreme noises that turn the ballot into a meaningless piece of paper.

Such aesthetic representations remind us that any truisms associated with "politics as-it-really-is" are worth an additional look. Moreover, in consulting works of art, our perspective on political phenomena such as elections, party affiliation, leadership recruitment, etc., may not only be broadened but become more critical. Viewing empirical research as the only representation of reality bears the danger of taking the political system as defined by those who lead and control it as a given, not as an object open to change. For example, the notion of citizen participation in democratic politics is the subject of much political rhetoric because it allows political elites to launch wars, accumulate wealth, and maintain power in the name of public consent. And nothing helps legitimize the power of those elites more than the acceptance of such political rhetoric as a mimetic reflection of reality.

Exposing popular consent as one among several plausible representations adds an element of criticism to political inquiry. I refer not to the criticism by committed artists producing posters to make a political point but to more subtle presentations of political phenomena and events in ways that make us think about them. The critical function of the arts and humanities has been discussed by Michael Mack, who emphasizes their "unique and underappreciated capacity to make us aware of how we can change accustomed forms of perception and action."[32] The aesthetic, he writes, has the unique capacity to help us explore different and so far unthinkable forms of action and interaction. Art can thus be seen as performing an "ethics of resilience which resists repetition and thus perpetuation of harmful practices."[33] Mack takes an active approach to literature, considering not only its cognitive and ethical contributions but its power as a major driver of social change.

> Representation here moves beyond what I call 'flat mimesis'. It does not only represent to us our world, but also places us within the world in new ways that allow . . . us to see alternative modes of adaptation. Literature's cognitive, religious and ethical dimensions are bound up with the

difference it can make in society if its imaginative coping strategies with change and its social consequences are more fully realized.[34]

This view of literature as providing resources through which we may become better prepared for future social adaptations brings us back to the cybernetic model of society. As I suggested before, this model originated in the belief prevailing in the 1960s that the modern social sciences would help societies adapt to their changing environments. Having realized the limitations of science in coping with the contingencies of the early twenty-first century, however, we may consider broadening the perimeters of the "knowledge unit" in the cybernetic model by incorporating political literature. Plays, short stories, poems, and especially novels absorbing us into fictional political situations may provide us with critical, creative, thought-provoking perspectives on our behaviour in the public sphere and perhaps also help us adapt to the contingent world we live in.

Paradoxically, the reliance on aesthetics as a possible source of political change comes at a time when literary scholarship is accused for abandoning it. Lindsay Waters, executive editor of the humanities at Harvard University Press, for example, complains about what he sees as the reduction of literature to ideas. Literary critics have abandoned the appreciation of aesthetics, he believes, focusing on the author's or reader's intention or ideology, which is not at all the same thing as art. "As a result," he writes, "literary critics are devoted to saving the world, not to saving literature for the world. . . . Instead of the erotics of art, we've got the neurotics of art: the meaning-mongering of interpretation for its own sake."[35]

This is an important warning for political scientists who may easily fall into what Waters calls "a legalistic parsing of the reduction of literature to an idea, a moral."[36] It is a trap that must be avoided, if only because literature is no substitute for the social scientist's quest for the truth; when literature turns into a political manifesto it loses the aesthetic qualities that make it valuable in the study of politics. As

Raymond Taras reminds us, "A political manifesto masking as a literary work is not a reliable narrative because it lacks the aesthetic qualities that entangle and entrap the reader. It is the aesthetic qualities that draw the reader into the complex, conflicting reality in which history encounters multiple branching points along which it may travel."[37] Marcia Eaton, concerned with the truth value of literary statements, concurs: "Literature, especially poetry, consists of pseudo-statements, statements the justification of which depends not upon their being true but upon the way in which they release or organize our emotions."[38]

This lesson has been acknowledged by scholars of aesthetics who point at the Kantian idea of aesthetic autonomy. In "Aesthetics and Politics," Lola Frost distinguishes between aesthetic objects and practices and reflective interpretation. The former, she claims, "resist unambiguous thought by mobilizing the interminate negativities of aesthetic effect (emotion, perception, sensation) and of aesthetic signifying processes which produce confusion, interminancy, ambivalence and irresolution."[39] She explains, however, that the disruption caused by the aesthetic experience "in turn provokes a determinate judgment, one which reassembles thought and invites reflection."[40] An example is Cerwyn Moore's attempt to trace violence in the first Chechen war not as part of the international political discourse of the state but by drawing on the use of hermeneutics and the literary arts, thus capturing non-overtly political forces which construct our representation of war. As Moore writes, "If contemporary IR [international relations] continues to be grounded in an abstract politico-ethical epistemology, the resultant approach to violence will have the effect of obscuring certain continuities displayed in discourses of cultural memory—the tragedy and sacrifice of contemporary violence."[41]

Another example is Michael Kochin's work on J. M. Coetzee's disturbing novel *Disgrace* as "a book about endings: the end of rape, the end of morality, and the end of humanity."[42] Analyzing the scene in the novel in which rape is used as a successful means to gain the rape victims' rights to the land, Kochin sees it as a demonstration of the end of rape because "we have lost the metaphysical beliefs in the soul and in freedom of the will from which we constitute rape as a moral and social category."[43] From the novel's often surrealistic scenes, Kochin derives insights on post-Apartheid South Africa in all of its brutal violence and the lack of power individuals have to protect their possessions as well as on what he calls "the apparent end of all distinctively human possibilities of a life worth living."[44]

Richard Devetak's work on Don DeLillo's 1985 novel *White Noise* also demonstrates how aesthetic forms, such as a novelist's ironic depiction of an event, serve as a source of insights on politics. The novel tells about the disruption of everyday life by an industrial incident which turns into a flood of reliable and unreliable conversations and rumours framing the event in ways that result in a violent response. The close relationship found in the novel between the way the event is handled and the narratives developing when it occurs and in its aftermath inspires an analysis of the construction of the September 11 event not only as an act of terrorism but as a world-changing act of war calling for (and justifying) the response devised by the Bush administration to attack Iraq. Devetak concludes by stating that literature is not so far removed from politics to the extent that both realms engage in narrativization of reality. "From literature," he concludes, "we can learn more about the means by which we make our worlds, not just the imaginary worlds of fiction, but the real worlds of politics and international relations."[45]

These examples point to a new trend which may or may not take hold in political science in which political phenomena are derived both from the literary text and from the aesthetic experience it generates. This trend reflects the acceptance by some political scientists of the lesson conveyed long ago by Erich Auerbach according to which we may approach reality by other means than its direct imitation. In his celebrated book *Mimesis*, Auerbach distinguished between the straightforward narration of Homer's myths and the Old Testament's writing of history as a godly plan, the latter leaving out elements of time, place, human motive, and the like which, however, makes it no less realistic. Here is a reminder of Auerbach's typology:

The two styles, in their opposition, represent basic types: on the one hand fully externalized description, uniform illumination, uninterrupted connection, free expression, all events in the foreground, displaying unmistakable meanings. Few elements of historical development and of psychological perspective; on the other hand, certain parts brought into high relief, others left obscure, abruptness, suggestive influence of the unexpressed, 'background' quality, multiplicity of meanings and the need for interpretation, universal-historical claims, development of the concept of the historically becoming, and preoccupation with the problematic.[46]

In the coming chapters, I attempt to show that the aesthetic qualities of literature may be used to enrich political inquiry. While I acknowledge the claim that "literature departments are literature departments, and not adjuncts to political science or cultural anthropology"[47] and agree that a literary text should not be chosen for analysis "because of some set of categorical properties it may or may not have,"[48] I propose an analysis of politics at the turn of the millennium based on my reading of several novels which can be shown to augment our understanding of the era we live in.

The novels are all concerned with phenomena of political significance: genocide, poverty, international conflict, terrorism, and others, but none of them is a political or ideological manifesto. In all the novels I chose for analysis, political phenomena are constructed within fictional frameworks that exceed their common representation, thus raising fresh ideas about the world of the early twenty-first century. They are all "political novels" insofar as this term refers to novels that have political relevance, though they do not necessarily provide a realistic representation of political figures, events, and processes.

Some of the novels discussed here are more explicit than others in their treatment of politics, but they all allow the derivation of political insights. My choice of the novels was based on their illustrative value;[49]

I chose novels which illustrate the contribution of fiction to political understanding by questioning, updating, and altering accepted political theories; by deepening our comprehension of otherwise incomprehensible political phenomena; by uncovering the past as a way to help us cope with the present; and by extrapolating from present political conditions where we may be heading and what alternative paths are available to us.

The novels include José Saramago's *Blindness*, analyzed as a literary response to John Rawls's theory of justice. Saramago, the Portuguese Communist, did not relate specifically to the liberal thinker Rawls, but the novel can be read as an answer to the question underlying the Rawlsian theory: How can we achieve a fair allocation of resources in society? By his forceful depiction of the allocation in an imaginary political context in which a society falls into a condition of blindness, Saramago brings up behavioural options that both enrich the theory and put it in question. He casts doubt on Rawls's principle according to which inequality in the allocation of resources becomes acceptable as long as the least advantaged in society are also benefiting. By describing a condition in which the least advantaged among the blind suffer much greater pain and humiliation than Rawls and his disciples account for, Saramago makes us rethink the theory and wonder about its application to the contemporary world.

I then discuss Cormac McCarthy's *The Road* as an updated version of Albert Camus's notion of the absurd. The grim tale of the father and child pushing a supermarket cart on the road after all the technological, economic, and political systems surrounding us have been destroyed is reminiscent of the revolt called for by Camus in the aftermath of the Second World War. In the face of the destruction brought about by the war, Camus put his faith in human consciousness, which he insisted would enable individuals to persist in spite of the Sisyphean nature of their life journey. This notion, however, requires an update in view of the events of the last sixty years, especially the massive development of information technologies such as cable television and the Internet, which, at the beginning of the third millennium, threaten to alter human consciousness. By turning off the lights on the world's TV and computer screens and exposing the violence and environmental destruction in the desolate universe behind them, McCarthy updates the Sisyphean revolt of the early twenty-first century.

Gil Courtemanche's *A Sunday at the Pool in Kigali* is an attempt by the author to help us comprehend an incomprehensible event: the Rwandan genocide. Courtemanche, a Quebecois journalist who covered Rwanda before and after the genocide, realized that, just as the world stood by in 1994 when the rulers of a small country in Africa managed to liquidate 15 percent of the population in three months, it would be incapable of understanding the events afterward, in spite of the many sources available for learning about them in detail. Indeed, no investigative report, eyewitness account, scholarly study, legal procedure, or work of art can fully represent genocide. The cruelty of the perpetrators, the fear of the victims, the cynicism of officials, the voice of hate radio, and the sights and smells of the killing fields will always be hard to grasp. Courtemanche chose the novel form in order to describe the Rwandan genocide from a unique perspective, that of the bystander, which every reader can easily identify with.

In *The Cripple and His Talismans*, the young Bombay-born Vancouver author Anosh Irani uses magical realism in order to help us enter into another incomprehensible world and get a picture (although still very partial and limited) of life in the poverty-stricken slums of his birth city. Irani proposes a careful and controlled shift from reality to fantasy and thus highlights some dimensions that are hard to represent in other genres depicting poverty, such as United Nations reports, urban studies, and documentary films. Once the poor, the beggars, and the homeless on the streets of Bombay become part of a fantasy in which their nightly dreams, for example, are described, we gain a new perspective on the physical environment of the slum, daily routine in the slum, the culture of death prevailing there, some hidden commercial practices, the politics of the slum, and the place of God in the life of the poorest of the poor.

The role of fiction in helping us cope with the past figures in three early twenty-first-century novels: *Kafka on the Shore* by Japanese writer Haruki Murakami, *Crabwalk* by German writer Günter Grass, and *The Rights of Desire* by South African writer André Brink. All three writers are concerned with the failure of their respective societies to come to terms with the evils they inflicted during the twentieth century and propose guidelines for a narrative of reconciliation. Many of the conflicts we experience today within states and in the international arena are seen as the outgrowth of conflicting narratives held by former perpetrators and former victims. The three novels, however, propose a nuanced narrative, one giving central place to remembrance of the evils of the past without turning past victims into present perpetrators.

John le Carré's *Absolute Friends* provides us with a unique perspective on the sources of contemporary terrorism. After describing Edward Said's prescriptive model of the postcolonial public intellectual as siding with the victims of oppression, I show how Le Carré, worried about the uncompromising approach taken by public intellectuals associated with the anti-globalization movement today, constructs a character embodying some of them and, as the story unfolds, turns the fictionalized public intellectual into a terrorist, thus raising awareness of the potential dangers of the "politics of victimhood."

I then discuss two novels – one by a Sunni Moslem Palestinian Arab living in Israel and one by an Israeli Jew – that problematize further the politics of victimhood and shed light on the complex relations in the Middle East. Sayed Kashua's *Let It Be Morning* is a creative attempt by a novelist to cope with the difficult issue of ethnic identity in the globalized world of the twenty-first century. I show how the protagonist, who, like the author, is an Arab living in Israel and writing in Hebrew, blurs common narratives pursued by the contending parties in the Middle East and exposes reckless ideas and policies pursued in the region. *To the End of the Land* by David Grossman is a literary effort to penetrate deeply into Israeli culture and, in so doing, reveal some of the root causes of the Israeli-Palestinian conflict.

I conclude by analyzing two novels whose strong depictions of present trends in technological development and international rivalry raise questions about the world's future. Margaret Atwood's *Oryx and Crake* is a "negative utopia" extrapolating present developments in genetic engineering and computing into the future so as to point out their dangers. But it goes one step further by situating the story of the future technological society within the age-old philosophical dichotomy of body and mind, thus providing a remarkably coherent explanation of the forces endangering that society today. Yann Martel's *Life of Pi* is also a utopian tale that warns us of the path we are taking in international affairs and points at a way out. I analyze the novel as a literary response to Samuel Huntington's "clash of civilizations" theory and show how Martel's literary image of a sixteen-year-old boy and a Bengali tiger on a lifeboat questions some of that theory's foundations and poses an alternative of coexistence between civilizations.

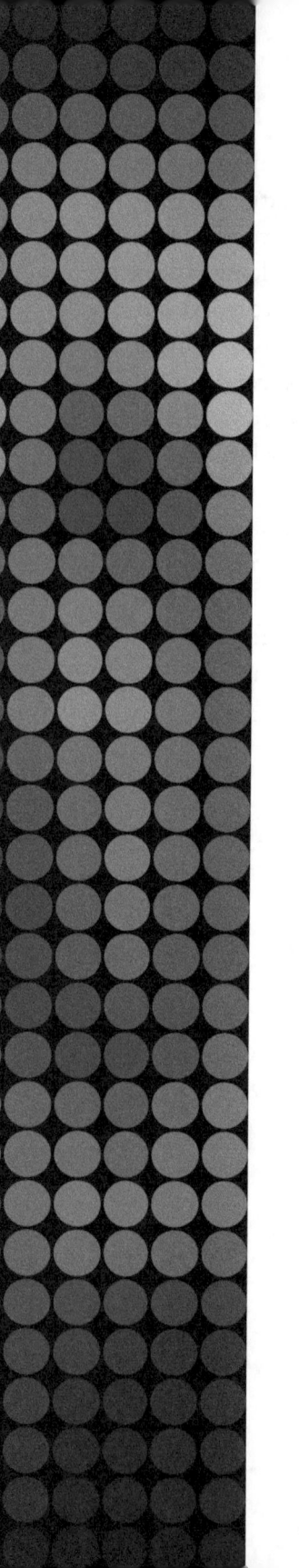

THE "ORIGINAL POSITION" IN JOSÉ SARAMAGO'S *BLINDNESS*

Following the tradition of social contract theories of the early modern age, John Rawls, in *A Theory of Justice*, renewed the idea of the "original position" intended to set up a fair procedure for the achievement of justice through bargaining between parties situated behind a veil of ignorance. "They do not know how the various alternatives will affect their own particular case," he writes, "and they are obliged to evaluate principles solely on the basis of general considerations."[1] The original position is a heuristic device for evaluating societies by their approximation to the principles achieved in an imagined bargaining process between rational actors stripped of knowledge about their relative positioning. Rawls proposes two principles that would be agreed upon in serial order behind the veil of ignorance: the liberty principle, in which equal liberty is assured, and the difference principle, based on maximin choice, in which inequality in the allocation of resources is accepted as long as the least advantaged are also benefiting.

This theory has rightly been considered one of the most important contributions to contemporary political thought. Whether or not one agrees with Rawls's rejection of utilitarianism (i.e., the assumption that rational actors behind a veil of ignorance would choose the public good), and with the version of distributive justice the second principle implies, the theory calls for considerations transcending particularistic interests and thus inspires a general ethical discourse in the Kantian tradition. Rawls pays tribute to Kant by claiming that the notion of the veil of ignorance was implicit in the eighteenth-century philosopher's ethics, but he also adds assumptions of his own about the parties in the original position, their knowledge, and their model of reasoning. For example, the parties in the original position are ignorant about their social, economic and intellectual status, the particulars of their plan of life, their psychological traits, and even the generation to which they belong. At the same time, they are knowledgeable of certain general facts: "They understand political affairs and the principles of economic theory; they know the basis of social organization and the laws of human psychology. Indeed, the parties are presumed to know whatever general facts affect the choice of the principles of justice."[2]

The original position, thus characterized, has led critics to question whether it allows the derivation of the two principles of justice and whether rational individuals behind a veil of ignorance would arrive at a priority for liberty and for a differential social order.[3] Benjamin Barber, for example, has claimed that there is nothing in the original position that suggests maximin as the most rational solution to the problem of choice under uncertainty. The question of what strategy would be most rational requires additional assumptions not provided by the formalistic conditions of the original position. Barber also doubts whether it is possible to conceive of individuals as having hypothetical knowledge of what it means to have interests and desires without having particular interests and desires themselves.[4]

Rawls and his disciples have responded to such criticism by arguing that the original position, being a heuristic device, had to be thinly defined and that stronger psychological assumptions about the behaviour behind the veil of ignorance are not needed because the theory is confined to conditions of moderate scarcity. Under these conditions, all that is required is the assumption that people are rational beings who would maximize primary goods and thus arrive at the two principles of justice.[5] While this response is effective in supporting the coherence of Rawls's theory, it is too limited if the theory is to serve as a guide for moral reasoning in the real world. If the original position is not seen as a sheer intellectual exercise but as a device for the derivation of principles of justice applicable to social and political settings, the assumptions about the behaviour of individuals in the original position ought to be, as Rawls puts it, "natural and plausible."[6]

Where can these behavioural assumptions be derived from? We could, of course, examine a variety of empirical political contexts, but Rawls's theory transcends such contexts in its attempt to propose universal principles of just behaviour by which societies in general could be evaluated. This is where literature comes to our aid in its depiction of human situations that may be complex, varied, and colourful but often devoid of specific political context. This is very apparent in José Saramago's 1995 novel *Blindness*, about a society whose inhabitants become blind and have to interact under the new circumstances. The novel by the noted Portuguese Nobel Prize winner provides rich insights on human behaviour by following the dynamics of a society that is not situated in any specific time or place.

The novel begins with the description of a busy intersection where a car does not move when the light turns to green because its driver is becoming blind. A Good Samaritan drives him home, steals his car, and becomes blind too. The first blind man is brought by his wife to the eye doctor's office, where other patients affected by blindness are in the waiting room: an old man with a black patch over one eye, a young lad who looks cross-eyed, a girl with dark glasses, and other characters whose names are never disclosed. Soon a blindness epidemic spreads, and the blind are directed by the government into quarantine in an abandoned insane asylum. The eye doctor, who also becomes blind, is accompanied to the asylum by his wife, who says she is blind in order to be with him, but is the only person in the novel who keeps her eyesight. As more and more blind people are brought into the asylum, the conditions there worsen and a group of hoodlums takes control over the food supplies, demanding jewelry, money, and women in return for food. Terrible violence erupts, the asylum turns into a fire trap, and the blind who rush out find out that the soldiers who guarded the place have disappeared because they have probably also become blind. A group of six blind characters and a "dog of tears" are then led by the eye doctor's wife through the streets of a chaotic city where all systems by which people feed and govern themselves have collapsed.

Not only are the characters unnamed but the city also remains unknown. This is a significant diversion from Saramago's earlier novels, which were strongly rooted in Portuguese historical and political reality.[7] *Blindness* has therefore rightly been classified as belonging to the genre of "plague narratives."[8] As in Camus's *The Plague*, writes José Ornelas, we are faced with an allegory of the body politic, which needs to apply more rational and ethical policies if it is to get rid of the metaphorical plague. Saramago was explicit about his concern with rationality: "With this book, I intend to question myself and my readers about our rationality, if we are, in effect, rational."[9]

Although the novel lacks the theoretical rigour of a political treatise and has probably not been written with *A Theory of Justice* in mind, its forceful depiction of human behaviour in an abstract but rich political context brings up behavioural options which, when applied to Rawls's original position, enrich the theory and help clarify some of the problems noted by its critics. The application is made easier by the structure of the novel which resembles social contract theories in conceptualizing a model of social relations and considering the choices expected in it as well as the political obligations implied by these choices. Let us now see how *Blindness* complements Rawls's theory by exhibiting some of the complexities of political experience.

THE NATURE OF THE ORIGINAL POSITION

Blindness helps overcome the difficulty of imagining an original position whose actors have no particular interests while they understand the meaning of these interests. This difficulty is overcome by the literary narrative's sensitivity to time. The blindness in Saramago's novel is described as a "white blindness," a condition in which individuals lose their orientation while maintaining a general memory of the functioning of society. Consulting his medical books, the eye doctor encountering the first cases of the pandemic considers it to be Agnosia, a rare neurological disease in which patients continue to see what they have always seen but lose the capability to relate it to any known information or to express what they see. At the same time, they do not lose their memory of what Rawls referred to as "the general facts about human society."[10]

Being confined to an asylum, the blind have to engage in the allocation of resources, such as food packages thrown at the doorstep, but most of their human attributes are gone. In a manner reminiscent of Primo Levi's description of his experiences in Nazi death camps, yet devoid of any spatial and temporal context, not only do the residents in the asylum fail to recognize each other but all their former affiliations are blurred: social and economic status, professional background, personal history, personality traits, education, resourcefulness, and the like. They also lose count of the days and the distinction between day and night.

These are individuals who have memories but lack knowledge about themselves and about others. As the doctor's wife puts it, "we're so remote from the world that any day now, we shall no longer know who we are, or even remember our names, and besides, what use would names be to us, no dog recognizes another dog or knows the others by the names they have been given, a dog is identified by its scent and that is how it identifies others, here we are like another breed of dogs, we know each other's bark or speech, as for the rest, features, colour of eyes or hair, they are of no importance, it is as if they did not exist."[11]

While they have lost their identity, Saramago's actors remain rational in the sense that they try to maximize whatever benefits are available to them. But as rational as they are, once stripped of knowledge about their identity, they do not bargain over matters of public concern. Ignorance is no trivial matter, and before individuals behind a veil of ignorance would engage in bargaining over the distribution of resources, we learn, they would make every effort to overcome the ignorance, and – if this turns out to be impossible – to hide it. If hiding also fails, they may simply panic.

When the first man becomes blind in his car, he does not accept his condition. A Good Samaritan brings him home and when he leaves, the blind man draws back the lid of the peephole and looks outside. He then sits on the sofa where he and his wife used to watch television. When they both leave the house to go to the eye doctor, their first instinct is to hide the blindness. "Wait for me here," says the wife in the lobby, "if any neighbor should appear speak to them naturally, say you're waiting for me, no one looking at you would ever suspect that you cannot see and besides we don't have to tell people all our business."[12]

The blind are constantly looking for ways to restore the self-consciousness diminished by their blindness. At night they dream they are blind, as if to regain control over their fate, and they do not give up easily on the knowledge of who they are. When the eye doctor himself becomes blind, he gets up in the morning and turns to where he knows the mirror was: "he simply stretched out his hands to touch the glass, he knew that his image was there watching him, his image could see him, he could not see his image."[13]

The uncertainty caused by the loss of knowledge about oneself and about others becomes a major concern. The blind have no way to know how long the condition of blindness will last and whether the resources they have to allocate, especially hospital beds and food, will suffice in a situation in which an increasing number of people are competing over diminishing resources, especially when more and more blind people are sent to the asylum. Rawls solved the problem by assuming moderate scarcity. Saramago enriches the theory by describing the dynamics that can be expected even when the scarcity is still relatively moderate, not to mention conditions in which it is growing:

The shouting had died down, now a confusion of sounds was coming from the hallway, these were the blind, driven like sheep, bumping into each other, crammed together in the doorways, some lost their sense of direction and ended up in other wards, but the majority, stumbling along, huddled into groups or dispersed one by one, desperately waving their hands in the air like people drowning, burst into the ward in a whirlwind, as if being pushed from the outside by a bulldozer. A number of them fell and were trampled underfoot. Confined in the narrow aisles, the new arrivals gradually began filling the spaces between the beds, and here, like a ship caught in a storm that has finally managed to reach port, they took possession of their berths, in this case their beds, insisting that there was no room for anyone else, and that the newcomers should find themselves a place elsewhere.[14]

While this behaviour exceeds anything Rawls had considered in drawing the model of the original position, it is worth looking at because even societies living in relative prosperity and seeking a fair distribution of resources may have gone through traumatic formative experiences. Saramago does not exclude the option of rational bargaining after the turbulence is over but reminds us that the formative trauma may have an effect on the bargaining process. He also reminds us of the difficulty rational individuals have in reaching agreement due to simple contingencies caused by the blindness. Rawls excluded such contingencies, which did not affect the normative structure he proposed, but Saramago instructs us that considering them may be helpful because individuals would have to navigate their way through contingencies if they are to achieve the normative goals set by Rawls. An example of such a contingency is the unforeseen and unnecessary quarrel that erupts when one blind man finds his bed occupied by mistake:

> Standing there, the doctor's wife watched the two blind men who were arguing, she noticed they made no gestures, that they barely moved their bodies, having quickly learned that only their voice and hearing now served any purpose, true, they had their arms, that they could fight, grapple, come to blows, as the saying goes, but a bed swapped by mistake was not worth so much fuss, if only all life's deceptions were like this one, and all they had to do was to come to some agreement, Number two is mine, yours is number three, let that be understood once and for all, Were it not for the fact that we're blind this mix-up would never have happened, You're right, our problem is that we're blind. The doctor's wife said to her husband, The whole world is right here.[15]

Let me clarify that the "white blindness" in Saramago's novel is not equivalent to ignorance (or to a "veil of ignorance"), but if we refer to it as a metaphor for a condition in which one loses recognition of self and others, then it points at the need to consider disruptions in the bargaining process that may lead to conflict rather than to agreement, especially when the actors are stripped of their particular affiliations and appetites. Consider the following paragraph:

> After a few minutes one of the blind men said, There's one thing that bothers me, What's that, How are we going to distribute the food, As we did before, we know how many we are, the rations are counted, everyone receives his share, it's the simplest and fairest way, But it didn't work, some internees were left without any food, And there were also those who got double rations, The distribution was badly organized, It will always be badly organized unless people show some respect and discipline.[16]

In other words, while it is possible to conceive of a normative model of the smooth distribution of resources, any concern with the application of the model to a human condition, however abstract, cannot ignore the need for some a priori set of norms assuring the smoothness of the process, which cannot be simply presumed. According to Saramago, without a normative foundation assuring a degree of trust between the members of society, no fair distribution system could be agreed upon. The following exchange demonstrates the importance of trust:

> What we should do is to take all the food to the refectory, each ward elects three of its inmates to do the sharing out, so that with six people counting there would be little danger of abuse and deception, And how are we to know that they are telling the truth when the others say how many there are in their ward, We are dealing with honest people . . . My dear fellow, I don't know about honest but we're certainly hungry.[17]

Saramago, then, adds to the theory of justice a note that without initial trust, even the most impartial system of distribution considered in the original position may seem suspect. Let us now consider the insights provided in the novel on the choices that can be expected in the original position.

CHOICE IN THE ORIGINAL POSITION

Social contract theory assumes that rational actors in the original position choose to abandon the state of nature for some constitutional arrangement. Hobbes's actors, fearing the war of all against all, consent to rule by the sovereign; Rousseau's actors choose fraternity; and Rawls's actors choose maximin, agreeing to inequality in the distribution of resources as long as the minimum payoff is improved. Saramago makes us face a difficult question in regard to the constitutional arrangement, especially when based on maximin: What if the payoff is so low that any controlled approval of it in line with the difference principle would prolong an unbearable, undignified, and immoral situation? How should we handle a human condition which is so unjust that only armed resistance would achieve Rawls's goal of giving "greater support to man's self-respect"?[18]

Rawls does not ignore the possibility that at times attention must be given to conditions of injustice, but he does not associate these conditions with the original position. He associates them with institutional arrangements in "near just" societies that may call, in very limited cases, for some form of resistance. He agrees we must ascertain how the ideal conception of justice applies to cases in which we are confronted with injustice, but he confines these cases to what he calls "nonideal theory," namely, "the theory of punishment and compensatory justice, just war and conscientious objection, civil disobedience and militant resistance."[19]

Militant resistance receives almost no mention. Rawls agrees that "in certain circumstances militant action and other kinds of resistance are surely justified"[20] but decides not to consider these circumstances. As to civil disobedience, he subjects it to very hard constraints: that it be used only after normal appeals to the political majority have been made in good faith and failed, and that it be properly designed to make an effective appeal to the wider community.

The marginalization of armed resistance in *A Theory of Justice* is related to the social contract tradition in which the evil that may justify it is considered either a primordial force to be overcome by human rationality or a product of discrepancies between contractual constitutions and real-world institutions. Saramago, however, presents ongoing evil as a major force to consider in any model of social relations. According to him, the more liberty is assured in egalitarian fashion in the original position in line with Rawls's first principle, the greater the chance that evil will affect the bargaining over the next principle. This is shown in a conversation about dead bodies in which it is said that the spirits of the dead "have never been as free as they are now, released from their bodies, and therefore free to do whatever they like, above all, to do evil, which, as everyone knows, has always been the easier thing to do."[21] Rawls is aware of the need to reconcile his theory of justice with common notions of good and evil. He does it by defining a good person as one who "has the features of moral character that is rational for members of a well-ordered society to want in their associates."[22] He recognizes the possibility of benevolent action, although he is careful to limit it to acts that are good to others provided that the sacrifices and hazards to the agent are not very great. He also devotes a paragraph in *A Theory of Justice* to people who are not good, whom he defines mainly by their excessive pursuit of power. He divides them into three types: the unjust, the bad, and the evil man. The first two types do not worry him; the unjust man seeks dominion for the sake of aims such as wealth and security which, when appropriately limited, are legitimate, and the bad man desires things like excessive mastery which, when duly circumscribed, are good. It is the third type who is less reconcilable with the theory, for he "aspires to unjust rule precisely because it violates what independent persons would consent to in an original position of equality, and therefore its possession and display manifest his superiority and affront the self-respect of others."[23]

Rawls, then, recognizes the existence of an "evil man" marked by "a love of injustice: he delights in the impotence and humiliation of those subject to him and he relishes being recognized by them as the willful author of their degradation."[24] But he assures us that "there seems to be no reason to fear that the numerous variations of moral worth cannot be accounted for."[25]

Saramago, on the other hand, makes us face the power of evil in full force. It is not clear whether the hoodlums who take over the food supply in the asylum are intrinsically evil or have only turned evil when the opportunity emerged, but in light of the author's hint in several places in the novel that immorality is the product of chance and opportunity rather than a personality trait (e.g., when the Good Samaritan who brings the first blind man home steals his car), it can be said that the appearance of evil in *Blindness* is reconcilable with the veil of ignorance assumption. A small group of rational actors who know no more than Rawls allows them to know behind the veil of ignorance, but do seem to know something about the way the distribution of resources has mostly ended up in human history, infuse old/new rules into the bargaining process.

To Saramago, these evildoers are not deviants to be discussed as part of "nonideal theory" but an immanent component of the human condition. As David Frier notes, "One of the key aspects of the presentation of the worst side of human nature in this novel . . . is the fact that this is no simplistic opposition of cruel oppressors and innocent victims. The lack of faith in others runs throughout this society, with the blind themselves calculatedly oppressing the blind."[26] As when landlords emerge ad hoc in refugee camps during the distribution of United Nations food supplies, the distribution process itself brings up opportunities to disrupt it in a way that may assure one's gains under all circumstances.

An early warning signal that this is going to happen is given after the residents of one ward are burying their dead. When the second ward's turn comes to bury their dead, a masculine voice says: "if you've buried some, you can bury the rest."[27] This "logic of collective action" is exactly what Rawls tries to prevent by placing the actors in a position in which they do not know, for instance, what ward they are in. But, even if they do not, Saramago makes us aware of ad hoc opportunities that may emerge in bargaining processes, leading to attempts to change the rules of the game. This happens when the hoodlums announce they are taking charge of the food, which from now on will be sold. Ironically, this simply leads to continued wheeling and dealing: "we must know how we're to proceed, where are we going to fetch the food, do we all go together, or one at a time."[28] The irony stems from the fact that the contemporary reader is aware that once a concrete element of evil is introduced into the bargaining process, such bargaining has little chance and the worst can be expected. Indeed, the next step is the demand that in each ward two people be nominated to be in charge of collecting valuables – money, jewels, rings, bracelets, earrings, watches, everything the people possess – and hand them over to the hoodlums.

This still does not stop the routine bargaining discourse: "A blind man from the second ward on the right asked, And what are we to do, do we hand everything at once, or do we pay according to what we eat."[29] Moreover, some victims begin to use rationalizations: "some protested that they were being robbed shamefully, and that was the honest truth, others divested themselves to their possessions with a kind of indifference, as if thinking that, all things considered, there is nothing in this world that belongs to us in an absolute sense, another all too transparent truth."[30]

At times, the rationalizations sound as if they were taken directly from *A Theory of Justice*. "The maximin rule," writes Rawls, "tells us to rank alternatives by their worst possible outcomes: we are to adopt the alternative the worst outcome of which is superior to the worst outcomes of the others."[31] Now consider this: "If things continue like this, we'll end up once more reaching the conclusion that even in the worst misfortunes it is possible to find enough good to be able to bear the aforesaid misfortunes with patience, which, applied to the present situation, means that contrary to the first disquieting predictions, the concentration of food supplies into a single entity for appropriating and distribution, had its positive aspects, after all, however much certain idealists might protest that they would have preferred to go on struggling for life by their own means, even if their stubbornness meant going hungry."[32]

Can such rationalizations be seen as warranted for actors following a rational decision strategy under the new conditions in the asylum? Saramago who, as we have seen, does not believe that liberty is a guarantee against evil, brings evil to such an extreme that all rationalizations turn into a farce. In one of the more horrifying tales in modern literature, we are led through ever-increasing demands on the population, which leaves it with no option but armed resistance.

The most horrifying moment comes when the hoodlums demand women in return for food. This demand does not stop the discourse in the asylum over such matters as how the food gained this way ought to be distributed, but it does shift the emphasis in the reader's mind to other questions: What is the value of dignity versus survival? Under what conditions is murder justified? What obligation do we have to fight evil even when it does not affect us directly? What right do bystanders have to condemn armed resistance by a desperate people? Saramago does not provide us with answers; he just hints that the answers would not be found by subjecting these questions to rational choice calculations. To him, an additional moral imperative is needed, which I will now discuss.

THE ORIGINAL POSITION AND POLITICAL OBLIGATION

One of the strongest critiques of *A Theory of Justice* concerns the difficulty of deriving from the original position a political obligation to abide by in the real world. As George Klosko puts it, "the natural political duty cannot be defended successfully from the 'original position,' the distinctive standpoint of Rawls's theory. Either the duty will not be sufficiently strong to ground moral requirements akin to political obligations, or if it will, it will not be a 'natural' duty."[33]

Ronald Dworkin explained the weakness of the natural duty in the theory by the lack of a contractual relationship between the bargaining parties. "If a group contracted in advance that disputes amongst them would be settled in a particular way," he writes, "the fact of the contract would be a powerful argument that such disputes should be settled in that way when they do arise." But he also notes that no such contract is provided for in the theory. "Rawls does not suppose that any group ever entered into a social contract of the sort he describes. He argues only that if a group of rational men did find themselves in the predicament of the original position, they would contract for the two principles. His contract is hypothetical, and hypothetical contracts do not supply an independent argument for the fairness of enforcing their terms."[34]

Saramago's *Blindness* is helpful in highlighting this missing theoretical link and its ethical implications. He does so with a literary shift in which the asylum is burned down and the blind find themselves in the street. They are now in a new situation in which the blindness is gradually diminishing. At first they still cannot see each other but former affiliations are restored. They search for their original homes and families and redevelop feelings toward them that had been suppressed in the asylum. Various forms of communication and organization are established and ultimately their eyesight returns.

The message is loud and clear: nothing that has been occurring before serves as a guide in the "real world." For example: "Say to the blind man, you're free, open the door that was separating him from the world, Go, you are free, we tell him once more, and he does not go, he has remained motionless there in the middle of the road, he and the others, they are terrified, they do not know where to go, the fact is that there is no comparison between living in a rational labyrinth, which is, by definition, a mental asylum and venturing forth, into the demented labyrinth of the city, where memory will serve no purpose, for it will merely be able to recall the images of places but not the paths whereby we might get there."[35]

The plans, calculations, and agreements made before cannot serve as an effective guide for those having now to walk the turbulent roads of the city. This becomes clear early in the book when the car thief dies from an infected wound in his leg, unintentionally caused by a girl with dark glasses when he tried to molest her. When the girl sobs that the death has been her fault, the text reads as follows: "It was true, no one could deny it, but it is also true, if this brings her any consolation, that if, before every action, we were to begin weighing up the consequences, thinking about them in earnest, first the immediate consequences, then the probable, then the possible, then the imaginable ones, we should never move beyond the point where our first thought brought us to a halt."[36]

Indeed, how could one calculate in advance how to proceed once everybody is free to go home? No rational decision about the ordering of the dispersal procedure, say, according to considerations of distance from the homes, could account for the spontaneous, erratic, unpredictable feelings that are now rising, like the longing by the girl with dark glasses, who also happens to be a prostitute, for her parents:

> If they were to go from house to house, from the one that is closest to the one furthest away, the first house will be that of the girl with dark glasses, the second one that of the old man with the black eyepatch, then that of the doctor's wife, and finally the house of the first blind man. They will undoubtedly follow the itinerary because the girl with dark glasses has already asked that she should be taken to her home as soon as possible, I can't imagine what state my parents will be in, she said, this sincere preoccupation shows how groundless are the preconceived ideas of those who deny the possibility of the existence of deep feelings, including filial ones, in the, alas, abundant cases of irregular conduct, especially in matters of public morality.[37]

Rawls's second principle of justice could be applied to this situation by the actors behind a veil of ignorance deciding to give priority to those who will have a sudden emotional outburst in the real world, but such feelings are hard to account for in advance. Saramago believes in the existence of authentic feelings that cannot be simulated. This is conveyed by the doctor's wife, who says that "the feelings with which we have lived and which allowed us to live as we were, depended on our having the eyes we were born with, without eyes feelings become something different."[38] In a conversation with the girl with dark glasses, she explains that their new experience in the city requires the development of new feelings instructing them who they are, for at present all they have are memories, which are insufficient as an ethical guide.

The memory of who they were in their former state of existence does not provide the blind with a sense of who they presently are as moral beings. Saramago believes that the only effective force obliging us to do good and resist evil is our moral conscience: "The moral conscience that so many thoughtless people have offended against and many more have rejected, is something that has always existed, it was not an invention of the philosophers of the Quaternary, when the soul was little more than a muddled proposition."[39] He does not tell us where that moral conscience is to be found. All we are left with is a statement by the girl with dark glasses, who says: "Inside us there is something that has no name, that something is what we are."[40]

Even when asked about it in interviews, Saramago has refused to spell out his notion of morality. Interviewed by Anna Klobucka, he preferred to stick to an epigraph from *The Holy Family* by Karl Marx and Friedrich Engels: "'If the human being is shaped by his circumstances, then it is necessary to shape those circumstances humanely.' This contains all the wisdom I needed in order to become what it seems I am considered to be: a 'political moralist'."[41]

Yet Saramago's focus on moral conscience helps build up the link between the original position and political obligation in the theory of justice. Rawls assumes that individuals in the original position are moral persons, defined as "creatures having a conception of their good and capable of a sense of justice."[42] Both components of this definition are related to the assumption of rationality. Moral persons are presumed to have ends not ranked in value and the requisite ability to understand and to act upon the principles adopted in the original position. The moral duties to be expected of individuals, such as the duty of mutual respect, are also deduced by Rawls from the assumption of rationality. For example, individuals are expected to do small favours and courtesies and acknowledge those done to them because "although the parties in the original position take no interest in each other's interests, they know that in society they need to be assured by the esteem of their associates."[43]

Saramago's conception of moral conscience is also strongly rooted in rationality. In his Nobel lecture, for instance, he spoke about his illiterate grandparents who raised pigs and on cold winter nights would go to the sty and fetch the weaklings among the piglets, taking them to their bed. He made clear that it was not just a compassionate soul that prompted them to act in that way but the rational need to protect their daily bread. In similar fashion, the doctor's wife, the only person who does not become blind and serves as the author's model of the moral person, remains rational and calculating all along. She never loses her sense of purpose and even cuts the throat of the hoodlums' leader with scissors when there is no other way to save her and her companions' life and dignity.

But there is an added element here. Like Saramago's grandparents in the above tale, the doctor's wife combines rationality with compassion. When she invites a group of poor and hungry blind people to her home, the scene is described as a pilgrimage into paradise, both because, as a practical person, she took care of the house before leaving for the asylum, and because the "small favors and courtesies" she is involved in are accompanied by tenderness.

This has been noted by reviewers of *Blindness* such as Tim Parks, who stresses the contrast between the eye doctor who constantly talks about the need to organize and his wife's realization that no amount of organization will ever be enough to guarantee the most basic requirements of food and hygiene. She embodies an additional quality needed on the road to survival: "a growing physical tenderness toward the other members of the group, a sort of desperate respect for the human body, her own and others', which she transmits to her companions by simple acts of practical love."[44] Even her killing of the hoodlums' leader has been interpreted as an act combining rational and moral elements. That act, José Ornelas writes, "cannot really be framed by any specific conceptual system. Her action is not based on some sort of abstraction; rather it is an act of humanity or an act of solidarity with other human beings to re-establish reason, the very fabric of dialogic human interaction."[45]

Complementing Rawls's rigorous and coherent theory of justice with a vague and fuzzy concept like "moral conscience" is not easy but may be useful in light of the difficulty in otherwise understanding why individuals, such as Saramago's blind who emerge from the asylum into a devastated city, maintain a degree of mutual respect toward each other and toward the social and political order (epitomized in this novel by void and meaningless speeches given in public squares). The difficulty in incorporating the concept stems from the lack of criteria for distinguishing between moral conscience and the reasonable rules proposed by Rawls, or accounting for those, like the hoodlums, who ignore it. However, no rational calculation can, in itself, explain the effectiveness of the doctor's wife in maintaining a degree of order and cleanliness among the blind roaming the streets of the city unless it is accompanied by what Parks has referred to as "deep awareness of their now radical interdependence.[46] It is this awareness that makes individuals agree on rules of conduct in the first place and respect them, to a degree, when the conditions change.

The doctor's wife appears sometimes as a saint. The meal she serves to the poor and hungry, for instance, resembles a biblical rite: "In the middle of the table, the lamp was like a sun surrounded by shining stars."[47] But this should not mislead us. Saramago, the Portuguese Communist, is not putting his faith for survival of the human race in saints but in rational persons with practical interests who are nevertheless endowed with a degree of compassion needed for the initiation and maintenance of the social contract. He sees the combination of rationality and compassion as an authentic human quality embodied in the doctor's wife who sees the world while others fail to see it. As she says: "I am not a queen, no, I am simply the one who was born to see this horror, you can feel it, I both feel and see it."[48]

This quotation implies that the combination of rationality and compassion could become a significant social-political force once the eyes of others will also open up. Saramago does not develop this idea in *Blindness* but it can be found in his later novel *Seeing*, published in 2004. The story takes place in the same unnamed city four years after the blindness epidemic. Now, the doctor's wife is accused of treason because the qualities attributed to her in *Blindness* seem to have passed over to others. A majority of the population has taken a stand against an evil and corrupt government by casting a blank ballot in the elections, and the doctor's wife is investigated and ultimately shot for instigating what the government perceives as an organized rebellion (but has actually been a spontaneous act).

This literary exercise points at Saramago's belief that most people are too blind to see the need for compassion and tenderness as a means of survival but also at the possibility that the horrors surrounding them may generate an awareness of their radical interdependence. This awareness, when applied to Rawls's theory, may explain why moral decisions and political obligations are sometimes taking hold in the real world against all odds.

CONCLUSION

Living at the beginning of the twenty-first century, we owe a great deal to John Rawls, who renewed the discourse on justice and provided the language for its consideration in such a way that the desires of individuals, groups, and nations are not allowed to serve as the only guide for action. Many of the horrors that occurred in the twentieth century stemmed from the definition of crude interests as moral imperatives, and Rawls's theory of justice provided an alternative by guiding us to view our actions in separation from such interests. Although no theory can be expected to change the way decisions are made in reality, Rawls provided a standard for the evaluation of policies in a wide range of areas such as social welfare, international intervention, and human rights. A fair and just policy is one that exceeds particularistic notions of the private or public good, however noble they seem, and accounts for those who may benefit the least from the policy. In a world that has largely given up on egalitarian aspirations in the social, economic, and political spheres, *A Theory of Justice* became a reminder of the need to respect not only our own liberty but also that of others.

We also owe a great deal to José Saramago, who singled out the difficulties we face on the road to justice: memories of the past that haunt us, contingencies that disrupt the process, and the presence of extreme evil in politics, business, and other areas, infringing on the fair allocation of resources. Saramago's *Blindness* is a thought-provoking novel that raises hard questions on the value of dignity, the right of self-defence, the role of bystanders who observe evil, and similar questions asked today all over the world in regard to massacres, armed conflicts and many other occurrences of violence. In this chapter, I tried to show how, by relating *Blindness* to Rawls's theory of justice, we may clarify some of the problems raised by the theory's critics and enhance its application to social and political settings. This may also serve the more general purpose of realizing the combined contribution of political philosophy and literature in coping with the hard moral questions of our time.

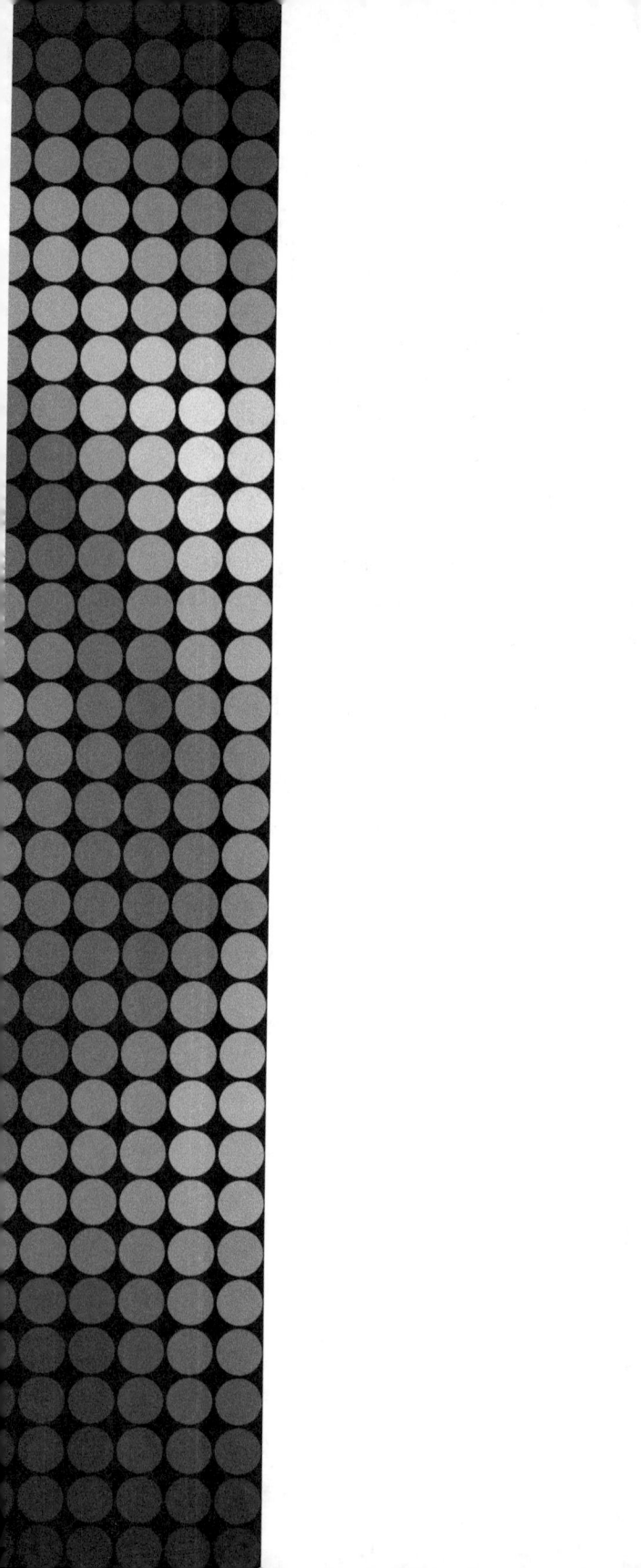

ABSURDITY AND REVOLT IN CORMAC MCCARTHY'S *THE ROAD*

In this chapter I identify four major themes of absurdity and revolt at the centre of Cormac McCarthy's 2006 novel *The Road* – transience, existentialism, reality's precedence with respect to storytelling, and trans-generational commitment – themes first developed both theoretically and literarily by Albert Camus and others in the crucible of the Second World War and its aftermath, more than half a century ago. These themes remain with us in this powerful twenty-first-century novel and continue to be useful standards for the evaluation of our lives both in the private and public spheres, especially with respect to our subjugation to technology and its electronic interpenetration of our interpersonal lives. In what follows, I analyze *The Road* within the framework of Camus's notions of absurdity and revolt, spell out the four themes, and discuss their usefulness as contemporary standards of evaluation.

THE ROAD **AND CAMUSIAN THOUGHT**

In *The Road* we follow the journey of a father and child pushing a supermarket cart on the road after the technological, economic, and political systems surrounding us have been destroyed. The reader is left wondering why the two continue, what allows them to endure, and why suicide is not the preferred option. The unnamed father and child walk through the grey-black remains of cities, villages, and forests burned to ashes, with dead bodies all around. "They passed through the site of a roadside hamlet burned to nothing. Some metal storage tanks, a few standing flues of blackened brick. There were gray slagpools of melted glass in the ditches and the raw lightwires lay in rusting skeins for miles along the edge of the roadway."[1]

The causes of the destruction are never given. *The Road* thus differs from didactic tales like Aldous Huxley's *Brave New World* that issue warnings of authoritarian control, domineering scientists, and the like. What we are faced with is what Camus, in his 1942 essay *The Myth of Sisyphus*, called "a universe suddenly divested of illusions and lights."[2] The setting is one in which all aspirations and illusions associated with the world as we know it have dissipated and the political, religious, and commercial rhetoric glorifying them have been silenced. Scrabbling through the charred ruins of a damp, rotten house with a corpse floating in the black water of the basement, the father sees for a brief moment "the absolute truth of the world. The cold relentless circling of the intestate earth. Darkness implacable. The blind dogs of the sun in their running. The crushing black vacuum of the universe."[3]

Why is the earth seen as dying intestate and why does the destruction not entail at least an ethical lesson? The answer lies in the difficulty of attributing meaning to the universe, which is the core of Camus's notion of the absurd. We are trying to attribute meaning to a world whose meaning escapes us. As Camus notes, "I don't know whether this world has a meaning that transcends it. But I know that I do not know that meaning and that it is impossible for me just now to know it."[4] But Camus also challenges us to face the absurd and not to commit either "philosophical suicide" by speculatively positing meaning without proof, or actual suicide as a result of the recognition that life is meaningless. Sisyphus, who rolls a stone up the mountain only to see it roll down, thus becomes a symbol of revolt. The Greek mythological hero is observed at a moment of agony, when he descends from the mountain to the plain. "A face that toils so close to stones is already stone itself! I see that man going back down with a heavy yet measured step toward the torment of which he will never know the end."[5] This is an "hour of consciousness,"[6] one in which Sisyphus, conscious and defiant of his fate, is free.

> I leave Sisyphus at the foot of the mountain! One always finds one's burden again. But Sisyphus teaches the higher fidelity that negates the gods and raises rocks. He too concludes that all is well. This universe henceforth without a master seems to him neither sterile nor futile. Each atom of that stone, each mineral flake of that night filled mountain, in itself forms a world. The struggle itself toward the heights is enough to fill a man's heart. One must imagine Sisyphus happy.[7]

The Myth of Sisyphus inspired many in the Second World War era with its call to overcome despair at a moment of great agony, allowing a ruined world to face its conditions with open eyes and rebel against illusory religious, political, and ideological doctrines. Camus warned a whole generation of the illusory nature of doctrines attributing fundamental values to an ineffable universe and called for a revolt against such doctrines, a revolt which gives life its value. "Spread out over the whole length of a life, it restores its majesty to that life."[8]

In 1947 Camus published *The Plague*, a strong literary representation of revolt. Variously interpreted as an allegory drawn from the Nazi occupation of France and as a statement of the human condition, the novel describes the Sisyphean efforts of a few individuals to help a population stricken by plague. Dr. Bernard Rieux, the medical doctor, and Jean Tarrou, the visitor who organizes sanitary squads, as well as a few others, are aware of the overwhelming power of the plague but refuse to give in to it. They know that all religious and political institutions have failed them and that their individual actions promise only inescapable defeat, but by refusing to give in to either illusory promise or the plague itself, they rebel. As the doctor says, "since the order of the world is shaped by death, mightn't it be better for God if we refuse to believe in Him, and struggle with all our might against death, without raising our eyes towards the heavens where He sits in silence?"[9] Camus insists that the rebellion stems not from virtues like courage and devotion, definitely not from Christian love as Father Paneloux, the priest, preaches in the novel, but from "comprehension,"[10] that is, understanding the absurd human condition.

In the post-war era, one could easily identify with the plague-stricken town of Oran, "hitherto so tranquil and now, out of the blue, shaken to its core."[11] The destruction caused by the Second World War and the disappointment with the religious and political systems that failed to prevent it led to reactions similar to those of the residents of Oran. "At such moments the collapse of their courage, willpower, and endurance was so abrupt that they felt they could never drag themselves out of the pit of despond into which they had fallen."[12] And yet Camus shows a way to persevere through the conscious application of common decency in human affairs. As Rieux says, "That's an idea which may make some people smile, but the only means of fighting a plague is—common decency."[13]

Although *The Plague* is a gloomy tale of death and suffering, Camus never gives up on recovery; the wartime loss of courage, willpower, and endurance is temporary. Even at the peak of the plague, when the town is at the mercy of the epidemic, the doctor considers the possibility that the pestilence may die out of its own accord, and when it does, the people of Oran still have a strong enough memory of their former life to look ahead toward restoration. The whole town, Camus writes, "was on the move, quitting the dark, lugubrious confines where it had struck its roots of stone, and setting forth at last, like a shipload of survivors, toward a land of promise."[14] At the end of the novel, the narrator, Dr. Rieux himself, while not approving of official declarations of victory over the plague, admits that "the dominion of the plague has ended."[15]. In other words, while the Sisyphean curse is never lifted, as the gods show no mercy and offer no salvation, the people of Oran do regain their consciousness and find the courage to keep going.

In his 1951 book *The Rebel*, Camus developed the earlier solitary character of Sisyphus into "the rebel," who feels solidarity with others. The rebel puts his whole being into the revolt and is willing to die as a consequence of the act of rebellion, which demonstrates that there is a common good he considers more important than his own destiny. The affirmation implicit in every act of rebellion, writes Camus, is extended to something which transcends the individual insofar as it withdraws him from his supposed solitude and provides him with a reason to act. Rebellion can only find its justification in solidarity with others. "In order to exist, man must rebel, but rebellion must respect the limit it discovers in itself—a limit where minds meet and, in meeting, begin to exist."[16] Although the nature of the meeting is elusive, it singles out Camus as a moralist.[17]

An important dimension of Camus's morality is his insistence upon a revolt that recognizes limits. Surveying historical revolutions which were motivated by nihilism and led to absolutism, he believes that there exists a moderate way of acting and thinking that does not expect to attain absolute political forms. Politics is no religion, and history should thus not be seen as an object of worship but as an opportunity that must be rendered fruitful by a vigilant rebellion. The most vigilant rebel, however, cannot achieve perfection; children will still die unjustly even in the best possible society because no individual can eliminate the suffering of the world. In recognizing such limits, the rebel differs from modern revolutionaries – be they fascists or communists – who pretended to change the course of history. The Rousseauian wish to reverse the advance of technology, for example, seems useless to Camus because, as he puts it, "The age of the spinning-wheel is over and the dream of a civilization of artisans is vain."[18]

The moderate rebellion he proposes is consistent with the notion of the absurd, as it does not propose a revolutionary scheme which turns the world over but sees the revolt in the willingness to move forward in spite of the absurdist conditions.

As I shall argue, the father and child in McCarthy's novel, who have no illusions about the void universe but persist in their journey on the road, may be seen as figures in a literary representation of Camus's notions of absurdity and revolt.

ABSURDITY AND REVOLT IN *THE ROAD*

Camus's notions of absurdity and revolt remain relevant in the twenty-first century,[19] especially with respect to the growing influence of electronic and digital mass media. The events of the latter half of the twentieth century, and first years of the twenty-first century—the wars, the political crises, the social movements—have been accompanied by the development and massive dissemination of information technologies, especially cable television and the Internet, which have become the main filters through which events are received and interpreted. And at the beginning of the third millennium, new technologies threaten to alter human consciousness. When Tarrou is asked in *The Plague* what he means by "a return to normal life" he speaks with a smile of "new films in the picture houses."[20] Sixty years later, films, soap operas, reality shows, video games, social media, and other forms of communication not only mark normal life but seem to dominate it. Certainly the Sisyphus who in the 1940s was happy at the foot of the mountain because of his non-illusory comprehension of the human condition faces new challenges in the present age of political, commercial, and media spin and information overload. Non-illusory comprehension, beyond the ubiquitous rhetoric of happiness, may be slipping beyond our grasp.

In his 1985 book *Amusing Ourselves to Death*, Neil Postman noted the collapse of the discourse of reason in the television age, showing how television made entertainment the natural format for the representation of all experience. Our television set keeps us in constant communion with the world, he writes, but it does so with a face whose smiling countenance is unalterable. Entertainment has become the supra-ideology of all discourse on television, and even news shows depicting tragedy and barbarism are part of a format for entertainment, not for education, reflection, or catharsis.[21] And it is clear that the entertainment format has also enframed Internet culture.[22]

In *The Age of Missing Information*, Bill McKibben showed how television encourages a non-reflective culture by making individuals lose their orientation to both space and time. Electronic media have become an environment of their own, he writes, a global village in which local and regional consciousness is supplanted and "placelessness" prevails due to the fact that electronic content makes sense across virtually all regions and cultures; it is dubbed and copied around the planet.[23] Television leads us to ignore the progression of time by expecting us to shift entirely each half hour from fear or sadness to laughter and back. There is no rhythm, McKibben writes, nothing like the image of summer following spring to help you orient yourself over the course of a lifetime, which in turn makes it very strange to grow old and die. "Television never grows old, never ceases that small talk that may be innocuous when you're thirty but should be monstrous by the end of your life."[24]

Cultural critics have noted the impact of television on the human consciousness through its use of artificial means like dazzling studio lights, smiling news anchors, recorded laughter, and the like to create a false sense of happiness which blurs the distinction between information and entertainment and desensitizes us to the tragedy, barbarism, and death we are exposed to in large portions. These observations, however, become even timelier in the age of the Internet. Communication experts have often expressed enthusiasm about computer-mediated communication technologies seen as supporting human traits such as "the desire to communicate, the desire for freedom from arbitrary authority, a resistance to uniformity and a preference for diversity, a love of the unexpected and the serendipitous."[25] Yet the Internet often seems to weaken, not strengthen, the human sense of reality. Individuals engaged in blogging, chatting, tweeting, or interacting with Facebook friends do indeed satisfy their human desire for self-expression and free communication, but these activities are mostly confined to cyberspace, where comprehension is challenged by noise, social discourse by chatter, politics by public relations, friendship by electronic interaction, and consciousness of the absurd by an unending quest for happiness. A blogger's announcement that "spring is in the air and that means leafy green Web sites are popping up all over the web" hardly reflects the change of seasons. A site like "if i die" (www.ifidie.net), allowing Facebook users to record a message to be posted to their Facebook page posthumously, does not enhance a genuine consciousness of life and death. When Sisyphus is imagined climbing the mountain with an iPad and headphones, he cannot be understood as comprehending the futility and sterility of the universe.

The Internet is more detrimental than television to a non-illusory comprehension of reality because television viewers are generally aware of the escapist nature of the medium, even when watching "reality shows," whereas Internet users may easily be led to confuse virtual reality with actual reality. For example, the enthusiasm among communications scholars over new media has made some of their writings resemble the ideologies of the interwar era in their promise of a redemptive political future. Millions of individuals sitting at their computers were taken to represent a democratic public sphere, while new media may encourage a politics of solitude that is more consistent with totalitarianism than with democracy.[26] The Internet is an effective tool for the mobilization of support for important causes, but it often creates the illusion that computer-mediated communication among virtual publics may substitute for political activism in the real world, an illusion allowing wars and atrocities, inequality and injustice, political corruption, environmental destruction, and many other social ills to continue undisturbed.[27]

In *The Road*, McCarthy turns off the screens, exposes the violence and destruction in the real and ineffable universe, and sets the parameters of the twenty-first century's revolt. The novel was not necessarily designed to turn us away from the mass media's amusements, or to show us how to live conscious lives devoid of illusions, but in very real ways it does do those things. The father and child's walk on the road with no illusions about the absurdity of the world may be seen as an updated version of Camus's revolt. To show this, I shall now identify four major themes of that revolt at the core of McCarthy's novel: the realization that life is transient, the precedence given to existence over essence, the refusal to substitute storytelling about reality for reality itself, and a genuine commitment to succeeding generations.

1. Transience

The Road begins with the following words: "When he woke in the woods in the dark and the cold of the night he'd reached out to touch the child sleeping beside him. Nights dark beyond darkness and the days more gray each one than what had gone before."[28] These words are reminiscent of the second sentence in *Genesis*: "And the earth was without form, and void; and darkness was upon the face of the deep." The universe in *The Road* is presented in its bare, unilluminated state with the lights over grocery stores and gas stations shut off. Significantly, the dark setting involves change, growth, and transformation, as when the father counts each frail breath of the shivering child and the two of them look at bare strands of second-growth timber. This stands in contrast to media images whose mostly fast and hasty movement fails to represent change, growth, and transformation. Electronic and digital media provide us with more information than we have ever had and expose us to a larger variety of events than we've ever experienced, but the magnitude of the information and the speed with which the events are passing through us lead to a media phantasmagoria with little room for subtle and sensitive observations of the kind attributed in this novel to the father and child. Consider the following exchange between them:

> Are we going to die?
>
> Sometime. Not now.
>
> And we're still going south.
>
> Yes.
>
> So we'll be warm.
>
> Yes...
>
> I'm going to blow out the lamp, is that okay?
>
> Yes. That's okay.[29]

This simple exchange involves recognition of the distinction between light and darkness, warm and cold, north and south, life and death. These basic distinctions have always been of concern to humans but are getting blurred in the contemporary world in which electronic and digital technologies allow us to enjoy everlasting lights on our computer screens without worrying about dawn or sunset (which we may not even notice when we are online), to keep a constant room or office temperature, to follow a GPS with no clear sense of where we are going, and to construct for ourselves a virtual "Second Life." *The Road*, on the other hand, serves as a reminder that no virtual construct or other illusion will allow us to overcome the constraints of reality. In the father's dreams, some visions appear to him in white, but when he wakes up he realizes the falling snow is not white but grey. He knows that his and his son's survival depend on hard work in the real world and he therefore wakens himself from the siren worlds coming to him in his dreams: "He said the right dreams for a man in peril were dreams of peril and all else was the call of languor and death."[30]

The Road not only dismisses illusions but highlights the importance of facing the transience of life in a sober and straightforward way. Only when we face reality and recognize that life is transient can we sense movement and growth. Without turning death into a moving force of life,[31] McCarthy shows life to be enriched by the recognition that death is part of it. Once humans do not pretend to be immortal by building pyramids or creating posthumous Facebook pages, they may share in "the minutes of the earth and the hours and the days of it and the years." The novel's two protagonists live in time and do not believe in eternity for, as the child puts it, "ever is no time at all."[32] Nor do they believe in promises of a happier world made by politicians, advertisers, and talk show hosts. As the father warns the boy: "When your dreams are of some world that never was or of some world that never will be and you are happy again then you will have given up. Do you understand? And you cant give up. I wont let you."[33]

2. Existentialism

The father's warning not to give up on life by abandoning reality for dream and survival for promise contains a significant existentialist echo. Existentialism has many definitions and interpretations,[34] but *The Road* can be read as a fundamentally existentialist tale in its emphasis on the precedence of existence over essence. I refer to the claim that individual action matters, and whatever determinants we attribute to it, we are shaped by what we do rather than by God, nature, or society. We interact with our environment, which is often threatening and hostile, but our fate is the product of our own making. As Sartre writes, "man first of all exists, encounters himself, surges up in the world – and defines himself afterwards. . . . Man is nothing else but that which he makes of himself. That is the first principle of existentialism."[35] Following Nietzsche, Sartre recognized the contingencies within which we live, but unlike Nietzsche, he put his faith not in heroic affirmation but in what John Duncan calls "a necessarily imperfect and often messy Sisyphusian activism uninterested in romantic posturing."[36]

McCarthy's characters never abandon a non-illusory view of their surroundings. They act and hardly talk. They move forward even though there is no vision to follow and no lighthouse to point the way in the darkness. In the first part of the book the father and child are walking south toward the sea, but when they reach it, they are disappointed to find that the sea is not blue but grey. Yet, the two keep going because it is not the blue sea or any other destination that gives meaning to their journey. What we become is the outgrowth of what we do. This idea is demonstrated when the two find their own footsteps on the ground and conclude that by following them they will be going in the right direction—they will be doing what they are doing. Similarly, when they arrive at the ruins of the house in which the father grew up, the latter realizes that his childhood dreams had no chance of fulfillment because life consists of our activities, not our dreamy plans. "This is where I used to sleep. My cot was against this wall. In the nights in their thousands to dream the dreams of a child's imaginings, worlds rich or fearful such as might offer themselves but never the one to be."[37] In *The Road*, existence always precedes essence; even the names given to things are seen as void. People have always called the things they see by names, which has endowed these things with higher qualities and meanings, as when certain species of birds are called "songbirds." In this novel, however, all names fade in the father's memory: "The names of things slowly following those things into oblivion. Colors. The names of birds. Things to eat. Finally the names of things one believed to be true. More fragile than he would have thought."[38] By making names fade, the author demonstrates the fragility and futility of the attempt to attribute additional meanings to things. Also, when the father and child assure an old man they meet on the road that they are not robbers and he asks them what they are, the author writes: "They'd no way to answer the question."[39] It is then the old man himself who, responding to the father's questions, articulates the idea that reality is indifferent to the plans designed by humans and to the meanings they attribute to it:

> How do you live?
>
> I just keep going. I knew this was coming.
>
> You knew it was coming?
>
> Yeah. This or something like it. I always believed in it.
>
> Did you try to get ready for it?
>
> No. What would you do?
>
> I don't know.
>
> People were always getting ready for tomorrow. I didn't believe in that. Tomorrow wasn't getting ready for them. It didn't even know they were there.
>
> I guess not.
>
> Even if you knew what to do you wouldn't know what to do. You wouldn't know if you wanted to do it or not.[40]

Here, then, lies the second theme of absurdity and revolt. There is no world besides what we make of it. The meanings we mistakenly assume to arise from our surroundings are fragile. We are the product of our deeds rather than of our visions. And we keep going.

3. Storytelling and Reality

The Road leaves no room for any story to be told besides the life story that unfolds at any given moment. In every conversation with the child, the father focuses entirely on the mundane tasks of survival. For example:

> Are we going to die now?
>
> No.
>
> What are we going to do?
>
> We're going to drink some water. Then we're going to keep going down the road.
>
> Okay.[41]

The focus on the mundane tasks of survival does not stem from dismissal of the larger spiritual issues brought up by the child but rather from necessity. There simply is no story to tell unless one is willing to invent lies; there is no tale other than the one occurring at present. The father therefore dismisses all tales, visions, and dreams, including his own dreams about his late wife, which represent to him a futile attempt to escape reality:

> In his dream she was sick and he cared for her. The dream bore the look of sacrifice but he thought differently. He did not take care of her and she died alone somewhere in the dark and there is no other dream nor other waking world and there is no other tale to tell.[42]

How then can he cope with the child's need for stories? What stories can he tell him when he inquires about the past, as children do? As much as the father wants to satisfy that need, he finds no story to tell.

He thought hard how to answer. There is no past. What would you like? But he stopped making things up because those things were not true either and the telling made him feel bad. The child had his own fantasies. How things would be in the south. Other children. He tried to keep a rein on this but his heart was not in it. Whose would be?[43]

The author does not grant us the privilege to invent stories, such as the mythologies explaining the creation of the earth or the learned essays of philosophers. This privilege is apparently no longer available to us after the horrors of the twentieth century; if we were to tell the true story of that century, it would fail to capture the voice of the dead, the smell of the butchered, and the sight of the oppressed. At times it seems as if the author is expressing his own difficulty in telling the story of a world that has lost its sense of life, as when the father realizes that any story about the past would be suspect. "He could not reconstruct for the child's pleasure the world he'd lost without constructing the loss as well and he thought perhaps the child had known this better than he."[44]

Toward the end of the novel, the child no longer asks for stories as he realizes that storytelling cannot change his fate. The value of life lies in living it, not in painting it pink. When the father asks whether to tell him a story, he says no:

Why not?

Those stories are not true.

They don't have to be true. They're stories.

Yes. But in the stories we're always helping people and we don't help people.

Why don't you tell me a story?

I don't want to.

Okay.

I don't have any stories to tell.

You could tell me a story about yourself.

You already know the stories about me. You were there.[45]

A common story which persists over time and across cultures is that of a supreme being whose presence provides people with a sense of direction and allows them to unburden themselves of responsibility for the evils they inflict on others. Yet, in spite of many religious elements in *The Road*,[46] the author does not grant us this comfort: "On this road there are no godspoke men. They are gone and I am left and they have taken with them the world. Query: How does the never to be differ from what never was?"[47] This approach is consistent with the refusal of existentialist thinkers to substitute the will of God for the human imperative to act (and the responsibility this imperative entails).[48] The two main characters do not make this point themselves. It is brought up by the old man they meet, who tells them: "There is no God and we are his prophets,"[49] adding that "where men can't live gods fare no better."[50] McCarthy keeps the role of God ambivalent. A supreme power is definitely not absent from the novel; the father feels he has been appointed by God to protect his son. What the author does not accept are common religious interpretations and morals. For example, the descriptions of the world's destruction resemble doomsday prophecies but are not related to theological notions of sin. "Within a year there were fires on the ridges and deranged chanting. The screams of the murdered. By day the dead impaled on spikes along the road. What had they done? He thought that in the history of the world it might even be that there was more punishment than crime but he took small comfort from it."[51]

The lack of common religious morals does not abolish the distinction between good and evil; the father and son aspire not to do evil. They will always be good, the father promises, and evil is not going to afflict them because they are "carrying the fire." The Promethean myth of the fire stolen for mankind and carried by the torchbearer from generation to generation is applied here to a man and boy who have not given up (as the boy's mother did) on life. There are no special attributes that prepared them for the task other than their endurance on the road, which stands in contrast to the mother's reliance on visions of the future. "Sooner or later they will catch us and they will kill us," she said before committing suicide.[52] The fire, however, is given to those who carry on, even if for no apparent reason. In the morning after the mother disappears, never to be seen again, the father and child get up and set out upon the road. They both realize she may have been right, but their existence is not the outgrowth of calculations about right and wrong or deliberations about the value of life held "with the eagerness of philosophers chained to a madhouse wall."[53] They simply endure, and their endurance becomes a major literary representation of revolt in the face of the absurd.

4. Trans-generational Commitment

In *The Rebel*, Camus emphasizes the strong relationship between rebellion and solidarity. "Man's solidarity is founded upon rebellion, and rebellion, in its turn, can only find its justification in this solidarity."[54] For Camus, human solidarity is the inner meaning of rebellion; rebellion is meaningless unless embodied in solidarity[55] This strong relationship is a major theme of *The Road*. The father and child walking on the road may raise comparisons to the father and son in Christianity or in the biblical story of the sacrifice of Isaac, but at no point in the book does the option exist of sacrificing the boy's life for a higher ideal. The father's welfare cannot be separated from the health and well-being of his son, and it is inconceivable to define his individuality without considering the two's interdependence.

The Road not only highlights the interdependence but shows it to be a condition of survival. In the harsh world described in the novel, there is still a slim chance of survival as a result of the father's love and care. As mentioned before, the book begins with the father in the dark and cold woods reaching out and touching his child. "His hand rose and fell softly with each precious breath."[56] There is little to add to this beautiful description, as if the full commitment involved in the relationship can only be conceived in the world after its destruction. In the contemporary world in which we consume the next generations' resources, destroy the planet on which they will have to live, and often define love and care by the number of "likes" on our Facebook pages, it is unusual to follow a relationship consisting of a father's hand moving to the rhythm of his child's breath, with very few words exchanged between them. The novel includes many instances of a father's tender care. "He woke in the dark of the woods in the leaves shivering violently. He sat up and felt about for the boy. He held his hand to the thin ribs. Warmth and movement. Heartbeat."[57] The father looks at the boy in his sleep, comforts him when he is cold and hungry, and protects him in all circumstances. The land they walk in is "Barren, silent, godless,"[58] but the boy is a godly gift. "He knew only that the child was his warrant. He said: If he is not the word of God God never spoke."[59] He takes the need to take care of his son as a godly imperative: "My job is to take care of you. I was appointed to do that by God. I will kill anyone who touches you. Do you understand?"[60] When the boy becomes ill, the father gives him the most devoted and tender care. "He held him all night, dozing off and waking in terror, feeling for the boy's heart. . . . He wiped his white mouth while he slept. I will do what I promised, he whispered. No matter what. I will not send you into the darkness alone."[61]

But the father is not immortal and becomes ill himself. "In some other world," the author reminds us, "the child would already have begun to vacate him from his life. But he had no life other."[62] When the boy realizes his father is dying, he begs him to take him along. This cannot be done, because the fire has to be carried on, but the father promises he will always continue to be there for his child. "If I'm not here you can still talk to me," he says. "You can talk to me and I'll talk to you. You'll see."[63] Although he is mortal, the boy will always be able to hear his voice. "You have to make it like talk that you imagine. And you'll hear me. You have to practice. Just don't give up."[64] And the boy does not give up. When the father dies, he kneels beside the body wrapped in a blanket and cries. "He cried for a long time. I'll talk to you every day, he whispered. And I won't forget. No matter what. Then he rose and turned and walked back out to the road."[65]

At the end of the novel, a man and woman come out of the woods and take the boy under their care as the journey continues. This unexpected turn is consistent with the theme of trans-generational commitment that endures a father's death. The child continues to be protected because the commitment by a mortal person is no less assuring than the belief in an immortal entity. As we learn about the boy: "He tried to talk to God but the best thing was to talk to his father and he did talk to him and he didn't forget."[66]

The Road places commitment at the centre of revolt. *The Plague*'s protagonist, Dr. Rieux, is also fully committed to his patients, whom he nurses day and night, but Rieux separates himself emotionally from his patients in order to fulfill his tasks:

> Indeed, for Rieux his exhaustion was a blessing in disguise. Had he been less tired, his senses more alert, that all-pervading odour of death might have made him sentimental. But when a man has had only four hours' sleep, he isn't sentimental. He sees things as they are; that is to say, he sees them in the garish light of justice; hideous, witless justice.[67]

For the father in McCarthy's novel, however, the child's fate is not a task to be fulfilled because it is just and righteous but because the child is an inseparable part of his own being. He simply knows that his existence and that of the child are inseparable, "that the boy was all that stood between him and death."[68] He realizes that their survival is not assured, that the mother may have been right in preferring suicide over the uncertain walk on the road, but he pursues the journey, knowing that by living a life of full bond with the boy, life is fulfilled to the utmost: "He sat the boy down and pulled off his shoes and pulled off the dirty rags with which his feet were wrapped. Everything's okay, he whispered. Everything's okay."[69]

This theme of trans-generational commitment is one of the most important themes to be considered in the context of the twenty-first century. Existentialist and other thinkers have not neglected the elements of love and commitment,[70] and individuals often show commitment to others, but can we really say that "everything's okay" when our existence on this planet involves an exhaustion of resources and environmental destruction or when we have no idea what the electronic and digital media we disseminate in uncontrolled quantities may bear for future generations? Will they lead to an expansion of consciousness or rather to a closing of the mind? Like Camus, McCarthy does not provide us with normative guidelines, but neither does his novel allow us to neglect trans-generational commitment as a major component of our existence.

CONCLUSION

McCarthy's *The Road* updates Camus's notions of the absurd and revolt in the context of the early twenty-first century. The post-apocalyptic tale of a father and child walking on the road serves as a timely reminder that life is worth living not only when we immerse ourselves in transcendental hopes, redemptive ideologies, and virtual reality but when we recognize the futility of these constructs and yet endure. This reminder is important in an age in which new media of mass communication threaten to alter human consciousness. With cyberspace turning into a major arena in which we receive political information, conduct economic activities, get educated, play games, make friends, etc., we may become less sensitive to the distinction between reality and its virtual representations. In this chapter, I identified four major themes of absurdity and revolt in McCarthy's novel: the realization that life is transient, the precedence given to existence over essence, the refusal to exchange storytelling about reality for reality, and a genuine and concrete commitment to the next generations.

These four themes may serve as useful standards for the evaluation of our present life both in the private and public spheres. Human life is, of course, too complex to be placed within a simple typology separating conscious and unconscious existence. There are lots of variations to consider besides the authenticity of the rebel who recognizes the absurdity of life and the enslavement associated here with new media that blur our conception of time and space, challenge our freedom and privacy, and mistake superficial interactions for human commitment. There are obviously many options open to us for conducting our private and public affairs in the age of new media, and it would be wrong to search for a free and authentic existence only in a world that has experienced a major catastrophe.

The Road, however, makes us aware of the need to evaluate every step we take on the road of life in terms of the degree of consciousness we maintain. The massive introduction of communication technologies into society and culture today is accompanied by a redemptive rhetoric which does not differ much from the language of past ideologies. And like the public intellectuals who served as "fellow travellers" of these ideologies, communication researchers are often serving the producers and marketers of new communication technologies in their willingness to prematurely attribute to those technologies social values such as freedom, democracy, and civil engagement. It would be safer to assume that today's digital revolution will follow every other technological revolution in the past in having both positive and negative social implications. Therefore, as we go through today's revolution, we must ask ourselves at every turn whether we exist as free, creative, committed individuals or are deluded by a false rhetoric of happiness, whether our awareness of the world's problems as a result of the flood of information in the electronic and digital media involves a concrete attempt to solve them, and whether our political associations are based on genuine civil solidarity or on superficial ties that involve no real commitment to anything – least of all to the next generations. By making us think about these Camusian themes in the contemporary world, *The Road* demonstrates rather forcefully the contribution of the literary imagination to existentialist thought.

CHAPTER 4

THE BYSTANDER'S TALE: GIL COURTEMANCHE'S *A SUNDAY AT THE POOL IN KIGALI*

When it comes to genocide, most of us are bystanders. The bystander is someone present, but not involved, in an event demanding involvement, such as an individual ignoring a street fight or a nation-state refraining from humanitarian intervention. The role of bystander is unrelated to the specific conditions of the event. Whether we have full information about the genocide or just scattered fragments, whether it occurs close to home or in some remote country, whether we have the will to intervene but not the power, or the power and not the will, we cannot escape a degree of responsibility for it.

Gil Courtemanche's *A Sunday at the Pool in Kigali*[1] is a novel about the Rwandan genocide of 1994, in which an estimated 800,000 Tutsis were brutally murdered within a period of three months by the Hutu-controlled state with little to no interference by individuals, states, or international organizations. The novel joins a long list of works on the Rwandan genocide: books by journalists and scholars such as Linda Melvern's *Conspiracy to Murder*[2] and Philip Gourevitch's *We Wish to Inform You That Tomorrow We Will be Killed With Our Families;*[3] eyewitness accounts, such as Immaculee Ilibagiza's *Left to Tell;*[4] reports by international organizations, such as the Organization of African Unity's "Rwanda: The Preventable Genocide";[5] legal documents, such as the minutes of the United Nations' International Criminal Tribunal for Rwanda;[6] films such as "Hotel Rwanda" and "Sometime in April"; documentaries such as "Triumph of Evil" and "The Last Just Man"; J. T. Rogers's play *The Overwhelming*; and many others.

The lengthy reports, learned treatises, detailed accounts, horrific pictures, earthshaking testimonies, retrospective reflections, and works of fiction and art attempt to cope with the hard questions raised by the events of spring 1994: What motivated a small, poor state in Africa to plan, execute, and devote substantial resources to butchery of 15 percent of its citizens? What accounts for its success in killing, over a three-month period, close to a million people with machetes and other simple weaponry? What went through the minds of those who killed, raped, and tortured men, women, and children who were often their next-door neighbors? What went through the minds of those who sold the Hutu regime the machetes? What kept the international community silent? What explains the stonehearted policies of France, Belgium, Great Britain, the United States, and other signatories of the Universal Declaration of Human Rights? How could United Nations officials stay idle in face of detailed information on the genocide coming in on a daily basis? Why did other international organizations, NGOs, missionaries, and human rights watch groups turn out to be so ineffective? And why did the world media devote so little attention to the Rwandan genocide?

These questions will always remain open, and Courtemanche's novel does not provide more answers than other works on the Rwandan genocide but stands out in the light it sheds on the bystander's role. This explains the interest the novel sparked in Canada following its publication in French in 2000 and in English in 2003. Novels such as Franz Werfel's *The Forty Days of Musa Dagh*, Primo Levi's *The Monkey's Wrench*, or Eli Wiesel's *Night* have been very effective in bringing the reality of genocide to the attention of large publics. This novel, however, has become a national bestseller not only because of the decision by the author, a Montreal journalist, to use the genre of the novel to convey the story of a genocide,[7] but because *A Sunday at the Pool in Kigali* is to a large extent the bystander's tale, and, as such, it hit a nerve in Canada, a country tormented by its failure to make a difference in Rwanda.

Canada has long been engaged in controversy over the failure of UN forces to slow or halt the genocide. Some have criticized General Roméo Dallaire, the Canadian commander of UNAMIR (United Nations Assistance Mission in Rwanda) for sticking to rules and procedures when bold action was needed, while others have emphasized the impossible position Dallaire found himself in, lacking the experience, authority and capability to make a difference in the crisis. Whatever one's stand in this controversy, it has sensitized Canadians to the Rwandan genocide and made them realize the magnitude of the international community's failure in preventing it.

In his memoir *Shake Hands With The Devil*, Dallaire wrote that "the international community, through an inept UN mandate and what can only be described as indifference, self-interest and racism, aided and abetted these crimes against humanity."[8] These words resonate with Canadians who have always taken pride in their country's international peacekeeping missions and were therefore bewildered in the 1990s when these missions failed in Somalia, Rwanda, and the former Yugoslavia. These failures led to revisionist conceptions of peacekeeping among Canadian historians[9] and to a shift in the public image of the peacemaker from saviour to bystander. "The traumatized peacekeeper, an important Canadian icon," Sherene Razack wrote, "is a man who bears witness to the savagery and who is overcome by it."[10] Many Canadians concurred with Dallaire's summary of the tragedy and felt they too had "watched as the devil took control of paradise on earth and fed on the blood of the people we were supposed to protect."[11]

Courtemanche is also very critical of the failure of Canada and other members of the international community to intervene in Rwanda but insists it was not the devil we were watching that spring of 1994 but real people killing other people. This is a central assumption made by the author, which turns the Rwandan genocide from an event occurring on a different planet inhabited by devils to one occurring in the political reality we are part of and share responsibility for.

In this novel, the Rwandan genocide is not occurring in the "heart of darkness," Joseph Conrad's 1902 metaphor. When Conrad's narrator, the steamship captain Marlow, sails to Africa, he leaves civilization behind: "The rest of the world was nowhere, as far as our eyes and ears were concerned. Just nowhere. Gone, disappeared; swept off without leaving a whisper or a shadow behind."[12] And Conrad's main character Kurtz, the European colonialist, is the manifestation of evil. "His was an impenetrable darkness. I looked at him as you peer down at a man who is lying at the bottom of a precipice where the sun never shines."[13] Conrad's readers thus join Marlow in an adventurous journey to Africa, where they observe the manifestation of evil before returning safely to the shores of Europe, where they can indulge in what Nigerian novelist Chinua Achebe has ironically called "those advanced and humane views appropriate to the English liberal tradition which required all Englishmen of decency to be deeply shocked by atrocities in Bulgaria or the Congo of King Leopold of the Belgians or wherever."[14]

Achebe accused Conrad of making Africa "a metaphysical battlefield devoid of all recognizable humanity."[15] This critique is not without foundation; cultural historians have shown that the myth of Africa as a remote, dark continent devoid of recognizable humanity had strong roots in Western thought.[16] This myth can still be detected in reports on the Rwandan genocide at the end of the twentieth century. For example, in 1995 journalist Philip Gourevitch went on a series of trips to Rwanda, where he gathered testimonies about the genocide. His reports, published in the *New Yorker* and later in book form, reflect his difficulty in telling the story from other than an outsider's perspective. As he admits, "I took Marlow's condition on returning from Africa as my point of departure."[17] He realizes there is a difference between what happened and what he imagines to have happened and settles for the latter, writing that the horror as horror interests him "only in so far as a precise memory of the offense is necessary to understand its legacy."[18] In other words, we are faced with reports which frame the genocide in those familiar terms ingrained in our memory (mostly derived from the legacy of the Holocaust) while leaving out much of the specific reality.

This is where *A Sunday at the Pool in Kigali* comes in. Courtemanche disapproves of his fellow journalists who, "ignorant as tortoises,"[19] arrive in Rwanda after the genocide to produce quarter-hour human interest pieces, being led by local guides "from one common grave to the next."[20] Having not been in Rwanda himself during the genocide, he realizes the difficulty in representing the horrors from the perspective of the perpetrators and victims. He does, however, provide a rather authentic account of the events by constructing the character of Valcourt, the ultimate bystander who lives in Rwanda "without getting involved or taking sides in anything."[21] By telling the Rwanda story from Valcourt's angle, he puts a mirror to his own face, and to ours.

Once we observe the events from the bystander's perspective, they no longer occur within the "heart of darkness" but become part of a mundane political reality. In what follows, I show some of the insights we gain from this novel on that reality, especially on the political context of the Rwandan genocide, its dynamics, its rhetoric, and the international response to it. I then comment on the novel's contribution to the question of the bystander's responsibility.

1. THE POLITICAL CONTEXT OF THE GENOCIDE

Conrad's Kurtz, the product of an era in which the colonial project was treated with fascination even by its critics,[22] has a romantic aura to him. He is identified with "vigorous action";[23] he is part of "the heavy, mute spell of the wilderness";[24] and is seen as a "remarkable man who had pronounced a judgment upon the adventures of his soul on this earth."[25] Courtemanche's Valcourt, on the other hand, is anything but vigorous. He is, rather, a product of the postcolonial context in which this novel (and the Rwandan genocide) is set.

The novel's events unfold in Kigali after independence, with the obligatory symbols of decolonization: Constitution Square, Development Avenue, Boulevard of the Republic, Justice Avenue. The colonial past is mentioned at length, but the tale is about evil stemming from present realities, not from past memories. This is what "postcolonialism" refers to here: a condition in former colonies affected by the colonial past but not identical with it, one of social, economic, and political patronage by a nexus of local and global agencies.[26]

The story begins at the pool of Hôtel des Milles Collines (known as "Hotel Rwanda"), where we meet a collection of cultural representatives, including "international experts and aid workers, middle-class Rwandans, screwed-up or melancholy expatriates of various origins, and prostitutes."[27] The author describes the "artificial paradise"[28] that emerges when global agencies concerned with "development" launch projects that enrich corrupt elements inside and outside the country but are mostly irrelevant to the Rwandan population.

Postcolonialism is a new game, and the players do not resemble their colonial forefathers; their skin is of all colors and they often come to Africa to assist rather than to exploit. Valcourt is a clear example. A Radio-Canada producer, he has been commissioned to establish an educational television station in Rwanda that would spread information on prevention, hygiene, and dietary matters. To the Canadian development agency financing the project, this activity was expected to lead to "democracy and tolerance,"[29] but the Rwandan government would not allow the disclosure of undesired information about the conditions of its citizens and Valcourt thus ends up sipping beer for two years at the pool in Kigali.

Valcourt is no colonialist, and his attraction to the land does not stem from an economic or political interest or from a fascination with Africa. He is an actor in a new postcolonial scene which lacks the romantic glory that had sometimes been associated with colonialism. "Valcourt was as arid as a desert, like dead earth that rejects seed. He was being eaten away by the hopelessness of living, the malady that afflicts only those who can afford the time to think about themselves. Valcourt was dead though alive."[30] This barren existence stems from the replacement of Valcourt's Quebecois identity with the identity of a global citizen, which is all but surreal due to the futility of the postcolonial project he is involved in: "The plot is heavy-handed and the characters behave as predictably as in a TV soap opera."[31] Many development initiatives in Africa are hopeless. A third of Kigali's adults are HIV positive, but at the hotel pool we find the president's nephews, one of whom – a former political science student in Quebec – organizes death squads, while the other controls the sale of condoms donated by international aid agencies. The abolishment of colonial rule, according to Courtemanche, has not helped the African people. Globalization provides new opportunities for some local forces but not for the masses. A Rwandan just back from Paris, for instance, is portrayed by his sporty outfit, sunglasses, a crocodile attaché case, and an import licence for some product of secondary necessity in his pocket, which he will sell at a premium price.

The author describes the well-intentioned yet ineffective policies by international organizations which result in poverty and misery. The story of one AIDS patient shows the difficulty of complying with the dictates of the International Monetary Fund, which demands that the sick pay for hospital costs plus the cost of food and nursing. Another story of a local entrepreneur shows the difficulties involved in microcredit initiatives; he tries to sell anti-tuberculosis medicines only to find out that they are handed out by missionaries for free.

The hopelessness of the postcolonial project is illustrated by a love story between Valcourt and a twenty-two-year-old Tutsi girl named Gentille. Valcourt makes a commitment to save her, but it is clear from the outset that this commitment will not endure once things turn nasty. To him, Gentille is an exotic fantasy representing the vigour he misses in his life, while to her, Valcourt represents the lover from the movies she likes to watch for the long kisses, bouquets of flowers, and men with broken hearts. In other words, the postcolonial relations are too illusory to make us trust a foreigner's commitment to a local girl. Valcourt and other agents of international agencies working in Africa remain bystanders, "close enough to talk about it, even to write about it. But at the same time so isolated with their portable computers in their antiseptic rooms, and in their air-conditioned Toyotas, so surrounded by little Blacks trying to be like Whites that they think Black is the smell of the perfumes and cheap ointments sold in the Nairobi duty-free shop."[32]

The author reminds us that these bystanders – missionaries, aid and development experts, NGO activists, and the like – have not prevented the outburst of over one hundred wars in Africa since the end of colonialism. Moreover, in order to advance their noble causes they often co-operate with corrupt regimes, support ruthless dictators, and refrain from taking sides in local conflicts, which turns them, according to the author, into collaborators. Such collaboration is not surprising when governments are involved, for instance, when the Chinese government finances a highway allowing Rwanda's president to return from Kigali to his native region in comfort. It is more surprising when non-governmental bodies are involved, as in the case of Belgian nuns co-operating with the president's wife on the selling of babies for adoption. As one missionary tells Valcourt, there is hardly anybody who escapes the evils associated with the bystander's role:

> There are thousands of us missionaries in Africa who have chosen the path of silence, staking our faith on our presence and endurance. . . . We're not the only ones who think this way. Your humanitarian organizations would rather collaborate with a dictator than denounce him. . . . If I could testify before a court, I would have all the members of this government put in prison, plus at least half the international experts from the International Monetary Fund and the World Bank who, without the slightest scruple, feed the insatiable appetites of all the dictators in Africa.[33]

The social, economic, and political reality in Rwanda, then, is not seen as a simple extension of the colonial condition but as part of a new reality in which global and local agencies committed in theory to development of the African continent fail to save it from sickness, hunger, and genocide. By placing the events in this postcolonial context, the novel turns the death of Africans from a local to a global matter and the Rwandan genocide from an event occurring "out there," in a remote country in Africa, to an integral part of our political world. No country today, Courtemanche writes, belongs only to its soldiers and rabid patriots; the occurrences in any country affect the entire world. As one drunk Tutsi warns Valcourt when the genocide begins: "You still don't understand. Good little Westerner that you are, all tied up with fine sentiments and noble principles, you're witnessing the beginning of the end of the world."[34]

2. DYNAMICS OF THE GENOCIDE

At the beginning of the novel, we read about jackdaws as big as eagles and as numerous as house sparrows that caw all around the gardens of the Hôtel des Milles Collines. Such early warning signals of terrible things to come accentuate the sense of the vulnerability of the victims and the weakness of the bystanders. This is the chronicle of a death foretold; nothing will save Gentille, the Tutsi waitress, from torture and death. We are led into the genocide very slowly, and with every step it becomes clearer how helpless she is, and how useless Valcourt (who ultimately finds his way to Nairobi while she is forced to stay behind) becomes.

This is as much the story of Valcourt, the bystander, as of Gentille, the victim. Courtemanche avoids the tendency, found in several writings on the Holocaust, to place the events outside the sphere of politics.[35] To the contrary, the atrocities occur in a very real political setting, which raises important political questions: Why are decisions to commit ethnic cleansing carried out so precisely and enthusiastically?

How could a few hundred men planning the elimination of a segment of humanity believe that the majority of the population would agree to go along? How could they believe that the people would agree to turn into killers by the thousands? And how could they have been so sure of it? Though they remain unanswered, we are forced to consider these questions from a concrete political foundation rather than that of Achebe's "metaphysical battlefield devoid of all recognizable humanity."

These questions become even more concrete in light of the description of the genocide as an interruption of a vibrant, colourful, resourceful way of life. The Kigali market is "a lurid, spectacular tableau saying in its fashion that an indestructible Africa exists, an Africa of close proximity, elbow-rubbing, small business, resourcefulness."[36] By placing the tale in such a scene of endurance and persistence, the novel makes the reader recognize the often forgotten fact that the victims, while already doomed by the time we read about their "orgy of colour and noise, of bustle and loud, cheery voices," have not been born to be victims but rather to play what the author calls "a concerto to life. Small life, undistinguished, ordinary, wretched, boisterous, simple, rough, dumb, merry, life of whatever kind."[37] In history books, documentaries, and reports by international organizations, the perpetrators usually have faces while the dead victims are faceless. In this novel the reverse is true; the vibrant noises of the market are silenced when two anonymous militiamen wearing a cap of the president's party are twirling their machetes. "The market's cheerful, noisy anarchy had ceased, the way the birds in a forest fall silent when a predator creeps near."[38]

One of the rationalizations made by bystanders in horrific events is that they could not have known what was going on, but the author claims that information about the Rwandan genocide was readily available. A project of such magnitude, he explains, in which a government decides to liquidate a large part of a country's population, requires substantial planning and preparation, and certain signals could be detected long before the operation got underway. He describes, for example, trucks filled with militiamen beginning to arrive in the city. "They were being billeted in different neighborhoods with party sympathizers, and at night were throwing up roadblocks and checking the identity of anyone passing."[39]

The killers' intentions are not kept secret: "We're going to cut throats, chop, butcher. We're going to cut open women's bellies before the eyes of their husbands, then mutilate the husbands before the wives die of loss of blood, to make sure they see each other die."[40] Nor do the killings take place in hiding. Courtemanche describes how hundreds of killers – like that little bearded fellow in a Chicago Bulls sweater with Michael Jordan's name on the back – are on the prowl, noisily carrying out their work. Many of the atrocities are committed by drunk hooligans, "Beers in one hand, machetes in the other, eyes rolling up in their sockets, legs unsteady."[41]

The perpetrators are often known to the victims. A neighbourhood roadblock, for instance, in which a couple is brutally abused and killed is manned by a dozen of their neighbours under the command of a policeman who happens to be a cousin. The scene resembles a suburban block party. "The men were having a ball at the roadblock. A radio with the volume on full was diffusing disco to the farthest corners of the neighborhood. Shadows danced and leaped crazily, silhouetted against the lurid light of two fires lit in big metal barrels."[42] The party ends, as many block parties do, without enthusiasm when "the two bodies looked like abattoir refuse, carcasses clumsily cut up by unskilled butchers. The men had had their fill of pleasure and violence."[43]

3. RHETORIC OF THE GENOCIDE

One of the strongest expressions of the bystander's role can be found in the lengthy dialogues between Valcourt and Hutu officials taking place while the atrocious events proceed without interruption. This is also where the dynamics of the genocide are effectively placed in the postcolonial context, as the officials are all well-educated individuals versed in the political and legal language of globalization and skilled in using it as a tool of deceit and manipulation.

The condition in which one decides to file a complaint with the police only to face an official pouring himself a glass of beer and responding by "Name, address, profession, nationality and civil status, please,"[44] which promises endless harassment rather than a solution to the problem, is familiar from other bureaucratic contexts. Here, the author shows how this practice is effectively applied by mass murderers. Witnessing the killing of a prostitute by a Belgian in the hotel, and the cover-up of the murder by the Belgian Embassy, whose security people hijack the dead woman's body, Valcourt and Gentille go to the public prosecutor's office to lodge a complaint. In the novel's ironic language, "The assistant chief prosecutor received them out of respect for Valcourt, the citizen of a donor country and above all a neutral country like Canada, a country that asked no questions and gave with its eyes closed, a perfect country in short."[45] The long sermon by the official indicates a deep understanding of the postcolonial soul, especially the emphasis on democracy and the rule of law, while being willing to compromise both in the name of relativism and political correctness. "We too are seeking the path to greater democracy," he says, "even if we have not been practicing it as long as you. We too believe in the rule of law and practice it, although sometimes in our own ways that may surprise others but must be respected."[46]

We later learn that the official has gained this understanding during his studies at a Canadian university. This has not made him less ruthless, just more capable of manipulating the truth and doing so in a seemingly polite manner: "Since you are alone in wishing to go to law, as my learned colleagues say, I will ask you to remain here to comply with the formalities and answer the questions of our investigators."[47] The official's use of such expressions as "my learned colleagues" or "we are rushed off our feet today" becomes petrifying when we learn who the colleagues are and why they are rushed off their feet, as "from the next office came hysterical laughter. In the waiting room a group of militiamen . . . were amusing themselves hitting a teenaged boy. Some policemen were standing by, laughing. Three civil servants sat behind small school-type desks, slowly pushing pencils."[48]

The deceit and manipulation accompanying the genocide is not attributed only to local officials but also to foreign consuls and journalists who help the Hutu government spread false versions of the events either for political reasons or simply due to ignorance and laziness. And in contrast to the expectations raised by the Truth and Reconciliation Commission in South Africa, Courtemanche draws a gloomy picture of the ability to learn the truth even after the massacre ended. When Valcourt bribes his way among the Hutus who fled the country in order to meet the sergeant who imprisoned Gentille, he encounters the same deceitful rhetoric as before. The sergeant, who has now been promoted to lieutenant by the government in exile, does not even remember the affair. "He was a handsome man who looked you straight in the eye and never raised his voice. Why care about the disappearance of a single person when an Anglo-Saxon Protestant plot was going to eliminate every last living Hutu?"[49]

According to this novel, then, there is little chance for the victims of ethnic cleansing to have their "day in court" even in an age of open information. This is largely the result of the easiness with which false rhetoric can be used to conceal the worse of criminal offences. When faced with authentic documentation spelling out in detail his abuse of Gentille, the lieutenant, we are told, did not even flinch, just opened another beer, spat, and made long speeches about the plot he and his comrades had to fight off. As the author concludes, "propaganda is as powerful as heroin; it surreptitiously dissolves all capacity to think."[50]

4. THE INTERNATIONAL COMMUNITY

The author singles out three international actors for their role in the Rwandan genocide: foreign governments, the United Nations, and the world media.

The role of the Belgian and French governments is well known. Courtemanche describes the colonial era when the Belgians brought European racism to the region and disrupted the coexistence between Hutu and Tutsi. European racism has not been diminished, however, with African independence and with globalization. The author contends that it was racism that led Belgian, French, and Italian forces to evacuate white foreign nationals from Rwanda when the massacre began, leaving all others to die. "Make no mistake," says a priest when the foreign troops are about to arrive, "they're not coming to stay and save the country."[51] The French are described as feeding the inhumanity of the killing of hundreds of thousands of men, women, and children with arms and military advisers. Occasionally we are reminded of the weapons used in the massacre: Chinese machetes, Uzi automatic rifles (courtesy of Israel, arriving via France and Zaïre), or French grenades that had travelled via Cairo through Zaïre.

The explanation given by the Quebecois author for the French role in the genocide is both political and cultural: "In the great designs of the great powers, these Rwandans were of negligible weight, people outside the circle of real humanity, poor, useless types whom the glorious French civilization, with monarchical arrogance, was ready to sacrifice to preserve France's civilizing presence in Africa, a presence already threatened by a major Anglophone plot."[52] The combination of political interest and cultural arrogance is manifested in the character of "Madame the consul," the French consul who is more concerned with her golf tournament than with the murder of a cardinal she is actually helping to cover up.

While UN officials are not accused of active collaboration, one of the most negative characters in the novel is the unnamed Canadian general commanding the United Nations troops in Rwanda. In a review of Dallaire's *Shake Hands With The Devil*, Courtemanche admitted his difficulty in handling the character of Dallaire, the UNAMIR Commander, in the novel, especially after he learned of the general's attempt to commit suicide over his failure to stop the genocide.[53] But in the novel he takes a harsh position with regard to the unnamed general: "Meticulous, legalistic, a civil servant and exemplary bureaucrat, as virtuous as 'le Grand Machin' itself (as General De Gaulle was pleased to call the United Nations). What he knows of the world is airports, the grand hotels of Brussels, Geneva and New York, and strategic studies centres. Of war, he knows what he has seen on CNN."[54]

This description makes the general a symbol not only of the UN but of the entire postcolonial project. Many of the behaviours attributed in this novel, rightly or wrongly, to the general can be seen as illustrations of the contemporary international community which fails to act on behalf of persecuted minorities in the Third World, adheres to routine when bold decisions are needed, and settles for empty rhetoric that helps rationalize failures to engage in humanitarian intervention when necessary. An example of such rhetoric can be found in the following statement made by the general: "The international community would not remain indifferent, but for the moment the UN forces could only intervene peaceably, in the hope that their presence alone would bring those responsible for these excesses back to reason."[55]

Much of the international community's indifference is blamed on the world media. Courtemanche shows the discrepancy between the events taking place on the ground and their representation in the media. When the besieged refugees in the Hôtel des Milles Collines begin to drink the pool water, the media is not troubled:

> That day in its major international bulletin CNN spent twenty seconds on the recurrence of ethnic problems in Rwanda, giving assurances, however, that foreign nationals were safe. Even the perspicacious BBC said little more. Radio-France Internationale talked about recurrent confrontations and ancestral tribalisms, wondering if Africans would ever be able to rid themselves of their ancient demons that kept provoking the most dreadful atrocities.[56]

Courtemanche claims the media's failure to report accurately and responsibly on the killings was partly due to the primitive methods used by the killers, which do not look good on television. One Rwandan says when the massacres begin:

> We'll have the savage efficiency of the primitive and the poor. With machetes, knives and clubs we'll do better than the Americans with their smart bombs. But it won't be a war for television. You won't be able to stand fifteen minutes of our wars and massacres. They're ugly and you'll think they're inhuman. It's the lot of the poor not to know how to murder cleanly, with surgical precision, as the parrots of CNN say after their briefings from the generals.[57]

CNN and other media outlets have never been known for insightful reporting on Africa. "The media don't show dead bodies cut up by men and shredded by vultures and wild dogs," Valcourt says. "They show the pitiful victims of drought, swollen little bellies, eyes bigger than TV screens, the tragic children of famine and the elements – that's what moves people."[58] When he sends off an article on the looming genocide to a dozen newspapers, only one – a small Catholic weekly in Belgium – accepts it for publication. He recalls that he himself had not been sensitive to cries of alarm during the drought in Ethiopia in 1983, arriving there to report on the situation only after the famine had already triumphed. In one of the hardest statements made in this novel, he notes that the disclosure of the atrocities of 1994 is probably not going to change the nature of reporting on Africa, for "it takes ten thousand dead Africans to furrow the brow of even one left leaning White."[59]

CONCLUSION

The mix of genres in *A Sunday at the Pool in Kigali*, being both a novel and a chronicle of events, detracts from its value as a literary work; the narrative is burdened with names, historical facts, and lengthy explanations more common in work by journalists than novelists. The value of the novel, however, lies in its unique perspective. Through the character of Valcourt, a journalist, Courtemanche, a journalist himself, highlights the role of the bystander in the Rwandan genocide. And since this role has been played by most individuals, governments, and international organizations in 1994, the questions raised in this novel are widely applicable.

The main question is that of responsibility. Once the atrocities committed around us are seen as occurring not in some remote planet but as part of political reality, we share in the responsibility for them. This is so even when we lack the power to change the course of events, which is mostly the case. As this novel illustrates, preventing a well-planned, well-orchestrated massacre covered up by manipulation and deceit is close to impossible, even for international agents facing a relatively weak state. On the other hand, powerless actors may not be excused from their responsibility. This point is often overlooked in public and media discussions. In the Canadian discourse on Roméo Dallaire, for example, the general's supporters point at the little power he had while his critics claim he had the power but failed to use it.[60]

Responsibility, however, is not merely a function of power. Valcourt, who is both well-intentioned and powerless, reflects the complexity involved. Although he does everything in his power to save Gentille, he feels responsible when he fails to do so. This feeling goes beyond the well-known survivor guilt[61] or the tendency to become an "ethical bearer of truth and responsibilities to the victims of human rights abuses."[62] Valcourt bears a clear ethical burden, which greatly problematizes the bystander's role.

The complexity added here to the bystander role is quite timely; researchers of genocide have recently argued that the way bystanders were treated in the past must be updated. Tony Kushner, for example, calls for a more nuanced study of Holocaust bystanders.

> Put bluntly, we like our bystanders to be as bifurcated as the categories of victim and perpetrator . . . this is a

> dangerous if understandable development. For rather than nuancing our understanding of the complexity of human responses during the Holocaust, the bystander category is in danger of aiding the tendency to see the subject in Manichean terms, as a symbol of mass evil alongside much less prevalent absolute good (with the emphasis put on the latter to enable hope for the future)."[63]

Kushner believes that a widening of the bystander category is called for. While in the past, it included a limited number of people who knew about the Holocaust and did not act; in today's genocides, everybody falls into that category. The bystander is no longer an easily distinguishable type. In an age of almost instant global communications, he writes, "we are all co-presenters witnessing, even if only through the media, the genocides, ethnic cleansing and other manifestations of extreme racism that besmirch the contemporary world."[64]

Ethicists concerned with responsibility have generally accepted this widening of the bystander category but have not given up the attempt to attribute varied ethical obligations to different bystander types. In an article on the responsibility of bystanders in Bosnia, for example, Arne Johan Vetlesen admits that today, for every person directly victimized in a genocide, there are hundreds, thousands, perhaps even millions of bystanders who are cognizant of the events through the mass media. He distinguishes, however, between passive bystanders and bystanders by assignment, that is, professionals who, by formal appointment, are situated closer to the scene of the genocide and can thus be attributed greater responsibility. "Responsibility for what is now unfolding . . . must also be seen to rest with the party not itself affected but which is knowledgeable about – which is more or less literally *witnessing* – the genocide that is taking place."[65]

It is the blurring of such distinctions in *A Sunday at the Pool in Kigali* that contributes to an updated view of the bystander's responsibility. There were simply too many forces that stood by when Hutus massacred Tutsis to allow us to single out certain officials. In a chapter titled "Silence," Linda Melvern surveys the international actors who should be accountable for the genocide, and the list is endless. From start to finish, she writes, all governments continued to recognize the interim government of Rwanda as legitimate, and international organizations allowed its representatives to serve in such bodies as the UN Commission on Human Rights. She tells about the major role played by British Prime Minister John Major and American President Bill Clinton in shaping a passive policy toward the crisis and in abandoning UNAMIR. She also talks about the press, especially in Great Britain, which described the mass killings as incomprehensible to outsiders and as not amenable to reason. "The newspapers described 'hopeless, helpless horror', taking place in a relatively unknown country, far away."[66]

But all these forces could not have been so successful in preventing intervention in Rwanda were it not for world public opinion, which settled for the framing of the crisis as a tribal war in Africa. The global, postcolonial world of the late twentieth century, while no longer fascinated by far-away continents, largely adopted the early-twentieth-century "heart of darkness" metaphor, which allowed the genocide to go on for three months, as if such killing was unavoidable, and underlined the search for the sources of evil in some metaphysical sense when it was over. In this novel, however, evil is seen as political rather than metaphysical, and the burden of responsibility shifts to all citizens of the new global world.

This raises a hard question: What can be done in a world in which we may recognize our responsibility to halt atrocities we hear about on an almost daily basis while also recognizing how little power we have to make a difference? It is Gentille who raises this question in the novel. At one point, Valcourt regains his vibrancy and begins to ply his trade again, trying to explore "what's hidden behind the bogeymen, the monsters, the caricatures, the symbols, the flags, the uniforms, the grand declarations that lull us to sleep with their good intentions." "Can't we do anything?"[67] Gentille asks timidly and Valcourt admits that very little can be done but that it is still one's duty to stay, observe, denounce, and report. Realizing that his efforts to knock at embassy doors and bring denunciations before the representatives of established powers had only been futile agitation, he nevertheless believes that he must continue recording the events so they are not forgotten. Courtemanche is aware that this minimalist task is less than heroic. Nor can its success be assured. Valcourt, he concludes, "would write for those willing to read, speak to those willing to lend an ear, even half an ear, but that was all."[68]

CHAPTER 5

FICTION AND THE STUDY OF SLUMS: ANOSH IRANI'S *THE CRIPPLE AND HIS TALISMANS*

Since 2001, UN-Habitat, the UN program in charge of promoting socially and environmentally sustainable human settlements, publishes reports on the condition of urban centres throughout the world. These reports convey striking data. Today, half of the world's population lives in cities, with about half of them lacking reasonable housing conditions. In Africa, only a third of the homes are connected to water and sewage. In Asia, where most of the cities with more than ten million inhabitants are located, over 60 percent of the households lack the necessary infrastructure for decent living.

One report discredits the common assumption that urban populations are healthier, more literate, and more prosperous than rural populations. Slum dwellers in developing countries, it says, are as badly off if not worse off than their rural relatives.[1] Another report deflates recent expectations that globalization would be a blessing to urban dwellers because financial liberalization would move savings from developed to developing countries, lower the costs of borrowing, reduce risk through new financial instruments, and increase economic growth. In reality, the opposite has happened: savings flowed from poor to rich countries, interest rates have generally increased, risk has risen, and economic growth has slowed, with the poor in the cities paying much of the price.[2] And a 2014 report on the state of African cities notes that despite recent overall growth, the continent continues to be plagued by massive urban poverty and many other social problems.[2a]

Similar information can be derived from urban studies by scholars and journalists. In *Planet of Slums*, Mike Davis provides important data on the slum dwellers of the world. He defines slums as urban areas characterized by overcrowding, poor or informal housing, inadequate access to safe water and sanitation, and insecurity of tenure. Based on this definition, slum dwellers constitute a staggering 78.2 percent of urbanites in the less developed countries (and only 6 percent of urbanites in developed countries). This equals fully a third of the global urban population. Davis claims, however, that accurate statistics are difficult to come by because poor and slum populations are often deliberately undercounted by officials and such phenomena as informal housing are hard to trace. Moreover, even if the statistical data were accurate, it would be hard to grasp their meaning. Learning that a billion inhabitants of the earth are crowded into about 200,000 slums does not even begin to comprehend the reality of these crowded areas in which all the ills known to the human race are concentrated: violence, drugs, prostitution, gangs, police and government corruption, health hazards, ecological neglect, and an "alternative economy" in which women, children, and even bodily organs turn into merchandize.[3]

Nor do other sources of information provide a full picture of life in the slum. Occasionally, sensitive movies and documentaries like *City of God* or *For the Love of Children* provide important insights into the back streets of the developed world. Modern tourism also gets us closer to the Rio favelas, the Johannesburg townships, etc. But even the most curious tourist remains in the dark. We are exposed to the sights of poverty, such as the beggar I saw in Bombay holding her crippled baby, but we know nothing about what we have seen: Where does that person come from and where is she going? Who is she working for?

Has the baby been crippled intentionally? Where does she sleep and what are she and her baby dreaming about at night?

An important source of information are first-hand reports, such as *Maximum City* by Suketo Mehta, a New York–based writer and journalist who lived in Bombay as a young man and records his return to the city. *Maximum City* is an engaging account of life in a city of 19 million inhabitants – more than the number of inhabitants of 173 states. Mehta describes the beauty of the city with its sea, colonial buildings, and palm trees. He discusses the role of the city as a financial and commercial centre, and its attraction to Indians impressed by the shining lights and sweet songs of Bollywood. Bombay is likened to a golden bird whose voice appeals to millions.

The author does not ignore the city's slum, Dharavi, the largest in Asia, with its high mortality rate, huge population density, and a ratio of 1 toilet seat to every 100 persons,[4] but the slum is not described with the same vividness with which other parts of the city are, as if the genre here is too limited. It seems that a wholly new dimension is needed to record life in the slum: a mystical dimension that none of the agents of reality – UN statistics, urban studies, tourist guides or journalistic reports – can provide.

This is where Anosh Irani's novel *The Cripple and His Talismans* comes in as a literary device throwing light on life in the Bombay slums. The novel is written in the genre of "magical realism," that is, a representation of reality that mixes the mundane with the imaginary. While literary critics mostly use the term to depict fiction that applies a matter of fact, realistic tone when presenting magical happenings,[5] I refer to literary narratives that cope with a complex social or political reality by transcending it temporarily and in a well-controlled manner.

Irani, a young Bombay-born writer living in Vancouver, transcends the real Bombay for a dark, terrifying, and nauseating picture of the city's slums, which is partial, one-dimensional (and thus quite unjust to their inhabitants) but also instructive as it highlights phenomena otherwise discarded. "Things that make perfect sense are false and should not be trusted," he writes. "You must be illogical to understand the world."[6] Irani proposes a careful and controlled shift from reality to fantasy and thus highlights some dimensions missing in the other genres. The fantasy he creates shows Bombay to be operating by a wholly different logic than Vancouver, for example, a logic reserved for those places where "trees are few, men are many, smoke is mistaken for air, prayers are mistaken for threats and answered with blood."[7]

Irani makes us listen to the unique song of a city filled with "magic, poverty, thievery, music, pollution, dancing, murder and lust,"[8] a song we otherwise fail to hear. As the protagonist, a man in search for his lost arm in the streets of Bombay, says: "It surprises me how much I do not know about this city. Tomorrow I might meet a midget who is ten feet tall, a butcher who sells newborn babies, a boxer who works as an anesthetist in a hospital by knocking patients senseless."[9] While we occasionally meet these characters in the crime chronicles, their becoming part of the fantasy makes us meet them in a fuller sense. Let me now show how the novel's magical realism contributes to our understanding of six dimensions of the Bombay slums: the physical environment, life of the poor, the culture of death, commercial practices, the politics of slums, and the role of God.

1. PHYSICAL ENVIRONMENT

In this novel, the slum is not portrayed as a distinct area separated from the city. "In this city," the author writes, "one minute you are in a garden and the next you are in a slum. It is most natural. Ask me to retrace my steps and I will be unable to do so. A person travels in this city like a bad smell – over here now, strong and pungent; then gone suddenly, only to reappear in another part of the city a few moments later"[10] The well-documented phenomenon of improvised housing and entrepreneurship in the slum is vividly described: "Beyond the tracks is the underbelly of the poor, houses hand-built by husbands and wives, with stolen roofs, under whose heat run five or six children. Some are custom-made gambling dens where the little ones serve liquor and boiled potatoes to the card players."[11]

We get a feel for the presence of children everywhere as part of the urban setting: "The sari shops are all closed for the night. Beside them is a makeshift temple with oil lamps in its hutch. They are still burning because there is no wind. Five children sleep near the shutters of the sari shop. They snore in peace; they do not hate the world. Only those who have beds hate the world."[12] The wide presence of children in the streets is matched only by the presence of mosquitoes: "There are so many mosquitoes here that it looks as if the mosquitoes have formed a net to trap humans."[13] But nothing represents the physical environment better than the dark sky: "It happens a lot in this city. The sky forgets that it is blue. It sees the dusty winding streets, the naked children, the withered dogs, the widows, the drug-selling temples and it turns sad. It takes away its own light in shame."[14]

The author tells us about the railway platforms in the city by showing us hell: "In fact, hell's design is loosely based on a railway platform: no urinals, lots of people, and you have to buy a ticket even though you do not want to be there."[15] The bus is not much different: "Old people, children, and cripples are damned. The god of public transit does not indulge in frivolity. For sentiments and mush, please visit your local cinema hall."[16]

And we do. The sweet songs and bright lights of Bollywood, as well as the price paid by many who are attracted to them, are presented in a dialogue between a young woman who wishes to become a big star and a fortune teller who seems to know where the movie dreams may lead her: "I imagine that along the way her legs will spread like cheap butter, her breasts will come out as often as moons do, sheets will crumple, and the scent of paisa will fill her heart. . ."[17] The author has a harsh view of Hindi melodramas: "We deserve all the melodrama we get," he writes. "We are always greedy for more. Look at our movies. They are melodrama dipped in a tub of full honey, evil, stupidity, golden skin and happy endings."[18]

2. LIFE OF THE POOR

The novel provides the means of listening to the poor in an intimate way. At the beginning of the novel, the protagonist is instructed to listen to the sounds of the street, for only by listening to the sounds can the meaning of it all become clear. For example, "in the bicycle bell of a little boy lies the wail of his mother, for she knows he will leave her soon when he is crushed by a speeding truck."[19] In similar fashion, we learn to listen to the sounds and watch the sights of poverty. The protagonist admits that before he became crippled, he used to pass by the houses of the poor and blindfold himself, while now he sees the sights and hears the sounds: "Young boys smoke ganja in dim light. Men blindfolded by a dark sky sleep on the footpath in neat rows. These are men who walk the earth, build houses in the shade and smuggle in traces of warm light when life is not looking."[20]

When the poor, the beggars, and the homeless are made part of a fantasy, some of the puzzles are answered. We learn, for instance, what the beggar we saw on the street during the day dreams about at night: "Everyone is sleeping but their dreams are wide awake. People are laughing, singing, bouncing off the buildings, flying into each other's arms and kissing their own hands, because for the first time in their lives, they love themselves." We also learn how the morning looks like for those stricken by poverty: "Dawn breaks. It breaks the poor first. Get up, dip piece of bread in tea, shit outside, brush with fingers, leave fallen hair in dust, have gentle chat with neighbor about dying, live for nothing."[21]

The fictional elements arouse our sensitivity to this existential state of affairs even more than the explicit descriptions of poverty in the novel: "Little boys and girls sit in a row on the street and pluck out their teeth one by one. They strongly believe in the tooth demon. They have not eaten for days and he has told them he will exchange teeth for bread. The children seem quite happy with this barter. But then a girl, no more than two years old, breaks out of the line and tells the others that they must not trust the tooth demon. His plan is to buy *all* their teeth. Without teeth, they will not be able to eat. They will die."[22]

3. CULTURE OF DEATH

The novel is filled with references to death. The author represents the hopelessness of his characters' lives through their death wish. Consider the following description: "Even though it is night, Mr. P's coffins enterprise is open. This makes sense to me. People die at all times. At night, all of us leave our bodies and visit our loved ones in the spirit world. A few of us do not come back. We look at our body from up above and wonder why we would want to repossess it. That is how we die in our sleep."[23]

The characters are obsessed with suicide, but even suicide, we learn, is a privilege of the rich: "The rich succeed at suicide but not because they are adept at it. They have the facilities: the guns and expensive rope. They live in tall buildings from which they can jump."[24] Poor people, on the other hand, encounter many problems in their attempts to commit suicide. When the cripple decides to jump from a roof and carries a heavy stone to the top of the building because his body is too light, the stone is stolen from him. On another occasion we learn of a spot near railway tracks which is useful not because the train can be caught there but because people can throw themselves in front of it. "A few years ago, policemen were stationed here to prevent suicides but then one day the policemen killed themselves. The city does that to us all."[25]

Such black humour introduces us to the death wish attributed to the inhabitants of slums. This may be quite unjust, as studies have shown the vibrancy and survival skills of slum dwellers. There is no reason to accept the author's assumption that an entrepreneur operating a rickshaw at the centre of Bombay and having therefore to dwell on the street is more suicidal than a limousine driver in Beverly Hills, or for that matter, the customer riding the limousine. But the novel emphasizes the nonchalant way in which death is treated by those who have lost hope. "Some people crave death as they do cigarettes."[26]

4. COMMERCIAL PRACTICES

One of the first encounters of the man in search of his arm is with a woman selling rainbows. This is a good introduction to a commercial world in which everything is being bought and sold. Nothing, however, prepares the reader for the scenes in the novel in which the selling of body organs is described, especially the story of the kidnapping of a man in order to detach his arm and give it to someone willing to pay for it.

The story provides a lucid picture of that practice. It is presented as a routine venture, very similar to the sale of many other products, which may also involve some discomfort when one reads about it, or about its consequences, yet is conducted quite routinely and without interruptions. The organization of the human limbs in Baba Rakhu's warehouse is meticulous. Neatly packed in plastic sheets, they hang shamelessly, like suits and shirts waiting to be picked. They are labelled with names in alphabetical order; they even shine a little, coated with a substance to preserve them.

Particularly striking is the escapist attitude of the protagonist, who is appalled yet willing to go along with the practice in order to get a new arm. "I try not to imagine how Baba must acquire these limbs." His initial reaction, and the response that follows, are rather funny. He asks: "So you do sell arms and legs. . ." "You act as though I am selling arms,"[27] is the answer. And elsewhere: "Where do you get these arms?" "Do you check where the vegetable vendor gets his stock? Do you know every detail about the fish that are sold at your doorstep?" "This is different." "Only if you let it be."[28] The macabre scenes in which people's organs are cut out by force are set in a way very similar to descriptions of other commercial enterprises. The economic philosophy expressed by Baba, the organ vendor, sounds familiar: "Think of it as an orange. It might grow in someone else's garden, but if you are hungry you will eat it."[29] The question whether the organs are donated or stolen is reduced to a minor technicality. Baba does not recommend thinking too much on the morality of the enterprise. "Talk is for politicians. We simple folk must simply exchange arms."[30]

The story highlights the connection between the theft of organs and police corruption. "If you go to the police, there is a special place reserved for your other arm right there in the corner,"[31] the cripple is warned. The reader is confident that he will not go to the police, not only because it is dangerous but because it is easy to find rationalizations for the gruesome activity of organ theft, reminiscent of the rationalizations accompanying international arms sales (e.g., "if we don't sell, someone else will"). The abduction of a taxi driver whose organs are taken is accompanied by rationalizations that he beats his wife, supports Pakistan in its cricket matches against India and that part of the cash generated by the sale of his arm will go to his widow. Such evasions become a way of life: "I look away, I look at the closed ration shops, at the mosque in the distance, at the faces of politicians slapped onto the walls, at the stall of the coconut seller, at the open-air garbage dump, at the car we came in, its steering wheel, its seats, its trunk. I look back."[32]

5. THE POLITICS OF SLUMS

What are the political factors responsible for the conditions described in the novel? One factor is the exhaustion of resources as a result of the India–Pakistan rivalry: "One day this city will burst. There will be so much sadness it will be unbearable. Waves of misery will sweep the neighbouring countries as well. We will all drown together, holding hands, being laughed at by the rest of the world. Only in death will we know that we could have been friends, helped each other by burying our nuclear weapons in our deserts until they were forgotten. We have brains, we have guts, but we have left our hearts under the hut of the poor."[33]

The main source of the harsh conditions, however, seems to be the preference given to matter over spirit. In a powerful fantasy, the author leads us back to the sixteenth century. The protagonist is now the cook in Emperor Akbar's palace. The cook is a sworn enemy of the palace singer, who sits on the highest dome in the palace. His voice travels over pink rivers, blue trees, and orange groves. When the emperor goes to war and the singer is left in charge, he issues decrees stating that if drought were to hit, all birds could be killed except nightingales – the birds of song. But the cook kills the nightingale because "when there is famine, hunger overtakes common sense and when the stomach grows, so does the heart. It laps up wood and poison with the same delicious tongue."[34] He knows that "if the bird of song is eaten, all men shall hunger for music forever,"[35] but the material needs prevail.

Our willingness to satisfy our material needs at any cost and sacrifice spiritual assets for material gains leads to the gloom we experience throughout the novel. As the cook realizes after the kill, "The garden glows like some cheap stone. It rises and looms above my head, waiting to descend upon me. It comes lower and lower. Something is terribly wrong."[36]

6. THE ROLE OF GOD

In asking what is wrong, Irani does not put all blame on humans but also on God, who has abandoned the slum of Bombay. God is sought throughout the novel. In a particularly disturbing scene in which two lepers fight each other, the question is being asked: "Is there a spirit world up there? Is there a separate one for lepers?"[37] This is not an obvious question to ask in a culture believing in many gods, but the author mocks this belief. "It is only natural that in this country people believe in a hundred gods. One God is not enough. One God has failed them, so they invent their own and worship them with words, milk and flowers in the hope that at least a few of these gods will come to life and help. I do not think it is stupid at all. Let people in other countries laugh. They would not last even a day in this hut. The mosquitoes would peel off their soft skin while they wondered what happened to the toaster and dishwasher, and why the smell of fresh paint has been replaced with the smell of shit."[38]

God has abandoned the city of Bombay, but the author hints that this is the result of God having been abandoned by man. This hint is given in a beautiful story, which can be seen as the book's credo, about a little boy who was alone in the universe and saw the vision of a tree. He made the roads of the world like branches of the tree, created all creatures and allowed them to walk the roads, but nobody walked toward him. Disappointed, he turned to man, but man asked him to go away and never to return. The little boy then asked the man what the place he stood on is called, so he remembers never to visit it again, and the man said: "Bombay."[39]

CONCLUSION

The fictional tale discussed here can obviously not replace the UN reports, urban studies, journalistic accounts, and other means by which we study the complex phenomenon of life in the slums. It points, however, at the contribution of fiction to coping with that complexity. The difficulty of grasping the meaning of data informing us that millions are living, as this is being written, in unbearable conditions calls for new approaches to the subject matter, and Irani's dark fantasy of Bombay, the "global capital of slum-dwelling,"[40] complements the more traditional means by which we approach slums.

Studies of poverty provide important data on the causes and dynamics of the phenomenon, but Irani's fictional description of a beggar's dream allows us to identify with her and her misery on some higher level of humanity. We know quite a lot about the destruction of the environment and its consequences, but by being placed in the position of a palace's cook during a drought we face the tension between the material interests of globalization and the spiritual values discarded on the way to their fulfillment in full force. And by leading us through a pristine store selling human organs, the author makes us aware of the rationalizations we use to allow commercial practices known to be utterly immoral when it comes to Third World countries.

Again, I do not to argue that fiction is more helpful in solving the world's problems than other intellectual endeavors. Yet novels such as *The Cripple and His Talismans* point to the elements lacking in more standard approaches to the study of society and to the contribution of magical realism to our understanding of twenty-first century poverty.

CHAPTER 6

NARRATIVE AND MEMORY IN HARUKI MURAKAMI'S *KAFKA ON THE SHORE*, GÜNTER GRASS'S *CRABWALK*, AND ANDRÉ BRINK'S *THE RIGHTS OF DESIRE*

In his seminal article "Life as Narrative," Jerome Bruner claims that we construct ourselves autobiographically, that is, the stories we tell about ourselves are not only forms of life writing but of life making. We create the culture we live in by our life stories, which themselves are constrained by that culture. As Bruner puts it, "I believe that the ways of telling and the ways of conceptualizing that go with them become so habitual that they finally become receipts for structuring experience itself, for laying down routes into memory, for not only guiding the life narrative up to the present but directing it into the future."[1] Both individuals and whole societies are steering their way into the future with the help of life stories in which the past is remembered and the present conceptualized.

Since only a few life stories told by individuals in society take canonical form, the cultural receipts constraining them may be seen as a scarce resource and hence as a source of political conflict. As Patterson and Monroe write, "The political importance of commonly shared narratives means they often become the focus of political debate."[2]

The debate over shared narratives lies at the core of the politics of memory, the political process by which we decide what personal narratives will be shared in the public sphere and which are doomed to oblivion. The modern state plays a major role in that process by building monuments and initiating commemoration ceremonies, and so do autobiographies. As Antonina Harbus writes, part of our shared cultural memory is derived from the generic and narrative schemas of published biographies and autobiographies, where the rhetorical management of material exerts a powerful shaping force not only for self-development but also for "contextualized interpretation."[3]

A case in point is Rousseau's *Confessions*, which played a powerful role in shaping the shared narrative associated with modernity. The confessions did so in their emphasis on the individual who believes in progress and is always on a journey from simplicity to complexity and from emotionalism to rationalism.[4] They also shaped the context of modernity by their search for moral perfection at the end of the road and their romantic fantasies about the future, which nourished both the French revolutionaries of the eighteenth century and the totalitarian movements of the twentieth century.[5] Moreover, Rousseau, as is well known, admired the "noble savage," an image linked to the justification of colonialism as a project bringing the fruits of European enlightenment to the natives of foreign lands.[6] Rousseau's life story thus inspired a narrative of modernity advanced with pride by Western thinkers for generations.[7]

Yet, over time, the narrative of modernity has raised concern, especially over its exclusionary nature. As Joel Kahn claims in *Modernity and Exclusion*, any conceptualization of modernity involves the construction of a model of the non-modern other, which may range "from notions of the other as a primitive version of the modern self to the other as irreducibly alien, from a visible and speaking other to one that is more or less completely invisible and silent."[8] Sidonie Smith talks about the "tyranny of the arid I" in Enlightenment life writings which have excluded anything that was "other, exotic, unruly, irrational, uncivilized, regional, or paradoxically unnatural."[9] Smith also shows, however, how more recent autobiographies have given voice to previously oppressed people and groups.

The voices of the oppressed have become a new canon in the public sphere, one challenging the shared narrative of modernity. The new canon has been conceptualized by Edward Said, who demanded that we not only listen to forgotten voices and persons but turn them into a shared narrative. For example, in his *Representations of the Intellectual*, Said demanded that contemporary intellectuals make the concern for the victims in their own nation-state a universal concern:

> To this terribly important task of representing the collective suffering of your own people, testifying to its travails, reasserting its enduring presence, reinforcing its memory, there must be added something else, which only an intellectual, I believe, has the obligation to fulfill. . . . For the intellectual the task, I believe, is explicitly to universalize the crisis, to give greater human scope to what a particular race or nation suffered, to associate that experience with the sufferings of others.[10]

With his demand to "universalize the crisis," Said sharpens the distinction between two conflicting narratives: the narrative of individualism, progress, rationality, and modernity commonly associated with the West and a narrative of victimhood pursued by the victims of slavery, apartheid, colonialism, genocide, and other oppressive forces attributed, rightly or wrongly, to the West. The intellectual, he claims, always faces a choice: "either to side with the weaker, the less well represented, the forgotten or ignored, or to side with the more powerful."[11] In other words, the narrative of victimhood is to be shared not only by the victims of colonial expeditions, for example, but by all those for whom the great evils of the modern era have shattered, to quote Dominick

LaCapra, "the image of Western civilization as the bastion of elevated values if not the high point in the evolution of humanity."[12]

The sharp distinction between the two narratives leads not only to intellectual debates but also to political conflicts within societies and in the international arena, for narrative and conflict are strongly related. "Every conflict is justified by a narrative of grievance, accusation, and indignity," writes Robert Rotberg. "Conflicts depend on narratives, and in some senses cannot exist without a detailed explanation of how and why the battle began, and why one side, and only one side, is in the right."[13]

An example of the relationship between narrative and conflict is provided by Robert Meister, who ties the origins of the Cold War to the conflicting narratives over colonialism and the refusal by the victims of colonialism to give up the revolutionary struggle against the former colonial states even after the latter have been defeated politically and morally. In an article titled "Human Rights and the Politics of Victimhood" he writes: "As the twentieth century's agent of revolutionary change, the unreconciled victim was not merely recalcitrant in both victory and defeat; he also remained a revolutionary because he continued to think as a victim after the perpetrators of past injustice had been dislodged from power."[14]

Meister discusses the unsuccessful attempts by political regimes such as the post-Apartheid regime in South Africa to cope with that polarization. The Truth and Reconciliation Commission, for example, attempted to define an appropriate public attitude toward the evils of the past. However, this is hard to achieve because the sought-after consensus on the moral meaning of the past comes at the expense of cutting off future claims flowing from it. "Putting the point crudely," he writes, "the cost of achieving a moral consensus that the past was evil is to reach a political consensus that the evil is past."[15] Thus, while political regimes recognize the need to reach closure or forgiveness, lay the past to rest, and empty the present of backward-looking political significance, this is not necessarily the interest of the former victims, who often turn to a militant and punitive form of rule. Meister warns us of such an option; the rule by victorious victims or their supporters would be worse than the status quo. The least just state, he argues, is that in which victors rule with the consciousness of victims.

A more nuanced narrative than the two narratives of modernity and victimhood is called for, one in which the evils of the past are remembered while past victims or their adherents do not turn into present perpetrators. I refer to a narrative of reconciliation not in the sense of bringing the holders of the two narratives together through dialogue and mutual understanding, as has often been proposed,[16] nor necessarily in the Freudian sense of "working through" by remembering and repeating the past.[17] What is needed is the construction of a shared narrative which may have healing power on the psychological level but would first and above all allow modern societies affected by past traumas to overcome the perpetrator-victim divide on the political level.

This is no easy task, as it is easier and more beneficial to confine political advocacy in the public sphere to the perpetrator-victim divide than to encourage those on both sides of the divide to partly transcend their roles as perpetrators and victims. This is why such a nuanced narrative may be found less in political rhetoric than in literary fiction. I shall now show how it emerges in three novels published in the early years of the twenty-first century by writers concerned with the failure of their tormented societies to come to term with the evils they inflicted upon others in the twentieth century: *Kafka on the Shore* from 2004 by Japanese writer Haruki Murakami,[18] *Crabwalk*, written in 2002 by German writer Günter Grass,[19] and the 2000 novel *The Rights of Desire* by South African writer André Brink.[20] Using fictional devices – a shadow, a fictionalized ghostwriter and a ghost – the three novelists point the way toward a narrative of reconciliation allowing Japan, Germany, and South Africa to move on, not by forgetting the past but by remembering it.

FICTION AND THE PAST

How can fictional characters such as ghosts fulfill such political tasks as showing societies how to cope with their past? This is where the turn to aesthetics is particularly useful. Consider Madhu Dubey's work on "Speculative Fictions of Slavery," in which the author realizes the important role realistic tales of slavery played in pressing the case for abolition but also notes their shortcomings. While forcefully representing the era of slavery in the first person singular, they may lead to a comprehension of slavery as an institution that has ended with the Civil Rights Movement and passed into the register of history. Dubey therefore turns to aesthetic genres such as fantasy and science fiction which keep the story alive. These genres allow an approach to the past as "something other or more than history."[21] While we do not tend to associate fantasy with history, Dubey writes, fantastic elements may reinforce rather than undermine historical authority. Speculative fictions overly situate themselves against history, suggesting that we can best comprehend the truth of slavery as a way to avoid such horrendous evil in the future by abandoning historical modes of knowing. "Refusing to regard the past of slavery as history, speculative novels suggest that the truth of this past is more fully grasped by the way of an antirealist literary imagination that can fluidly cross temporal boundaries and affectively immerse readers into the world of slavery."[22]

Ghost stories in particular serve as reminders of the horrendous evils of the past. This point has been analyzed in Avery Gordon's *Ghostly Matters*, a sociological analysis of ghost stories in which he notes the complexity and depth added by them to the realistic tales of the victims. Gordon reminds us that even those who live in the direst circumstances possess a complex and often contradictory humanity and subjectivity that cannot be narrowed down to a perspective that views them merely as victims. The ghost story provides a broader perspective:

> The ghost is not simply a dead or a missing person but a social figure, and investigating it can lead to that dense site where history and subjectivity make social life. The ghost or the apparition is one form by which something lost, or barely visible or seemingly not there to our supposedly well-trained eyes, makes itself known or apparent to us, in its own way, of course. The way of the ghost is haunting, and haunting is a very particular way of knowing what has happened or is happening. Being haunted draws us affectively, sometimes against our will and always a bit magically, into the structure of feeling of a reality we come to experience not as cold knowledge, but as a transformative recognition.[23]

It may seem paradoxical that a ghost story provides a deeper view of a historical experience than a realistic account, but this makes sense in light of the above-mentioned conflict of narratives in which the multifarious humanity of people subjected to the evils of slavery, colonialism, genocide, etc., is reduced to the notion of victimhood. The ghost, on the other hand, can be seen after Gordon as "a crucible for political meditation and historical memory,"[24] as are the ghostly figures in the three novels discussed here.

THE SETTING

Before discussing the novels themselves, let me state that the ways of political meditation in Japan, Germany, and South Africa differ, as does the degree to which historical memory takes shape in each of them. In a special issue of *Totalitarian Movements and Political Religions* devoted to reckoning with the past in former totalitarian societies, Anatoly Khazanov and Stanley Payne propose various approaches taken by former totalitarian countries to their history: honest reckoning and repentance, reconciliation and forgiveness, drawing a line between past and present, and forgetting the past or forging a new narrative about it. None of the three countries discussed here fits any of these types in pure form; political groups and parties within these countries advocate different approaches, and a mix of policies of memory – repenting, pretending to repent, disregarding the past, etc. – characterizes all of them.

Japan comes closest to a society trying to move on by merely putting the past to rest. As Khazanov and Payne claim, after the Second World War, Japanese nationalists portrayed their country not as an aggressor but as a victim; massive crimes, such as the 'rape of Nanking' and the vivisection of prisoners of war, were ignored and the dropping of the atomic bombs on Hiroshima and Nagasaki were stripped of all historical context and manipulated to fuel the myth of Japanese martyrdom. The failure to unsettle the scores of the past was unfortunate. "When scores remain unsettled, national narratives distorted, and collective memories sublimated," the two scholars write, "they may later re-emerge with surprising and unpredictable consequences."[25]

The case of Germany is the hardest to classify in any category, as it is filled with contradictions. West German leaders both on the right and left, such as Conrad Adenauer and Willy Brandt, understood the importance of repentance for the Holocaust and other crimes committed by the Nazis during the Second World War if Germany is to move toward prosperity, democracy, and international recognition. But the public at large, and the educational system, preferred in many cases to keep silent about the Nazi past, a stance made possible by the willingness of West Germany's allies in the Cold War to allow a rather moderate process of de-Nazification in the Federal Republic. The confusion over the past caused by the Cold War came to bear in 1986 with historian Ernst Nolte's comparison of the Nazi atrocities against the Jews to those committed by the Soviet Union, which sparked the "Historians' Controversy," an intellectual and public debate rightly defined as "a fight for memory,"[26] which has continued to the present day.

South Africa came closest to coping effectively with historical memory, in confronting the evils of the Apartheid era. Influenced by theological notions of confession and forgiveness, the Truth and

Reconciliation Committee (TRC) chaired by Anglican Archbishop Desmond Tutu called upon perpetrators of Apartheid – both white and black – to account for their crimes in return for being considered for amnesty. The TRC became an impressive historical experiment in coping with past evils as a way to move on but was criticized by those who felt that confessions were not always genuine, that perpetrators were let off too easily, and that the TRC, focusing on crimes committed by individuals, avoided dealing with the overall political system behind the crimes and thus missed the opportunity to build a new South Africa.

In spite of the variance in the ways Japan, Germany, and South Africa cope with their past, an overall narrative of reconciliation emerges in the novels produced in the three countries. Murakami, Grass, and Brink refer to the specific conditions in their countries, but each of them contributes to the construction of the narrative. Murakami uses a shadow of the past in order to warn modern Japan of the tendency to forget it, Grass uses a fictional ghostwriter to demonstrate the political consequences of Germany's failure to break the perpetrator-victim cycle, and Brink uses a ghost in the best tradition of South African ghost stories to show a way to emerge from that cycle in contemporary South Africa. Let me now show how that narrative evolves step by step.

HARUKI MURAKAMI, *KAFKA ON THE SHORE*

Haruki Murakami's novel *Kafka on the Shore* can be seen as a reflection on the failure of Japanese society to settle the scores of the past. The novel is filled with fantastic images: a rain of sardines and mackerels is coming down from the sky, cats talk, etc. This may partly stem from the fact that the novel has been written shortly after the 1995 Sarin gas attack in the Tokyo underground, as if Murakami were saying that if an ordinary Japanese can find himself on the way to work under a Sarin gas attack then everything is possible including the fall of sardines and mackerels from the sky. There is, however, more to it;

Kafka on the Shore deals not only with the present but with the past. The contingencies it leads us through may be seen as the outgrowth of a society marching into the twenty-first century before it has come to terms with its history in the twentieth century.

The cloud of the past is accompanying every step on the road taken by the protagonist, Kafka Tamura. Tamura is a fifteen-year-old Japanese boy whose father is a sculptor and whose mother left the house with his sister when he was four years old. He decides to go on a journey which, among other things, represents a search for freedom, serenity, and a sense of completion in modern industrial Japan. He puts some money, a watch, an old photograph, and a cellular phone into a backpack and leaves home. The first stop on the way is a quiet library on the island of Takamatsu. He has always loved to spend time in the reading rooms of libraries. "The library was like a second home. Or maybe more like a real home."[27] In the library, Kafka escapes into a thousand and one tales and feels free. But is he?

> I'm *free*, I think. I shut my eyes and think hard and deep about how free I am, but I can't really understand what it means. All I know is I'm totally alone. All alone in an unfamiliar place, like some solitary explorer who's lost his compass and his map. Is this what it means to be free? I don't know, and I give up thinking about it.[28]

The escape into books is not freeing the boy from anything, because no person is isolated; we are all linked by "prototypical memory."[29] In other words, we belong to communities tied together by shared memories. And although the inhabitants of modern Japan may hope to pursue their industrial endeavors with no concern for the evils inflicted by them in the Second World War, the war memories will keep haunting them. No matter how much time passes, Murakami writes, no matter what takes place in the interim, "there are some things we can never assign to oblivion, memories we can never rub away. They remain with us forever like a touchtone."[30]

The Second World War is present in every site on the boy's voyage. The journey of Kafka Tamura is accompanied by the story of Nakata, his shadow, serving as a constant reminder of the war and its consequences. Nakata is first introduced to us in the formal language of a top secret document produced by the U.S. Department of Defense about a B-29 airplane (the same make as the Enola Gay, which dropped the A-bomb on Hiroshima) that passed above the heads of Japanese children during a school outing in 1944. A teacher who accompanied the children describes the event as a slight diversion from the routine occurring in a pastoral setting.

> The glittering airplane we saw way up in the sky reminded us for a moment of the war, but just for a short time, and we were all in a good mood. There wasn't a cloud in the sky, no wind, and everything was quiet around us – all we could hear were birds chirping in the woods. The war seemed like something in a faraway land that had nothing to do with us.[31]

Everything soon returns to normal. While some of the children had collapsed with their eyes open, as if they were looking at something, all but one recover and the incident is forgotten (partly as a result of an American effort to keep it secret). The children's lives, we are told, were completely unaffected by the incident, which was fully erased from their memory. "Rather than a memory loss, it was more a memory *lack*,"[32] the author writes. One boy, however – Nakata – does not return to normal. By the time Kafka Tamura goes on his journey, Nakata is a man of over sixty who talks to cats. The author devotes every second chapter to this character who never mentions Hiroshima but does not allow us to forget it. After the B-29 incident, we learn, Nakata's shadow remained only half as dark as that of ordinary people. "I only have half a shadow," says the man who speaks about himself, "Nakata lost it during that war."[33] We soon realize that the other half belongs to Kafka Tamura, who shares his spirit with Nakata. For example, when

Nakata kills a man, Kafka, who is miles away, has blood on his hands. The two hardly meet, but as Kafka moves forward, so does Nakata, his "living spirit."[34]

At one point on his journey, Tamura finds refuge in a forest the Japanese army marched through during the Second World War. He bumps into two soldiers who got lost during manoeuvres sixty years ago and are now leading him to a small town in the woods where he has an opportunity to relive the past as we do when we indulge in nostalgia. In that town, the water is clean again, the milk has a natural taste again, the tune of "Edelweiss" from Rodgers and Hammerstein's musical *The Sound of Music* is playing in the background and the boy's lost mother appears as a living, breathing young girl standing in the kitchen at twilight, cooking him a meal. This return to the past is thrilling, and for a moment one gets the feeling that the journey has come to an end, as harmony has been found.

> I'm drifting away, away from myself. I'm a butterfly, flitting along the edges of creation. Beyond the edge of the world there's a space where emptiness and substance neatly overlap, where past and future form a continuous, endless loop.[35]

And yet, the thrill does not last and the boy is forced to leave the woods. Nostalgia does not help overcome the curse of the past. Murakami ties that curse to the godliness imposed on Japan in 1946 when General Douglas MacArthur, the American military commander in Japan, ordered the divine emperor to quit being God. "That curse is branded on your soul even deeper than before," the author writes. "That curse is part of your DNA. You breathe out the curse, the wind carries it to the four corners of the Earth, but the dark confusion inside you remains. Your fear, anger, unease – nothing's disappeared. They're all still inside you, still bothering you."[36]

Here, then, is the first building block of the narrative emerging from the three novels – the past remains with us however strong our desire to forget it. But Murakami may be saying more than that: once a modern industrial state like Japan faces reality rather than trying to escape it, it acquires the power to mobilize the creativity and resourcefulness needed to proceed. As Kafka Tamura is told at the end of the novel: "Let a bright light shine in and melt the coldness in your heart. That's what being tough is all about. Do that and you really *will* be the toughest fifteen-year-old on the planet. You following me? There's still time. You can still get your *self* back. Use your head. Think about what you've got to do. You're no dunce. You should be able to figure it out."[37] In other words, we need to acknowledge the past not only because it is impossible to forget but because in remembering there is a glimpse of hope for a better future.

GÜNTER GRASS, *CRABWALK*

German novelist Günter Grass offers us another building block of the narrative with his forceful demonstration of the consequences we may expect when the past is not remembered. *Crabwalk* shows how by ignoring history we stand a good chance of replaying the conflict between perpetrators and victims. The arguments made in this complex novel become even more complex in view of the revelation in 2006 (four years after the publication of *Crabwalk*) that Grass himself has failed to reveal his having been drafted into the Waffen-SS during the Second World War.

The novel is concerned with the following event. On January 30, 1945, a Soviet Stalinets submarine sailing in the Baltic Sea under the command of Captain Alexander Marinesko torpedoed and sank the German passenger ship *Wilhelm Gustloff*. The ship carried 1,000 sailors, 370 women serving in the German navy, and an unknown number of refugees who were trying to escape the Red Army advancing into East Prussia. The number of victims has been estimated at 7,000 to 10,000 (compared to 1,513 who lost their lives in the Titanic), mainly women and children who failed to elbow their way into the few life boats.

Grass was born in 1927 in Gdansk (Danzig) on the eastern shore of the Baltic, which explains his urge to write a novel about the sinking of the ship. Being part of the generation of post–World War II German writers, however, he realizes the difficulties this entails. Grass is aware that telling the story of the *Wilhelm Gustloff* may not be warranted because it might create sympathy for Germans of the Nazi era. He therefore uses a fictional device which seems at first like a gimmick but turns out to be rather meaningful. He introduces a fictional character, an elderly instructor in a Berlin technical school who has written a book titled *Dog Years* (one of Grass's own novels) and has an urge to investigate the *Wilhelm Gustloff*'s sinking but is unable to pull the project off. We learn that "around the mid sixties he'd had it with the past" and that "the voracious present with its incessant nownownow had kept him from producing the mere two hundred pages."[38] He therefore commissions someone else to write the story – a journalist named Paul Pokriefke.

Commissioning someone else to write German history is no trivial matter. Grass believes that his generation of writers had an obligation to engage in "*Vergangenheitsbewältigung*," the process of remembering and managing the past, but failed to undertake the task and left it with characters like Pokriefke, a journalist with a rather meagre profile, a pen-for-hire on his way downhill. He has once written for Axel Springer's right-wing newspapers, then for left-wing newspapers and is presently keeping his head above water by doing hackwork for a wire service and writing occasional feature articles on such topics as "What's Green about Berlin's International Green Week?" and "Turks in Kreuzberg."[39] This unflattering profile points at the scant hope Grass places in the present generation of writers conducting the intellectual discourse over Germany's past.

Crabwalk may thus be seen as an exploration of the fate of a country once its historical past is left unattended by educators and intellectuals and left to dubious characters, especially today when it comes to be negotiated on the Internet. When Pokriefke begins his research, he realizes that the story requires attention to the Internet where it unfolds. It unfolds by the sharpening of the existing perpetrator-victim narratives, which leads to murder.

Wilhelm Gustloff, after whom the ship was named, was born in Schwerin in 1895. Due to a chronic weakness of the lungs, he did not fight in the First World War. He was rather sent to recover in Davos, where he eventually joined the Nazi party and helped recruit new party members among German and Austrian citizens living in Switzerland. In 1936 he was assassinated by David Frankfurter, a Jewish medical student protesting the rise of Nazism. Frankfurter was convicted in Switzerland for the murder and pardoned in 1945.

Grass portrays Gustloff as a low-level Nazi operative and does not express much enthusiasm over Frankfurter's act either. Yet this assessment does not prevent the making of the two into larger-than-life characters on the Internet, where the assassination attains mystical proportions. The ship named after the Nazi operative began to sink on January 30, 1945, which happened to be the martyr's fiftieth birthday and twelve years to the day since the Nazis' seizure of power. In an imaginary website called "Comrades of Schwerin" (whose URL is that of the book's publisher), such coincidences are described as the result of the hand of Providence. The inconsequential question whether Gustloff was more of a socialist or a nationalist turns into a battle between right- and left-wing chatterers. As Grass puts it, "A virtual Night of the Long Knives took its toll."[40]

The Gustloff myth did not begin with the Internet; the Nazi party had already turned him into a martyr during David Frankfurter's trial in Switzerland in 1936. But in the age of the Internet, says Grass, it seems as though the case is being retried, "this time on a virtual world stage before an overflow crowd of onlookers."[41] Role playing on the Internet allows a continuous debate between some Wilhelm who represents the assassinated Nazi and some David who plays David Frankfurter. Instead of a serious discussion over the Nazi era we are now exposed to a return to the discourse of the Nazi era:

> The chat room promptly filled with hate. 'Jewish scum' and 'Auschwitz liar' were the mildest insults. As the sinking of the ship was dredged up for a new generation, the long-submerged hate slogan 'Death to all Jews' bubbled to the digital surface of contemporary reality: foaming hate, a maelstrom of hate. Good God! How much of this has been dammed up all the time, is growing day by day, building pressure for action.[42]

As the novel continues, it turns out that the website is run in Paul Pokriefke's own house by his son Konrad. Konrad is no skinhead, just an ordinary young German in the present age. As an adolescent he was in need of myths, and, failing to receive them from his father, who ignored the past altogether, he became a heir apparent to his grandmother, who has never given up the Nazi myths, even when she was a fervent Communist in East Germany. As an incumbent of the present generation, Konrad knows how to use his website to draw the right-wing circles' muddled attention to the forgotten ship and its human cargo. But the more preoccupied he becomes with the online game, the more he loses touch with the actual historical event of the sinking of the *Wilhelm Gustloff*. He becomes a Jew hater and ends up murdering a young man he meets online and believes to be a Jew.

Grass sees the resort to the Second World War narrative by a young German to be the natural outgrowth of the urge to forget. Konrad's hate, he writes, was not dramatic but a "matter-of-fact hate. Hate turned down low. An eternal flame. A hate devoid of passion, reproducing itself asexually."[43] In other words, the author attributes to contemporary German youngsters, whose parents failed to talk to them sufficiently about their country's past, a persistent, underlying restlessness which may explode in unexpected ways. To Grass, a country's history cannot simply be ignored; the unfinished business of the past must be coped with on the educational, cultural, and personal levels, for otherwise it will come to haunt future generations. *Crabwalk* leaves no doubt that as Germany steps into the twenty-first century without coping enough with its past, the mastery of new technologies and new media by Konrad and his like will lead them to inflict evil again.

ANDRÉ BRINK, *THE RIGHTS OF DESIRE*

"I rest my case on the rights of desire," says Professor David Lurie, J. M. Coetzee's main character in *Disgrace*,[44] a novel depicting an arid, cheerless post-Apartheid South Africa that, like the disgraced professor, has managed to repent for the evils of the past only in name. André Brink's *The Rights of Desire* may be seen as an attempt to question whether South Africa is indeed doomed to disgrace or whether in spite of the violence and injustice still present in the country, a vivid society has a chance to emerge, whose citizens could claim the right "to live, to move, to breathe."[45] This claim depends on finding ways to cope with the evils of the past, and the novel proposes a way to do so. By constructing the figure of Antje of Bengal ("Antje" meaning "grace"), an abused eighteenth-century slave girl whose ghost is present in a house in contemporary Cape Town, Brink steps into the discourse launched by Archbishop Desmond Tutu, claiming that South Africa's passage into the future demands a genuine dialogue with the past, which recognizes the difficulty of getting at the truth or reaching reconciliation yet enlivens the haunted society in complex and often unexpected ways.

The dialogue with the ghost in *The Rights of Desire* allows one household in Cape Town to transcend the perpetrator-victim divide, thus pointing at a model of life in post-Apartheid South Africa which, in contrast to Coetzee's pessimism, involves a degree of grace. As claimed by one of the characters in the novel: "The country is not just crime, and corruption, and failure, and whatnot. We must believe there's something more to it, something larger than all of us, a kind of hope, a kind of potential. It's something like Antje of Bengal."[46]

The novel's main character, Ruben, is a white Afrikaner who is concerned neither with the past nor with the present. "I did watch Mandela's walk to freedom from Victor Verster prison," he says," but I did not vote in the much-vaunted democratic elections of '94. Queueing was too tedious for my liking."[47] When the world held its breath in view of the earth shaking events in South Africa: the end of the Apartheid regime, Nelson Mandela's release from prison, the free elections of 1994, and the TRC hearings, Ruben remained unimpressed. Politics, he admits, has never been a topic to excite him. The former librarian finds refuge in books and tries to ignore his surroundings, but neither the past nor the present can be easily dispensed with. "The House is haunted,"[48] Brink writes. Ghosts are no longer fashionable, but the ghost of Antje of Bengal resides in Ruben's house "just to tell her story, perhaps."[49]

The story, apparently based on a true case or a series of true cases, is sad and gruesome. Antje of Bengal, a seven-year-old girl, had been brought to the Cape on a Dutch slave ship in 1696. In a slave auction, she had been separated from her mother and sold to a baker and, after his death, to a tavern keeper who abused her as part of his provocation against his wife. The man, who served as deacon and stalwart of the church, copulated with the slave girl on the mat at the foot of the wife's bed, deriving a perverse satisfaction from tormenting his wide-awake wife with the sounds of his fornication only a step or two away from her. The wife in turn beat the slave girl up so severely that she caused her to have a miscarriage.

When the tavern keeper poisons his wife, Antje is charged with the murder. Her master is never even summoned as a witness because, as one historian put it, "to place a member of the Cape's elite in the same case as criminal slaves, was obviously more than the Court of Justice could stomach. To declare them as equals before the law would be to undermine the structures of inequality which bound the Cape's colonial society together."[50] In spite of testimony by the other slaves in the household pointing at Antje's innocence, the slave girl is condemned to be taken to the place of public execution, be bound to a pole, branded with hot irons, and then strangled with a cord until dead. Thereafter her head and right hand were to be removed and fixed on stakes and the remains of her body fastened to a forked post and exposed until consumed by the air and the birds of heaven. Her ghost, however, remains in the house to tell her story.

In his study of ghosts in literature, Alec Marsh writes: "Historical ghosts are unquiet spirits, the dead walking the 'perturbed spirits' of the injured, the murdered, the dispossessed. They walk out of our bad conscience with their fearful summonses, demanding that we change our life. They are said to haunt places where suicides, massacres and atrocities have been perpetuated."[51] Marsh notes that these unquiet messengers do not speak but wait to be understood. "They wait sadly, patiently, helplessly—perhaps forever—haunting a room until the right person shows up."[52] In Brink's novel, the right person is Ruben's coloured housekeeper, Magrieta, who is more than capable of listening.

When Magrieta was a young woman, she lived in Cape Town's District Six, whose destruction has been one of the Apartheid regime's landmarks. It was a mixed district populated by liberated slaves, artisans, merchants, and labourers. In 1901, blacks were ordered out of the district, and in 1966 the turn of the coloured came when 60,000 of them were expelled and their houses demolished. "That's when it all began," writes Brink, "the day of the bulldozers."[53] Since then Magrieta's life has been miserable; violence finds her wherever she is. During the days of Apartheid she was too black for the whites, and when Apartheid ended she was too white for the blacks. She often speaks about her gloomy experiences but Ruben makes no attempt to listen. As he says in the novel, he and his housekeeper have no way to bridge their two worlds:

> There was only a kitchen table between us, but we might have been creatures from different worlds who just happened by the purest coincidence to be sharing the same space. She, the large mother from the township, in her shapeless housecoat and her slippers with the pink pompons, harbouring

somewhere inside her global body the violence and the rage, the raping and killing and burning of her everyday world, its poverty, its meekness, and patience and suffering, its anger and rebellion and despair, its affirmations and denials, its witches and with-hunts.... What did I know of her world? She was as unreal to me as any ghost.[54]

Antje of Bengal, however, bridges the gap. With the appearance of the ghost, we learn, "The house became, as it had been long before, a place of talk and imagination."[55] Her presence assures that the past will not be forgotten, and yet the abused slave girl appears not only as a victim but as a full person, which leads the house's residents to live a fuller life themselves. The dialogue between the ghost and Magrieta is a source of support for the housekeeper, giving her the strength to endure. "I take the word of a woman who knows what it is to be sucked out by a man like an orange en then throwed away," Magrieta says in her own lingo. "Because she was a slave en because she was coloured en because she was a woman they all treated her like shit."[56] The relationship is reciprocal; Antje has not remained in the house only to tell her story but also to listen, and a dialogue is held between these two women whose experiences they can only share with each other because historians have failed to understand their plight. As this dialogue goes on, Magrieta no longer talks only as a victim: "There was a constant stream of reports on celebrations, christenings, weddings, school sports . . . trips to Strandfontein or Cool Bay . . . heckling a visiting politician."[57]

The ghost also allows other residents of the house to develop a richer narrative. As Ruben's tenant, Tessa, realizes: "Maybe she isn't here for herself but for us . . . perhaps we need our ghosts as much as they need us."[58] Ruben, being a white Afrikaner, loses his job to a black man in the post-Apartheid regime and, trapped in the perpetrator-victim circle, realizes the wheel has turned, which leads to his apathy and escapism. But the ghost's presence in his house breaks this circle and he begins to realize that life may be worth living after all.

> I am not alone ... Antje of Bengal is here. She will help me—and, no doubt, also make it more difficult—to face what has to be faced, what all my life I've tried to turn away from. There is a world outside—how did Rilke phrase it?—which requires me and strangely concerns me. Antje will see to it that I do not avoid it.[59]

How capable are we of holding a dialogue with the voices of the past? Brink believes we are, emphasizing the role ghost stories have always played in African culture, stories about "ghosts of dead Bushmen crawling from their unmarked graves to plague whoever had unwittingly trodden on them, the ghosts of the murdered returning to bring the perpetrators to justice or drive them to their death; the ghosts of ancient warriors, black and white, rising from forgotten battlefields of the past to haunt the living who tried to grow mealies or pumpkins or whatever on the blood-drenched veld; ghosts of people hanged for crimes they had not committed."[60] In other words, attending to the voices of the murdered, tortured, and dispossessed is not unfamiliar in South African culture, and Brink believes in the healing power of such memory.[61] His own ghost story goes beyond the clash between perpetrator and victim, adding another building block to a narrative in which the memory of the past is central and does not prevent but rather encourages us to claim the right to desire: the right "to live, to move to breath."[62]

CONCLUSION

The three writers whose novels have been analyzed in this chapter, Murakami, Grass, and Brink, are sharp-eyed observers of present conditions in their respective countries of Japan, Germany, and South Africa. They draw a rather gloomy picture of these countries, whose economic prosperity and industrial growth have been accompanied by human alienation, political extremism, street violence, and urban terrorism. All three novels describe unsuccessful attempts to find refuge from these conditions, which are attributed, explicitly or implicitly, to the three societies' failure to come to terms with their past. The demilitarization of Japan, the de-Nazification in Germany and the end of Apartheid in South Africa have not ended the anguish caused by evils of earlier periods and no escape to a library, or a journey to the end of the earth, could erase their memory.

All three writers show how the curse of the past still haunts these societies and look for ways to cope with it. As they do so, they add important nuances to the two narratives prevailing in the public sphere in many countries and in the international arena: the narrative of modernity, individualism, progress, and rationality mostly associated with the West and the narrative of slavery, colonialism, genocide, and other evils largely attributed to the West.

Each of the three writers is concerned with a specific political setting, but together they point the way toward a narrative in which the evils of the past have a central place, as does the realization that by coping with the past in its full complexity, rather than by advancing the perpetrator-victim divide, societies have a chance to move toward reconciliation. Such a narrative is easier to follow in fiction than in reality due to the power of such devices as ghostly characters to tie together the present and the past. Moreover, political leaders often prefer to stick to the narrative of the victim, or the former perpetrator threatened by the victim, than to encourage their followers to emerge from these one-dimensional roles and develop a multifaceted political identity.

Victims of evil and their descendants may find it hard to rise beyond the politics of victimhood for emotional reasons or because of the benefits gained by a continuous status of victimhood. It is also hard for those responsible for the victimization of others to overcome their fear of the turning cycle. But coexistence in a modern industrial society haunted by its past is dependent, in my opinion, on an introduction of some nuanced narrative as identified in the three novels into the public sphere. In such a narrative, the story of past evils remains central but the roles of perpetrator and victim are surmounted and a full account of the historical conditions which gave rise to evil is given as part of a genuine commitment to avoid its return.

Japan, Germany, and South Africa are examples of countries in which the discourse about the past, or its avoidance, causes deep rifts, but the same is true of all other countries. As history is filled with evil, politics all over the world is affected by the demand to make good the suffering of former slaves, oppressed Aboriginals, victims of genocide, etc. World politics is also largely affected by the discourse on modernity and its discontents. It cannot be expected that existing narratives will be abandoned because, as I've said before, they are deeply rooted in political cultures and too beneficial to political actors. Nevertheless, it is worthwhile to look at the nuances proposed here in order to help countries tormented by their past to remember it in a way that would not sharpen differences but rather allow humans to live in peace and dignity.

THE POLITICS OF VICTIMHOOD IN JOHN LE CARRÉ'S *ABSOLUTE FRIENDS*

John Le Carré's novels have not always been praised by literary critics; such is the case with his 2003 novel *Absolute Friends*. Here, however, I would like to discuss this novel for its contribution to the conversation on the role of public intellectuals in contemporary society. Public intellectuals are persons concerned with symbols and ideas who comment on society's present condition and provide guidelines for the future.[1] Such persons have always been hard to place within well-defined social role categories, partly, perhaps, because public intellectuals themselves have done much of the categorization. It is easier to attribute a social role to another group than to your own. Indeed, the sociological literature has mostly followed the notion proposed by Edward Shils of the public intellectual as having some contact with the transcendental.[2] Public intellectuals were seen as burdened with a mission: to introduce society to a universal set of norms sanctioned by a higher authority, like the biblical prophet who speaks a divine truth to earthly powers and thereby spreads norms of peace and justice to all corners of the earth. The prototype of the prophet lies at the core of works by Mannheim,[3] Parsons,[4] and others who saw intellectuals as located in a given society yet versed in a universal culture, nurturing it and feeding its values back to society.

Writings on intellectuals have often been concerned with the preservation of that universal culture within a world of growing nationalism. This concern is mainly associated with Julien Benda's book *The Treason of the Intellectuals*.[5] Writing in the 1920s, Benda observed two passions – class passion and national passion – overwhelming intellectual life, which meant that the intellectuals no longer rose above the masses in preaching humanism rather than class or national consciousness. In past centuries, he claimed, the development of national movements by the masses were accompanied by "a whole class of men, regarded with the greatest reverence, laboring to thwart this movement … men of learning, artists and philosophers, displaying to the world a spirit which cared nothing for nations, using a universal language among themselves."

Confining the universal culture developed among intellectuals to European culture, Benda cherished "those who gave Europe its moral values preaching the cult of the human, or at least of the Christian, and not of the national." They were striving "to found, in opposition to the nations, a great universal empire on spiritual foundations." This trend, however, ended in the age of nationalism:

> To-day the game is over. Humanity is national. The layman has won. But his triumph has gone beyond anything he could have expected. The "clerk" is not only conquered, he is assimilated. The man of science, the artist, the philosopher are attached to their nations as much as the day-laborer and the merchant. Those who make the world's values, make them for a nation; the Ministers of Jesus defend the national. All humanity, including the "clerks," have become laymen. All Europe, including Erasmus, has followed Luther.[6]

Benda set up a clear mission for the intellectual: to defend universal values against national or class passions. This mission distinguishes the true intellectual who transcends all earthly boundaries from the false one who yields to them. True intellectuals are never at home in any country and are willing to criticize their own society from a perspective that transcends the customs and norms they acquired as its members. They are also willing to pay the price such criticism bears.

This mission appealed to intellectuals who felt more at home in global settings in which a universal culture seemingly prevails than they did in encounters with their compatriots. In an essay titled "Our Homeland, the Text," for example, Jewish literary critic George Steiner, at home in many literary cultures, praised the transformation modern Jewish intellectuals made from the pursuit of sacred texts to literary scholarship and challenged them with a clear-cut choice: either stay out in the cold as an outsider to the national effort and remain a "critical humanist," or go to Israel and become part of the closed fist of the nation-state. A true thinker, Steiner writes, must know that no nation, no body politic, no creed, no moral ideal and necessity, including that of human survival, is worth a falsehood, a willed self-deception, or the manipulation of a text. But the nation-state cannot avoid these ills because it is founded on myths of insaturation and of militant glory and perpetuates itself by lies and half-truths. The locus of truth, to Steiner, is always extraterritorial. "Locked materially in a material homeland, the text may, in fact, lose its life-force, and its true values may be betrayed. But when the text *is* the homeland, even when it is rooted only in the exact remembrance and seeking of a handful of wanderers, nomads of the word, it cannot be extinguished."[7]

The dualist demand that intellectuals either remain loyal to the pursuit of a universal truth or serve the nation-state has been criticized by Michael Walzer, who notes Benda's own deviation from this dualism. By being drawn to the defence of Dreyfus and to the fight against Fascism, Benda demonstrated his unwillingness to leave the world to his enemies. His detached intellectual may obscure but never entirely block out the image of the engaged actor, Walzer writes, adding that while Benda's peculiar view of critical detachment derives from his own detachment as an assimilated French Jew who abandoned his own Jewish heritage, one of his greatest heroes was Albert Einstein, a committed Zionist who chose to identify not only with the universal ideals of truth and justice but also with his fellow Jews. "The goal that Einstein set for his own life was not the loss of self but the establishment of a 'spiritual equilibrium' – and this he thought possible only through the shared life of a nation."[8]

In his critique of *The Treason of the Intellectuals*, Walzer provides an updated view of the public intellectual's role, claiming that there is no realm of absolute intellectuality. He agrees with Benda that truth itself may be universal and immutable but reminds us that every practical embodiment of it in philosophical doctrine or poetic vision is partial and ideological:

> Justice is embodied not only in doctrines and visions but also in conventions, customs, beliefs, rituals, and institutions. The mark of the intellectual is not that he is necessarily detached from these forms of 'real life' and critical of them – for sometimes he must surely defend them – but that he is never blindly bound and wholly uncritical. He stands somewhat to the side; he establishes a critical distance. But this is a distance that can be measured in inches. It's not a matter of living (spiritually) somewhere else, across a chasm, in a distinct and separate world; it's a matter of living here – and drawing a line.[9]

EDWARD SAID'S VIEW OF THE PUBLIC INTELLECTUAL

The two models at the centre of the conversation over the role of public intellectuals – the model of the truth-seeking intellectual who remains uncorrupted by political commitments and the model of the engaged intellectual who criticizes the nation-state but remains rooted in it and committed to the political narratives it produces – came under attack in Edward Said's 1994 collection of essays *Representations of the Intellectual*. In an essay titled "Holding Nations and Traditions at Bay," Said mocks Benda's view that intellectuals exist in a sort of universal space, bound neither by national boundaries nor by ethnic identity, claiming that Benda's concern with intellectuals was limited only to Europeans. By referring to transcendental values, those that were universally applicable to all nations and peoples, Benda takes it for granted that these values were European and not Indian or Chinese, writes Said. Today, however, travel and communication have made for a new awareness of "difference" and "otherness" which requires a concern with national, religious, continental and linguistic variations among intellectuals, none of whom writes in Esperanto. But Said also rejects the possibility of drawing the line while being part of a national language community:

> The particular problem of the intellectual . . . is that a language community in each society that is dominated by habits of expression already exists, one of whose main functions is to preserve the status quo, and to make certain that things go smoothly, unchanged, and unchallenged . . . The result is that the mind is numbed and remains inactive while language that has the effect of background music in a supermarket washes over consciousness, seducing it into passive acceptance of unexamined ideas and sentiments.[10]

Said is skeptical of any intellectual endeavour conducted within the boundaries of the nation-state. Any article in the *New York Times*, however well researched, is seen by him as reflecting a "national corporate identity,"[11] helping the national community feel a sense of common identity and allowing the view of other political units in grand generalizations. He claims, for example, that the view of Islam in the West as incompatible with democracy is enhanced by intellectuals. Here, writes Said, "corporate thinking has *not* made intellectuals into the questioning and skeptical individual minds . . . individuals who represent not the consensus but doubts about it on rational, moral and political, to say nothing of methodological grounds, but rather into a chorus that echoes the prevailing policy views, hastening it along into more corporate thinking, and into a gradually more irrational sense that 'we' are being threatened by 'them'."[12]

This critique rejects the two competing models of intellectuals. Intellectuals may be defined as cosmopolitans who shine a light unto the nations, but their cosmopolitanism is seen as none but an ethnocentric bias, mostly a Western bias. Or they may be defined as critical observers of their own nation-state, but their affiliation with its language community prevents them from being truly critical. Said comes up with a third model by offering the intellectual a choice: "The intellectual always has a choice either to side with the weaker, the less well represented, the forgotten or ignored, or to side with the more powerful."[13] Assuming that every nation-building process produces its victims, intellectuals are distinguished by their siding with the victims. Following Gramsci's view of social reality as divided between rulers and ruled, Said considers it the intellectual's task to show "how the group is a constructed, manufactured, even in some cases invented object, with a history and conquest behind it"[14] and "to consider [social] stability as a state of emergency threatening the less fortunate with the danger of complete extinction, and take into account the experience of subordination itself, as well as the memory of forgotten voices and persons.[15] His exemplary intellectuals who match this third model in the United States are Noam Chomsky and Gore Vidal.

Said then goes a step further, demanding that the concern for the victims in one's nation-state be turned into a universal concern:

> To this terribly important task of representing the collective suffering of your own people, testifying to its travails, reasserting its enduring presence, reinforcing its memory, there must be added something else, which only an intellectual, I believe, has the obligation to fulfill . . . For the

intellectual the task, I believe, is explicitly to universalize the crisis, to give greater human scope to what a particular race or nation suffered, to associate that experience with the sufferings of others.[16]

Said not only stated this demand but fulfilled it in his own writings in which he presented the Palestinian people, to which he belonged, as the ultimate victims of the Arab-Israeli conflict. In *Blaming the Victims* he portrays the Palestinians as "the direct victims of Zionist theory and Israeli policy."[17] The positioning of Israelis as the perpetrators and of Palestinians as the victims allows the consideration of acts of terrorism as "isolated and politically worthless acts of desperation."[18] And even when admitting that Palestinians resorted on occasion to "spectacular outrages," which Said considers a "political mistake with important moral consequences,"[19] it turns out that the political and moral consequences refer not to the victims of terror but to the fact that Palestinian violence has been magnified in world public opinion.

This trend is then being universalized, for instance, when Said criticizes "the almost unconditional assent of the media, intellectuals and policy-makers to the terrorist vogue,"[20] calling for a return to a semblance of sanity which, to him, consists of revising the American attitude toward terrorism:

> [T]he terrorism craze is dangerous because it consolidates the immense, unrestrained pseudopatriotic narcissism we are nourishing. Is there no limit to the folly that convinces large numbers of Americans that it is now unsafe to travel, and at the same time blinds them to all the pain and violence that so many people in Africa, Asia and Latin America must endure simply because we have decided that local oppressors, whom we call freedom fighters, can go on with their killing in the name of anticommunism and antiterrorism? Is there no way to participate in politics beyond the repetition of prefabricated slogans? What happened to

the precision, discrimination and critical humanism that we celebrate as the hallmarks of liberal education and the Western heritage?[21]

Said's demand of public intellectuals to determine in any given situation who is the perpetrator and who is the victim leads to a change in their role; having been traditionally signified by their capacity to transcend popular political sentiment, the intellectuals are now being politicized, drawn into "the politics of victimhood," always expected to side with those perceived to be the victims.

This role change called for by Said in the 1990s becomes immanent with much of today's intellectual discourse moving online. The ease with which sudden brain waves can be made public on the Internet, the anonymity allowed in cyberspace, and the sheer magnitude of information piling up online are conducive to the politics of victimhood in that the victims can be immediately, perhaps automatically, identified; victims who were previously reluctant to speak up can be encouraged to testify behind a veil of anonymity; and anti-establishment sentiments against political leaders or media organizations can snowball with great intensity across the globe.

Under these conditions, intellectuals cease to remain aloof as Benda hoped or to draw the line as Walzer advocated, crowding instead with like-minded individuals – often millions of them – who agree on the identity of the victims, thereby avoiding a careful consideration of the complexities involved in any political situation.

LE CARRÉ AND THE PUBLIC INTELLECTUAL

What are the political implications of public intellectuals' participation in the politics of victimhood? What is the meaning of a global public discourse lacking the independence of mind characteristic of the traditional models of intellectuals advanced by Benda and Walzer? What can be expected when millions of statements are made in the mass media and new media which follow a rather regimented distinction between good and evil? How useful is an intellectual dialogue between relatively stable camps of bloggers or tweeters fighting fiercely over who is the perpetrator and who the victim is in any given situation? What is the impact of a global discourse that encourages the politics of victimhood?

It is hard to answer these questions, but fiction can come to our aid by imagining scenarios in which the conditions we ask about prevail, so that we can then follow step by step the development of behaviours affected by these conditions and consider alternative behavioural scenarios. Le Carré's *Absolute Friends* is a good example in this regard because Said's vision is largely embodied in its literary narrative and the novel thus offers, as literary works often do, a roadmap for thinking through its implications.

Le Carré's protagonist, Ted Mundy, fits quite neatly the postcolonial world conceptualized, and to a large extent led, by Said: a world conscious of the evils of colonialism and searching for a new political and corporate structure that would give a voice to its former victims. The son of a British colonial officer who was kicked out of India after independence, Mundy epitomizes the unmitigated disorientation felt by many following the collapse of the colonial order. He is "a hybrid, a nomad, a man without territory, parents, property or example"[22] and consequently finds himself in the company of radical anarchists who provide him with love, sex, and a partial sense of belonging, while he cares little for their ideology, or for any other one. "Why should he care that he knows even less about Mikhail Bakunin than he does about the parts of the female anatomy?"[23] He thus agrees with the young men and women he occasionally meets that the state is an instrument of tyranny – even if the state is the last thing on his mind – and about such matters as "individualization," extolling "the rehabilitation of the I" or "the supremacy of the individual."[24] Mundy is undaunted by belonging to "a tiny band of gallant comrades" in the 1960s, which turns his participation in the student demonstrations, sit-ins, and marches of the era into an automatic response by a disoriented soul finding refuge in protests against the Vietnam War, the Greek colonels, etc.

The author emphasizes the clarity with which distinctions between the children of light and the children of darkness were made in that decade, which left no question what one's obligations were in all circumstances: "To oppose the Vietnam war by all means... To arrest the spread of military imperialism... To reject the consumer state... To challenge the nostrums of the bourgeoisie."[25] Such clarity was not only the result of Marxist ideas but also of the closeness to the Second World War. As Mundy is being told when he joins a band of young radicals in Berlin, "In Berlin we can lean out of the window and shout 'Nazi swine', and if the arsehole on the pavement is more than forty years old we shall be right."[26] But the automatic categorization of individuals and nations does not end with Second World War Germany, as can be learnt from the description of a sermon held by Mundy's friend Sasha, the relentless revolutionary:

> He has called for the Nuremberg Tribunal to be reconvened, and the fascist-imperialist American leadership arraigned before it on charges of genocide and crimes against humanity. He has accused the morally degenerate American lackeys of the so-called government in Bonn of sanitizing Germany's Nazi past with consumerism, and turning the Auschwitz generation into a flock of fat sheep with nothing in their heads but new refrigerators, TV sets and Mercedes cars. He has railed against the Shah and his CIA-backed secret police, the Savak, and spread himself on the subject of the American-sponsored Greek colonels and the "American puppet state of Israel."[27]

Distinctions between the good guys and the bad guys become difficult when coalitions have to be formed with those who do not necessarily belong to the righteous, as Mundy realizes when he shoulders in demonstrations against the Iraq War of 2003 with "The beastly

Germans. The perfidious French. The barbarian Russians."[28] Such coalitions are inconsistent with the purist aims set by the young revolutionaries of the 1960s: "As a first stage, we shall wipe the human slate clean. We shall detoxify the brain, cleanse it of its prejudices, inhibitions and inherited appetites. We shall purge it of everything old and rotten . . . Americanism, greed, class, envy, racism, bourgeois sentimentality, hatred, aggression, superstition and the craving for property and power."[29] This requires the formation of a harmonious society in which "Brotherly love, natural sharing, mutual respect"[30] would prevail. The author leads us through the stages in which this task is being pursued today by public intellectuals like Canadian Naomi Klein, Indian Arundhati Roy, British George Monbiot and Mark Curtis, Australian John Pilger, Americans Noam Chomsky and Joseph Stiglitz and Franco-American Susan George. One of the novel's characters proposes the common denominator of these globally renowned intellectuals inspiring the anti-globalization movement:

> From their varying perspectives, each of these eminent writers tells me the same story. The corporate octopus is stifling the natural growth of humanity. It spreads tyranny, poverty and economic serfdom. It defies the simplest laws of ecology. Warfare is the extension of corporate power by other means.[31]

Since the experience of the 1960s has proven protests against governments and corporations ineffective, a new line is chosen. The anti-globalization thinkers search for an alternative to existing systems of the production and dissemination of knowledge. The existing systems are seen as controlled by national and multinational corporations, which allows them to instigate wars and destroy the planet without effective resistance. The masses lack the ability to expose the lies spread by their leaders, a problem which reached a peak in the Iraq War. "This is a war of lies . . . Our politicians lie to the press, they see their lies printed and call them public opinion . . . By repetition, each lie becomes an irreversible fact upon which other lies are constructed. Then we have a war."³² In order to prevent the cycle of lies and allow different viewpoints to emerge, the control over knowledge must be mitigated. This is attempted in the novel by a character named Dimitri who represents the sum of ideas propounded by the public intellectuals mentioned above. His main concern is the corporate control over higher education:

> How do these corporations achieve their stranglehold on our society? When they're not shooting, they're buying. They buy good minds, and tie them to their wagon wheels. They buy students wet from their mothers, and castrate their thought processes. They create false orthodoxies and impose censorship under the sham of political correctness. They build university facilities, dictate university courses, over-promote the professors who kiss ass and they bully the shit out of heretics. Their one aim is to perpetuate the insane concept of limitless expansion on a limited planet, with permanent conflict as its desired outcome. And their product is the zero-educated robot known otherwise as the corporate executive."³³

The solution to the corporate corruption of young minds lies in the creation of "corporation-free academic zones."³⁴ The meaning of the project remains blurred but the language is borrowed from the deconstructionist discourse prevalent in many university departments today. Dimitri ventures to establish a counter-university which has no dogma. "We offer no doctrinal front for our corporate adversaries to piss on. Like them, we shall be offshore and responsible to nobody. We shall use stealth. We shall be intellectual guerrillas. We shall install ourselves wherever the enemy is encamped."³⁵ The language leaves no room for doubt; a new intellectual culture is emerging devoted to the salvation of the planet and placing itself in clear opposition to the forces blamed for its destruction. Following the purism of the 1960s but far more confident in its ability to reconstruct the world of knowledge in the spirit of postcolonialism, it promises to turn the world upside down. As Said, Fanon, and others have hoped, the colonized will be liberated and a new humanity devoted to preservation of the planet and the human race will emerge.

Le Carré warns us of that new purism. Once the intellectual dialogue gives up pragmatic deliberations of complex political situations for the sake of a clear distinction between the children of light and the children of darkness, once the world is morally divided between the supporters of the Iraq War and those who resist it, once Israel becomes the ultimate predator and the Palestinians the ultimate victims, when students and their professors in the West describe the United States as the Great Satan while self-righteously dismissing evils conducted by the former victims of colonialism, then the door opens up to violence. Thus, when the counter-university is established, and boxes filled with books are delivered to its library, the novel's protagonist Mundy finds out that these boxes contain more than intellectual works. Unpacking at first copies of Fanon's *The Wretched of the Earth* in nine languages, he comes across books which are far more advanced than Fanon's works:

> Their preferred subjects are how to make bombs out of weedkiller and how to kill your best friend with a knitting needle, or booby-trap his car or lavatory, or garrotte him in his bed, or drown him in his bath, or smash the horns of his larynx, or send a fireball up the liftshaft of his workplace.[36]

CONCLUSION

Intellectuals are not terrorists and terrorists are rarely intellectuals; thinking and killing stem from different sources and only meet occasionally when revolutionaries justify their violence by reason or when terrorists are indoctrinated by intellectuals. The politics of victimhood, however, which has become a *bon ton* in certain academic circles, must be seen not only for the righteous intentions underlying it but also for its political implications. An intellectual arena in which the careful analysis of complex political issues is replaced by an automatic response by a crowd is politically dangerous. True, intellectual dialogue has a limited political impact. Intellectual interventions in politics have mostly ended in failure, for politics is more inspired by considerations of *realpolitik* than by persons of letters crying *J'accuse* as did writer Emile Zola in the Dreyfus Affair in late nineteenth-century France. But such interventions have always served as important reminders of the distinction between good and evil, even when evil has abounded. And the danger exists that this distinction may be lost once it turns into a robotic response programmed by a simplistic postcolonial doctrine. The consideration of good and evil does of course involve a strong a priori element; any moral statement begins with axioms such as "Thou Shalt not Kill." Yet, morality – religious or otherwise – becomes dangerous when applied to a political field characterized by complexity and subtlety. Such application requires careful consideration of the conditions prevailing at any given time; yesterday's victims may turn into today's predators and victimhood can easily be reconstructed and serve as propaganda devise by forces that are anything but righteous. Apologies for evils of the past are a welcomed phenomenon in the postcolonial world but they should not be taken as justifications to terrorize the alleged colonists. Just like religious morality, history is a bad guide for political action, and those coddling in the evils inflicted upon them in the past can be expected to inflict evil in the future.

The Internet in particular provides an all too comfortable means to introduce religious morality and historical accounting into the public sphere. This may lead to a cheapening of the discourse held by public intellectuals. The growth of online venues has stimulated the diversity of public intellectuals, and some cyberspace actors have become rather prominent, gaining a much larger readership than traditional intellectuals ever had. There is no reason to believe that today's online actors produce texts of lesser intellectual value and political relevance than those written in the past. Yet it is hard to imagine Emile Zola's cry having the same moral impact were it published in the hyperbolic environment of the Internet. In a setting in which a flood of moral imperatives is sent into cyberspace by often anonymous figures who may exclaim "J'accuse" but who have no responsibility to produce well-conceived, prudent, self-reflective arguments considering political complexity and subtlety and are thus prone to follow the politics of victimhood, extremist and violent political forces have a good chance of winning attention. The conditions of immediacy, anonymity, and crowding on the Internet do not necessarily lead good people to seek evil. But as Le Carré reminds us in *Absolute Friends*, global actors with good intentions may use bombs rather than books in their construction of a pure, clean, and peaceful planet.

CHAPTER 8

THE QUEST FOR IDENTITY IN SAYED KASHUA'S *LET IT BE MORNING*

In 2011, Mohammed Saif-Alden Wattad expressed the identity crisis he experienced as an Arab citizen of a Jewish state:

> Like a school of dolphins, most Israeli Arabs have lost their way deep in a stormy sea. One wave throws them up; another pushes them down to the bottom of the sea. They struggle day and night for their identity. They keep swimming in that stormy sea wishing for the sunny day to come, thus enjoying the glory of the sea; but the sea refuses to accept them, and the stormy waves insist to throw them out to the shore, where they get suffocated and find their death.[1]

These words represent the feelings of many Palestinian Arabs who, after the establishment of the State of Israel in 1948, found themselves within its boundaries. Having become Israeli citizens, they were always torn between their national identity as Palestinians and their identity as citizens of the sovereign state of Israel. Many national groups live as minorities within sovereign states, but the situation here has been particularly hard because of the ongoing Arab-Israeli conflict and because Israel, while granting its citizens political rights, defines itself as a Jewish state, thus excluding non-Jews from the narrative developed as part of the nation-building process. That narrative views the Jews' settlement of the land of Israel since the late nineteenth century as a return to Zion and a restoration of Jewish independence, while the Palestinian narrative views Zionism as a colonial movement and Israeli independence, achieved after a war in which 700,000 Palestinians became refugees, as a *Nakba* (catastrophe). The Zionist narrative has been institutionalized in the state in a way that made it impossible for its Arab citizens to identify with the state's hymn, flag, national holidays, and other symbols, as noted by Yitzhak Reiter:

> The national goals of the state are . . . reflected very accurately in its values and symbolic representations. The state's principle values, as well as its culture, which dominate the public space, strongly express the national interests and cultural aspirations of the Jewish majority. The public atmosphere, national educational norms and reforms, and official ceremonies that have developed over the years are all built around the Jewish historical memory and accentuate a Zionist outlook that includes Diaspora heritage, the Holocaust and the revivalist movement.[2]

We are thus faced with a complicated situation in which Arabs living in Israel are defining their identity as citizens of the state within circumstances encouraging their exclusion from it. No wonder they have been compared to a school of dolphins lost in a stormy sea, a metaphor relating both to the overall condition of the Arab minority in Israel and to the often futile discourse held about it. In what follows, I discuss that discourse in an attempt to highlight a creative attempt by novelist Sayed Kashua to breach its boundaries.

THE DISCOURSE ABOUT THE ARAB MINORITY IN ISRAEL

The difficulties experienced by the Arab minority in Israel have been analyzed by sociologist Sammy Smooha, who emphasized the circumstances at their core. The relations between Jews and Arabs in Israel were forged in tragic circumstances of war, destruction, evacuation, and coercion. In 1948, Smooha writes, the Arab minority unwillingly became part of the enemy and was subjected to nineteen years of military rule. The Arabs and Jews saw themselves as the indigenous population and demanded almost exclusive rights over the same strip of land.

Smooha puts special emphasis on class differences; Arabs in Israel are a working-class community within a middle-class society. About 90 percent of them live in Arab villages and towns and the other 10 percent live in separate neighbourhoods in Jewish cities. They do not share power and suffer from discrimination in allocation of state budgets, in appointments, and in obtaining work and housing in the private sector. "To put it bluntly," he writes, "the Arab minority is a distinct national-religious-linguistic, non-assimilating and dissident minority, whose loyalty is suspect, who is discriminated against, does not accept its situation as a decree of fate, and is enlisted in a struggle to change its status."[3]

Many have shared in the portrayal of the Arab citizens of Israel as a distinct, non-assimilating, dissident minority. Shlomo Ben-Ami sees them as "Torn between their loyalty to their Palestinian brethren across the border and their Israeli citizenship;"[4] Joseph Ginat contends that Israel's War of Independence has left the Arabs bitter and wishing for revenge, thus bringing about "a bitter existential struggle which has continued for many years on the background of mighty historical myths, which essentially deny the right of the Jewish state to exist;"[5] Ra'anan Cohen writes that "continuation of the present situation sharpens and deepens the Arabs' alienation toward the State, to such an extent that it will not be long before they resort to extensive and open civil disobedience and even violence;"[6] Yitzhak Reiter stresses the divide between the Jewish narrative that underlines the children of Israel's primordial right to the land and the Arabs' view of the same land as an inheritance from their ancestors;[7] Laurence Louër claims that "Arabs and Jews are not so much irreconcilable enemies, wishing to annihilate each other, as the bearers of two very different visions of what Israeli society should be."[8]

Over the years, certain steps toward reconciliation between the Jewish majority and Arab minority in Israel have been taken, especially in the early 1990s when the Middle East seemed for a short while to advance toward peace. Economic conditions in Arab towns and villages improved somewhat, and the Arab communities developed effective political parties and civil society organizations. However, in October 2000 Israeli police killed thirteen Arab citizens who demonstrated in support of their brethren in the Palestinian occupied territories, which caused a major setback. Disenchantment and pessimism have replaced hopes for reconciliation, and the discourse about the Arab minority in Israel held by Israeli Jews and Arabs alike has been radicalized.

Hillel Frisch describes the backlash of October 2000 from the Jewish perspective: "Israel's relationship to its Arab minority is largely informed by a sense of threat and security fears. These emanate from the strategic environment in which the dominant community is a majority within its own state yet a threatened precarious minority in the region."[9] Dan Rabinowitz and Khawla Abu-Baker describe it from the Arab perspective:

> The Palestinian community in Israel is a collective loaded with external pressures and fraught with inner tensions. To begin with, Palestinians are a majority turned minority ... Currently numbering over a million, Palestinians now represent less than a fifth of Israel's population and are in constant search of empowerment and political expression. To complicate things further, their quest for equality and

genuine inclusion in Israel takes place even as they seek a clearer role within the Palestinian fold.[10]

The Rabinowitz and Abu-Baker book was well received by Jewish and Arab intellectuals in Israel, who were encouraged by the authors' championing of a new "Stand Tall Generation" of Israeli Arabs and their straightforward call for a new Israeli ethos that would recognize the irreconcilability of the Jewish and Palestinian narratives. "Israel reflects the national aspirations, collective memory, and cultural values of its Jewish majority," they write:

> Its dominant narratives stress the legacy of the Jewish Diaspora, the Holocaust, and the rebirth of the Jewish nation through the Judaization of physical, cultural, and spiritual space. But in the experience of Palestinian citizens, Israel's ascendance, seen by its Jewish citizens as a supreme manifestation of historic justice, is associated with grave familial and communal loss.[11]

Rabinowitz and Abu-Baker see the solution in the abandonment of the Jewish-Zionist narrative and its replacement by "an alternative, inclusive approach to history and destiny,"[12] which, they admit, lacks political efficacy. Their book thus joins the discourse about the Arab citizens of Israel held for years within a small circle of academics, writers, and journalists separate from the political aspirations of both peoples. The Jews could not be expected to abandon the Zionist narrative, just as the Arabs could not be seen merely as seekers of Palestinian identity.

As'ad Ghanem shows that, although after the October 2000 events many Arab citizens of Israel reported feeling closer to the Palestinians on the West Bank and Gaza Strip than to the Jews in Israel, survey results indicate that most of them see their future within the state and as its citizens, distinct from other groups of the Palestinian people:

> Most see their future as largely or somewhat different from that of their fellow Palestinians who live in a political entity to be established on the West Bank and Gaza Strip, or in the Palestinian Diaspora. The data indicate that most Palestinian citizens of Israel (77.2 percent) prefer to remain citizens of Israel and would not want to move to a state established alongside it and become citizens of that entity.[13]

A similar argument has been made by Amal Jamal, who claims that although the Arab population in Israel showed a low level of trust in the system after the October 2000 events, this does not mean that all members of this community are renouncing their Israeliness. The Arab community, he argued in 2007, is rather seeking to expand the space in which to manoeuvre within the Israeli system. It demands collective national rights and power-sharing as well as the instrumentalization of its indigenous status, but through legal means and from within the Israeli system.

> Arab political conduct aims at empowering citizenship and turning it into a political formula that accommodates Palestinian national identity on the one hand and Israeli reality on the other. Israeli citizenship, although deeply criticized, is still conceived of as the best grounds on which Arabs in Israel can promote their rights.[14]

Jamal believes that the dialectics of the relationship between the Israeli polity and its Arab minority demand structural changes in the Israeli state in order to incorporate Arab citizens into the state's identity and structure. He also recommends that Arabs be given greater control over some aspects of their collective life and assures his readers that "a full incorporation into the state does not mean that the Jewish majority will lose its dominant status in the public sphere and in state institutions."[15]

Such calls for power redistribution in Israel, which would allow its Arab citizens to fulfill their group aspirations within the structure of the Jewish state, have not been widely accepted. The Jewish–Palestinian divide has rather been considered a zero sum game, as demonstrated by David Grossman in *Sleeping on a Wire*, a book in which he recorded conversations he held with Jews and Arabs in Israel. At the outset, he describes his own difficulty as an Israeli Jew in opening up to his fellow Arabs and making room for them. He admits that "something like a nervous security guard began running around inside me . . . just how much room to make for them? And at whose expense?"[16] Both his Arab and Jewish interviewees express fear that coexistence would come at their expense. As Grossman puts it, "The aspiration to separate unites us."[17] Arab intellectual and activist Azmi Bishara, for example, feels "very foreign among Israelis,"[18] comparing his position in the country to that of an American Indian, while Jewish novelist Sammy Michael's vision of Israel's Arabs includes their holding of a Palestinian passport. "We have still not clarified for ourselves, Arabs and Jews, the meaning and requirements of terms like 'equality', 'coexistence', and 'citizenship',"[19] Grossman contends, expressing his disenchantment over the lack of support he detected for his own vision of the Arab minority in Israel as a national group free to pursue its national aspirations within the Jewish state.

Grossman's interviews bring to light some of the features of the discourse about the Arab minority in Israel, including what he calls "mutual evasion and abstention,"[20] the division of the world into perpetrators and victims, the endless deluge of words leading nowhere, and the tendency to put forward theoretical solutions to human problems without enough sensitivity to the people affected by them. For example, the complex set of ideas and practices composing the life of an Arab citizen of the state is reduced by many – including well-meaning members of the Israeli Left – to abstract theories about indigenous identity, as if people can be defined only by their national identity. This reductionism, which overlooks economic interests, professional aspirations, and other personal preferences, results in such reckless ideas as the offer of Palestinian passports to Israel's Arab citizens.

The following conversation recorded in Grossman's book depicts these features. It was held between novelist A. B. Yehoshua, a main figure on the Israeli Left, and Anton Shammas, a Christian Arab poet, translator, and writer, over an interview Yehoshua gave in 1986 in which he proposed a solution to the agony felt by Shammas and other Israeli Arabs about their identity:

> I say to Anton Shammas – if you want your full identity, if you want to live in a country that has an independent Palestinian personality, that possesses an original Palestinian culture, rise up, take your belongings, and move 100 meters to the east, to the independent Palestinian state that will lie besides Israel.[21]

Shammas responded by pointing at the broader context dismissed in Yehoshua's abstraction of the Arab as an identity seeker. Using the biblical metaphor of Abraham, who is commanded to leave his country, kindred, and father's house for a God-given land in which a new identity is to emerge, he reminds Yehoshua that he, Shammas, is part of a country, kindred, and father's house he is not eager to abandon for the sake of a Yehoshua-given land. While he does not join in the sharp critique voiced against Yehoshua's statement by some intellectuals who saw it as a call for expulsion, he exposes its dividing nature: "You see Israeliness as total Jewishness," he says, "and I don't see where you fit me in. Under the rug?"[22] At the same time Shammas himself proposes unrealistic and reckless solutions to complex political matters, as when he advocates "the de-Judaization and de-Zionization of Israel."[23]

Both intellectuals engage in a long exchange of ideas in which the Jewish and Arab citizens of Israel turn into theoretical entities with no common ground and in which odd solutions that lead mainly to fatigue are proposed. As Shammas says at one point about the conversation, "It is the best prescription for killing time and raising the blood pressure."²⁴ Grossman's summary of the debate captures the nature of the entire discourse about the subject:

> The two of them continue to circle within a circular wall, unable to find the proper distance from which they can relate to each other, one to the identity-in-formation of the other, bewildering each other like magnetic poles.²⁵

Sayed Kashua's writings represent an effort to cope with that circular wall by constructing an identity that is not based only on abstractions but accounts for his aspirations as an individual, by refusing to divide the world into "us" and "them," by exposing the absurdity of proposals such as Yehoshua's 100-metre move, and by his straightforward observations of a complex political reality. Let me now show how this is done.

UNDERSTANDING KASHUA

Some of the reasons for Kashua's attempts to breach the boundaries of the reductionist, dichotomous discourse about the Arab minority in Israel may lie in his life story. Kashua was born in 1975 to a Sunni Muslim Arab family in the village of Tira in central Israel, part of the so called "Triangle" region in which many of Israel's Arabs live. His father, a member of the extreme left-wing group Matzpen, was detained for two years after the explosion of a bomb in the Hebrew University's cafeteria in 1969. At the age of fifteen the boy was accepted to the Israel Arts and Science Academy in Jerusalem, a prestigious secondary boarding school for gifted students attended by very few Arabs, and after graduation he studied philosophy and sociology at the Hebrew University. He began a successful career as a columnist, first for a local Jerusalem paper and later for the liberal daily *Ha'aretz*. His weekly column in *Ha'aretz*, in which he portrays himself with wit and humour as an anti-hero within a Jewish society, a prime time TV sitcom titled "Arab Labour" he created, and best-selling novels *Dancing Arabs*

(2002), *Let It Be Morning* (2004), and *Second Person Singular* (2010), make him one of Israel's most celebrated writers today. He writes in Hebrew and lives with his wife and children in an upscale Jewish neighborhood in Jerusalem. His celebrity status as a Hebrew writer has raised accusations of his alleged betrayal of the Palestinian cause.[26]

Kashua, however, cannot be seen as advancing or betraying any such cause; his work is marked first and above all by the blurring of common narratives. This is why scholars trying to relate his work to given narratives have mostly failed. In a chapter titled "The No-Man's-Land of the Israeli Palestinian", for example, Karen Grumberg describes Kashua's literary characters as located in a "social, cultural, and spatial in-betweenness."[27] She views the confusion of these characters about their identity as a form of paralysis, failing to account for the possibility that their identity as Palestinians in a Jewish state is a category in itself that can be seen as authentic as any other category. "This confused and confusing identity," she writes, "suspended between a clearly Israeli one and a clearly Palestinian one, gives rise to a new identity that is not so much a hybrid but more a superficial collage of various components identified with 'authentic' Palestinian and Jewish Israeli identity."[28]

Grumberg therefore misses the deep irony in Kashua's novel *Let It Be Morning*, in which he brings Yehoshua's idea of transferring an Arab-Israeli village to a Palestinian state *ad absurdum* by allowing it to materialize. In her analysis, the villagers respond to this new development with acquiescence because of their eagerness to participate in "an authentic Palestinian narrative."[29] Not only does the text not support that interpretation, but Kashua's writings defy any such fixed categories.

In an article titled "The Jewish Works of Sayed Kashua: Subversive or Subordinate?," Adia Mendelson-Maoz and Liat Steir-Livny deal with the difficulty of classifying an Arab who writes in Hebrew within the common typology of "Hebrew" vs. "Palestinian." The difficulty is solved by placing Kashua in another fixed category, that of the postcolonial writer whose characters imitate the colonists' gaze either as a form of subordination or of subversion. There is no question in their minds about the author's intentions:

> Writing in Hebrew clearly positions Kashua at a post-colonial juncture. To speak a certain language implies acceptance of a particular culture and reality . . . As part of the attempt to approach the majority, Kashua consciously chooses to play the post-colonial game, which features the adaptation of Jewish stereotypes and images.[30]

The two scholars do not even consider the possibility that, having been educated in a Hebrew-speaking environment, Kashua feels most comfortable with Hebrew, or that his writings stem as much from literary inspiration and sharp-eyed observations of reality as from a conscious choice to play the "post-colonial game." Thus, when Mendelson-Maoz and Steir-Livny identify what, to them, seem like Holocaust themes in Kashua's writings, they attribute them to a conscious attempt by the author "to produce a comparison between Jewish and Arab victimization and national traumas."[31] This contention misses Kashua's refusal to divide the world into perpetrators and victims and to consider the condition of Arabs in Israel only from the perspective of victimhood.

A more convincing interpretation of Kashua's writings is provided by Batya Shimoni, in "Shaping Israeli-Arab Identity in Hebrew Words: The Case of Sayed Kashua." She realizes that Kashua's literary works are more nuanced than the socio-historical discourse about Palestinian identity. While that discourse focuses mainly on shifts between the "Israelization" and "Palestinization of Arabs living in Israel," Kashua adds a bold and innovative perspective by throwing into the cauldron of identities the Jewish-Zionist component and its dominance in shaping the identities of the Arabs in Israel. "Socio-historical discussions usually present this component as a national-political factor preventing Arabs from being citizens of equal status in light of Israel's definition as a Jewish state," she writes, noting, however, that as a writer, "Kashua has the freedom to deal with the influence of the Jewish identity over the complex combinations among identities of Israeli Arabs."[32] Thus, Kashua does not just place his characters in a "no-man's-land" between their Israeli and Palestinian identities but examines the option of another identity – that of the "Jewish Arab" – which is so foreign to the discourse that even Shimoni, who consummately exposes it, cannot help interpreting its literary articulation as subversive.

Whether or not one accepts that interpretation, the Jewish Arabs in Kashua's writings are characters who not only represent conflicting national symbols within Israeli society but also incorporate broader elements of that society. For example, in one of Kashua's *Ha'aretz* columns, the narrator, filled with national pride on *Nakba* Day (the day in which the Palestinian catastrophe of 1948 is commemorated), puts on traditional Arab dress and ventures to take his children out to the wild. He ends up, however, at McDonald's and Home Depot and watches with great pride the *Nakba* Day events on HD television, his pride stemming from the VIP status granted him by the cable company. This satirical tale is more than just a subversive statement; we are faced with an author's search for a peaceful and dignified life amidst the blend of national aspirations, ethnic strife, racism, violence, materialism, technological progress, corporate trickery, greed, and many other features of Israeli society, and many other societies, in the twenty-first century. *Let It Be Morning* allows a closer look at that search and points at the fresh alternative provided by Kashua to the current discourse about the fate of Arabs in Israel.

LET IT BE MORNING[33]

The book is written, like Kashua's other works, in the first person singular. It begins with the narrator's return to his parents' house in the village in which he was born. Lying in his old bed in the children's room left untouched since he and his two brothers left, he may be seen as fulfilling his indigenous identity. It is a wish many intellectuals from Rousseau on would expect him to have, but it is not this narrator's wish. He goes back home because of the difficulty of living as an Arab in a Jewish society, but the room in which everything has been frozen in place does not spark the sense of a "state of nature." He rather understands the Heraclitean truth that the old room is no longer the one he left, for the world is in flux. As he puts it, "I'm going home, to a new place."[34]

The returnee, who has a new house built for him and his family near his parents' home in the village, has no illusions about it. It might be nice to have a home of his own, he thinks, but the house is nothing but a hideout: "I could easily disappear, easily fix my life in such a way that nobody will notice I've come back to this lousy village. At least I have a big house to bury myself in."[35] He returns to his birthplace because he has run out of steam in his efforts to make a life for himself in the big city. He is employed as a journalist by a Hebrew newspaper, but his daily encounters have taken their toll, leaving him with a sense of apprehension.

The October 2000 events were a turning point in this regard. "Ever since those days, something has been broken, something has died."[36] Those two days, he feels, caused the delegitimizing of the Arab citizens of Israel, whose citizenship has been repudiated. They also served to stoke fires of vindictiveness among Jews that resulted in graffiti calling for the deportation of Arabs. As a journalist, the narrator was less concerned with such graffiti than with the difficulty of finding his place in society. The privilege of criticizing government policy, for example, has become exclusively a Jewish prerogative, while criticism on his part made him liable to be seen as a journalist calling for the annihilation of the Zionist state.

The author vividly depicts the relations between a member of the Arab minority and his Jewish colleagues in a professional environment in which the political tensions affecting them result in a default strategy of political correctness:

> I tried to survive. I'd always been a survivor. I knew
> how to adapt to my surroundings, working and doing what

I wanted. Except that ever since those two bitter days in October, the task of survival had become tougher. I had to be twice as careful, to listen to quips and jabs by colleagues who'd never spoken to me like that before. I smiled when the secretary asked, almost every morning, "So, did you throw any stones in the entrance?"[37]

The narrator returns to his village in a futile attempt to seek security, comfort, and dignity. "I needed to return to a place, however small it might be, where Arabs didn't have to hide."[38] His return, however, is not cheerful, because not only the narrator but even his wife – who is portrayed in the best tradition of Kashua's writings as a non-reflective down-to-earth person – hates the village. Nothing encourages indigenous sentiments more than music, but the journalist seeking refuge in his birthplace cannot stand the nerve-wracking Egyptian music accompanied by the sound of drums and mechanical clapping he hears on the street, or the songs on the Arab music channels broadcast via the many satellite dishes on every roof:

> The songs come as a shock to me . . . all of them seem the same and sound the same, about love, mostly, the same words, changing only slightly from one song to the next, the same rhymes, the same annoying melody, a pounding beat that I don't like at all.[39]

Despite the common image of *Al Jazeera* as representing freedom of speech in the Arab world, he resents the media network, which broadcasts news the Arab world is used to hearing and likes to hear. He notices it includes no mention of Arab leaders, refrains from investigative reporting about rulers, and does not upset anyone. Nor does he enjoy scenes associated with Arab villages such as the sight of old people sitting at the entrance to the village mosque, rolling their Arab tobacco and licking it tight, huddling there together all day waiting for the next prayer hour. Passing by a group of housewives, he feels only resentment toward them. He is particularly furious about the violence spread in Arab villages for which the Israeli authorities, who take a hands-off approach toward this spreading phenomenon, may be partly blamed but which is disturbing nevertheless. Here, for example, is one description given by his aunts over tea:

> By the time the tea arrives, I have heard more stories – about usurious moneylenders using thugs who don't think twice about shooting anyone who's behind on his payments, about a whole army of criminals who exact protection payments from businesses and rape the wife of anyone who turns them down, or force them out of their vehicle in the middle of the village and confiscate it in broad daylight like the tax authorities, and about one poor guy, owner of a grocery store, who balked and dared to cross them. His store was sprayed with submachine-gun fire and now he pays them like everyone else does.[40]

The novel takes a sharp turn when one day a police roadblock is set up at the village entrance, tanks are surrounding it, and the residents, citizens in a sovereign state, find themselves behind a barbed wire with no idea what has happened. From here on, we are faced with an existential tale of life managed in the shade of mythological tanks. Like the residents of Oran in Albert Camus's *The Plague* who have to cope with a mysterious plague affecting their city, Kashua leads us for many pages through the efforts made by the residents of the besieged Arab village to survive.

The initial response is one of disbelief, as the scene is familiar from other regions like Tulkarm in the occupied territories but is inconceivable within Israel's boundaries. "'The soldiers must have confused us with Tulkarm', someone blurts out, and manages to elicit some laughter."[41] Belonging to a democratic state, the narrator's father looks for a good reason for the siege, as punitive action in a democracy is not arbitrary but related to the rule of law. He therefore speculates that the Americans must have thrown Israel some important information about an operation in Syria, and that Israel probably wants to make sure that life inside the country remains calm. While such speculations seem pathetic in light of the absolute power the author attributes to the silent soldiers on the tanks, which erases any chance that the rule of law had anything to do with the curfew, the father keeps rationalizing. "Very soon, when they realize we haven't done anything wrong, they'll get out, the way they always do."[42]

Responses by radical elements are no less pathetic. Here, for example, is the ironic description of one procession organized in response to the siege by political activists in the village:

> The Islamic Movement activists lead the way, followed by the pan-Arabists, then the Communists, each group shouting different slogans . . . the Muslims are shouting *"Allahu akbar"*, and *"Khaybar, ya Yahud"*, and that the army of Muhammad will soon be back. The Communists are singing songs of solidarity and support of the Communist Youth Movement and the pan-Arabists are praising Nasser.[43]

The narrator is also not impressed by a procession of armed men with *keffiyehs* masking their heads and weapons held high, a well-known means of exhibiting strength in the Middle East, as the face coverings are not enough to conceal the men's identities. He knows them to be simple criminals. "The pitiful scene of drug dealers and thieves roaming the village streets like some kind of new heroes can only mean bad news,"[44] he mutters. So much for the book's treatment of the "Stand Tall Generation" mentioned before. The narrator does not attribute much power to that generation even within the boundaries of the village. The main response to the siege is decided by the village elders, who have no difficulty in securing the young people's co-operation.

Assuming that the siege is caused by illegal workers from the occupied territories who found refuge in the village, a decision is made to round them up and hand them over to the authorities. The illegal workers are rounded up, loaded on three buses, and brought to the village gate where the mayor is waving a white flag. In a scene resembling an ancient sacrifice to the gods, a plank is put on the barbed wire, one of the illegal workers is forced to climb up the plank, and as he staggers across he takes a bullet and drops to the ground. As if this scene is not cruel enough, Kashua makes the mayor and his aides decide to try again "apparently convincing themselves that the soldiers had only shot because they thought one of the workers was hiding explosives under his clothing."[45]

This is a tale of confrontation between unequal powers in which the perpetrators and victims are clearly defined, but the author adds a third dimension to that divide, which complicates the picture.

> The new turn of events scares me at first, then makes me happy for a few minutes. I'll finally have a good story, I think... I'm right on the spot, after all, in the heart of the story — a journalist and a resident of the besieged village. I might even get asked to appear on TV.[46]

The change of narrative from victim to journalist may be horrifying to the reader in light of the gravity of the situation, but it represents a refusal by the author to adhere to a shared narrative of victimhood, a tendency he attributes not only to his narrator but also to other young, educated Israeli Arabs in the story, such as a bank clerk with rectangular glasses and an official black suit complete with white kerchief. She expresses her wish that the Palestinians in the occupied territories simply leave her alone. "Don't we have enough problems already? They should leave us alone. We don't need to take part in this war."[47]

This approach may seem like a copout; it clearly does not fit the expectation advanced in learned treatises and popular culture that indigenous minorities unite against their perceived perpetrators. Kashua, however, provides a more nuanced perspective. As an incumbent of the Arab minority in Israel he articulates the increasing resentment toward that minority, which many Jews see as a "fifth column" threatening the Jewish fiber of the state, but he does not accept the return to the roots as a viable solution. Just like Zionism, which failed in fulfilling its original goal of giving shelter to persecuted Jews, the return to the village does not grant the narrator peace and security. When things turn really bad, he hates himself for having thought that coming back would solve anything.

As an individual of multiple identities – Palestinian Arab, Muslim, husband, father, educated young man, striving journalist, Israeli citizen, incumbent of the modern world, Kashua is unwilling to define his narrator by a one-dimensional attribute and turn him into a poster child of the Palestinian revolution. At the same time, the novel expresses great agony over the impossibility of realizing those multiple identities as a non-Jew in the Jewish nation-state.

This barrier is often attributed to the insistence of the Israel Ministry of Education on emphasizing the Zionist narrative over the Palestinian narrative in Arab schools. Kashua gets around this problem by exposing the actual consequences of such an educational policy. When the narrator visits his wife, a geography teacher, in school, he finds her sitting on a chair under one of the trees planted on Jewish Arbor Day, teaching the same material about the *halutzim* (Jewish pioneers) he himself was taught twenty or thirty years ago. "She writes the words on the blackboard – *swamps, eucalyptus trees, diseases, mosquitoes, children dying, sand, desert.*"[48] He doubts, however, whether the children even have an idea who those *halutzim* were:

> I had never understood they were Jewish immigrants. It was never stated in so many words. I was convinced they were wise heroes that all of us ought to admire because they invented important things like netting for windows and doors, to keep out the poisonous mosquitoes which used to kill babies.[49]

This is an important paragraph, reflecting what can be labelled a postmodern approach to the narratives dividing Israeli society. It hints at the possibility of the Zionist and Palestinian narratives loosening up, merging, and reconciling. Yet while in the contemporary world conflicting narratives can be expected to loosen up, merge, and reconcile, this is not happening in Israel, where the narratives of the past are piously adhered to by both Jews and Arabs. The adherence to outdated dichotomous notions, which makes it impossible for Arabs to feel part of the Jewish state, is attributed in this novel not only to Jewish extremists who write anti-Arab graffiti on walls, or to organizers of armed processions in Arab villages, but to the failure of Israelis in general to understand the complexity of the situation and thus realize the recklessness of the ideas about its solution floating around in the public space. This comes to bear at the end of the novel when the tanks disappear and a historic peace treaty between Israel and Palestine is announced. According to the treaty, most of the Jewish settlements in Palestinian territory will be dismantled and Israeli lands will be handed over to the Palestinians in return for those that will be annexed to Israel.

The narrator's response to the announcement is enthusiastic, as many of the barriers to realizing his multiple identities in Israel, such as the suspicions felt toward Arab citizens of the state, would now be lifted. But he then finds out that his village has been transferred to the Palestinian territory as part of the peace agreement. His quest for identity throughout his life is shut off. His entire being, as a person whose life is devoted to a search for a place in a society that he is part of in spite of the barriers it set for him, is ignored.

Kashua would probably not be surprised that the shocking ending of the novel, in which a whole generation of Arab citizens of Israel is denied its quest for a multifaceted identity, may not be understood by many, including well-intentioned souls on the Israeli left. This is hinted at in the scene in which the narrator, who first disbelieves the news, finds out that the village has indeed been transferred to the State of Palestine and listens to the chatter on TV, where a representative of the Israeli left has this to say: "This is a decisive and vital step for the democracy of the State of Israel. We have been freed of the curse of occupation and created clear boundaries for our tiny country."[50] In other words, the narrator, who like the author is an individual of multiple identities – Palestinian Arab, Muslim, husband, father, educated young man, striving journalist, Israeli citizen, and incumbent of the modern world – has once again been subjected to the rhetoric turning him into an indigenous entity free to pursue its one-dimensional identity across the border.

CONCLUSION

The present discourse about the Arab minority in Israel is largely inspired by the intellectual tradition set by Edward Said's politics of victimhood, as noted in the former chapter. It is easy to apply notions of victimhood to the intellectual discourse about the Arab minority in Israel, and this is where Kashua's contribution to that discourse comes in. Kashua's writings include strong statements about the vulnerability of the Arab minority in Israel, the arbitrariness with which it is treated, and the failure of the Jewish nation-state to construct itself as an inclusive community allowing both the majority and the minority to flourish. They also point to the futility of solutions brought up in the discourse about the Arabs in Israel.

However, as he enlightens us on these issues, Kashua refrains from the politics of victimhood that epitomize much of the discourse about the Arab-Israeli conflict. In that discourse, the world is divided into perpetrators and victims, and the multifaceted nature of the parties, and of the individuals composing them, is often ignored. This reductionist, dichotomous approach results in ideas that may seem righteous yet are all but reckless.

Kashua's contribution lies in his refusal to adhere to dichotomous narratives in a postmodern world and view the plight of the Arab citizens of Israel merely from the perspective of the victim. This point is particularly salient in *Let It Be Morning*, whose protagonist, an Arab citizen of Israel, is situated in a village surrounded by tanks but is given more agency and power than the politics of victimhood would allow. Rather than having him play the expected role of the victimized member of an indigenous minority, Kashua portrays the protagonist as a sovereign person who is capable of choosing his way freely and independently.

By so doing, Kashua raises an issue that often gets lost in the Israeli discourse, the issue of shared responsibility. The model of the young Arab emerging from this novel does indeed belong to a new "stand-tall generation." It is a generation marked, however, not by its success in turning past victims into present perpetrators but by giving rise to a cohort of individuals unwilling to yield their multifaceted identity to outdated narratives. And, as they steer their way freely and creatively within the hard conditions prevailing in the country, they willingly share in the responsibility for the construction of new, conciliatory relations between the Jewish majority and Arab minority in Israel.

CHAPTER 9

POLITICAL ESCAPISM IN CONTEMPORARY ISRAEL: DAVID GROSSMAN'S *TO THE END OF THE LAND*

In an article published in *The American Naturalist*, two zoologists discuss the following symmetry in the evolutionary process: "Natural selection favors predator efficiency in finding and capturing prey and, simultaneously, prey adeptness at avoiding or escaping predators."[1] This is a reminder of the importance of escape in the evolutionary process; the prey escaping its predator uses a strategy of survival. In observing the natural world, we distinguish between an effective and ineffective escape by the prey's success at avoiding a predator. But in nature we do not find escapism, namely, an escape strategy that is seen a priori as ineffective, as in the myth of the ostrich burying its head in the sand in view of a predator.

"Escapism," defined as a conscious attempt to find relief from reality, is a cultural phenomenon.[2] It refers to an escape that is seen as utterly ineffective, even by the escapee himself or herself, as in the case of Madame Bovary's coping with her miserable life in nineteenth-century France by escaping into a world of fantasy, and subsequently into suicide. The boundaries between "escape" and "escapism," however, are not always clear, as the effectiveness of an escape strategy cannot always be determined a priori. What seems like merely a relief from reality may turn out to be a means of survival. What, then, accounts for the difference between escape and escapism on the cultural plane? The effectiveness of an escape on that plane, I would like to suggest, can be measured by the degree to which the escapee is able to construct a new narrative that changes the prey–predator relationship. This is why Emma Bovary, who failed to construct such a narrative, became a symbol of escapism, while the retreat of British and French forces from Dunkirk in May 1940, for example, is often viewed as an effective escape. This view stems from the rewrite of the war's narrative in Dunkirk, reflected in Churchill's words in the House of Commons: "We shall fight on the beaches, we shall fight on the landing grounds, we shall fight in the fields and in the streets, we shall fight in the hills; we shall never surrender."[3]

The power such narrative change may have on individuals and groups has been noted by Jerome Bruner, who wrote that "the ways of telling and the ways of conceptualizing that go with them become so habitual that they finally become receipts for structuring experience itself."[4] In this chapter, I would like to discuss escapist tendencies identified in contemporary Israel and raise the question of whether these tendencies may be associated with the construction of a new narrative for Israeli society. I shall use David Grossman's *To the End of the Land*,[5] originally published in Hebrew in 2008 and titled *Isha Borahat Mibsora* (literally "a woman fleeing the tidings"), a thought-provoking novel on the Israeli condition, to explore whether these tendencies represent escapism or rather an escape from a state of hopelessness into a new political phase, especially regarding the relations between Israel and the Palestinians.

POLITICAL ESCAPISM IN ISRAEL

In a seminal article published in *Psychology Review*, psychologist Roy Baumeister offers a theoretical foundation of escapism by proposing six steps an escapee would go through on the road to suicide: the realization that current outcomes or circumstances fall far below expectations; self-blame over that dissonance; awareness of oneself as inadequate, incompetent, unattractive, or guilty; negative affect; an attempt to escape from meaningful thought into a relatively numb state of cognitive deconstruction (and the use of increasingly strong means of terminating the aversive thoughts and feelings when the attempt is unsuccessful); and finally, a reduction of inhibitions, which may lead to suicide.[6]

Although this theoretical construct relates to individuals, it is partly applicable to whole societies, including contemporary Israel. In 1973, Israel suffered a major trauma when it was taken by surprise and barely contained an attack by its neighbouring countries, Egypt and Syria. The dissonance between the expectations that the new territories Israel acquired in the Six-Day War of 1967 would grant it security and the vulnerable position it found itself in during the Yom Kippur War of 1973 led to severe self-blame, especially over the hubris that prevented its political leadership from exploiting opportunities to reach a peace agreement with its neighbours before the war.

Writings by Israeli public intellectuals after 1973 were marked by self-flagellation and endless guilt, which has become a mark of the public discourse in the country. That discourse became increasingly confrontational and, due to the more-or-less equal size of the adversarial camps – one advocating concessions to the Palestinians, the other opposing such concessions – it moved in circles and never went beyond a deluge of words over the status of the occupied territories, which has not substantially changed for decades. Gradually, Israel has fallen into a state of numbness. For example, election campaigns were often dull as a result of the two camps balancing each other out and a large chunk of the electorate losing interest in politics. So-called "centrist" parties came to power with no clear agenda, from the Dash party in 1977 to the Yesh Atid party in 2013. Thus, Israel was seen by many as an escapist society, one that tries – unsuccessfully – to escape its many problems by ignoring them.

For example, in "Escape from Politics," Yael Yishai suggests that escape is not manifested in what people think or how they feel but in what they do regarding civic life. She proposes four venues of escapism: remaining secluded from the political world, concentrating instead on personal well-being; voting for political parties claiming to be apolitical; replacing political activity with voluntary civic work; and rejecting the democratic rules of the game. Yishai is mainly concerned with the effects of these venues of escapism on democracy. Apathy, she writes, threatens legitimacy; escapist partisanship undermines the proper conduct of parliamentary politics; reliance on voluntary work can reduce government's accountability; and rejection of the rules of the game may threaten the very existence of the state.

Yishai identifies all four forms of escapism in Israel, claiming that they nourish each other:

> Indicators of voter turnout, party affiliation, and protests reveal a growing sense of apathy. Escapist parties have become ubiquitous in Israeli democracy. Reliance on the third sector to solve social problems has increased in recent years. NGOs not only supplement politics but actually substitute for authoritative allocation of essential goods, such as shelter and food. Challenge to the rule of law is manifested by political violence and disobedience, motivated by anti-democratic ideology.[7]

In "Escapist Parties in Israeli Politics," Bernard Susser and Giora Goldberg define escapism as the shying away from weighty and challenging problems. Escapists turn to issues that are "more amenable to their will, more emotionally satisfying, less demanding of mental and physical energies – at times even to concerns that are insubstantial, even capricious."⁸ And while escapist behaviour seems unlikely in Israel due to its security concerns, ideological fervour, and life-and-death reality, the authors point to the existence of escapist political parties, which, they claim, have been an almost permanent fixture of Israeli public life over the past forty years. They analyze ten Israeli "ideologically unfocused" parties marketing "bizarre, eccentric, personalized and 'non-political' agendas to alienated voters,"⁹ and describe those escapist parties as follows:

> Their answers to political dilemmas tend to be sensational, uncomplicated and ethically charged. They promise quick results and dramatic successes. They display a low threshold for political ambiguities. . . . Significantly, these parties do not present clear policies regarding the central issues of Israeli politics: war and peace, the Palestine-Israel conflict, territories, settlements, negotiations, etc. Indeed, these issues tend to be sidestepped. At times they are expressly set aside with the claim that, in any case, they are irresolvable.¹⁰

Since the publication of the above article, which surveys the escapist behaviour of political parties beginning in 1977, the phenomenon has become even more salient, most notably in the parliamentary elections of January 2013, when a large number of Israeli citizens cast their vote for Yesh Atid (Hebrew for "there is a future"), a political party headed by a TV presenter whose political positions were all but blurred. The vote for this party represented to many the tendency to avoid hard but necessary political decisions and actions, especially regarding the Israeli–Palestinian conflict.

Various commentators have referred to that tendency before and after the elections. In 2012, Mark Leonard, director of the European Council on Foreign Relations, wrote that Israel under Prime Minister Benjamin Netanyahu was indulging in a form of triple escapism: (1) Security: believing that somehow Israel can achieve security first, and only afterward deal with the unresolved political issues that are the cause of insecurity and resistance. (2) Geopolitical: dismissing the solidarity of Arab leaders for the Palestinians as rhetoric that will not come to anything. (3) Economic: accepting the "start-up nation" myth created by the governing elite of Israel, which in practice means that it is economics rather than the peace process that takes centre stage.[11] Many commentators raised an eyebrow over the fact that, in the 2013 elections, the occupation hardly featured as an election issue, not even as a minor preoccupation.[12]

The question is whether these escapist tendencies can lead to the construction of a new narrative for Israeli society. Are these tendencies a form of escape or of escapism? In other words, can they lead to narrative change that may be seen as enhancing security and peace in the country? Was the 2013 vote for Yesh Atid sheer escapism or rather an escape from a state of hopelessness into a new political phase, as claimed in Yesh Atid's slogans? A preliminary answer to these questions can be found in Grossman's *To the End of the Land*, the story of Ora, a mother who sends her younger son Ofer off to battle and escapes to the Israel National Trail (INT), a 1,000-kilometre set of hiking trails crossing the country from north to south, in order to avoid the notification of his death.

This is presented as a clear case of escapism, reminiscent of hopeless attempts to escape one's fate in ancient Greek tragedies. As in those tragedies, Ora knows the announcement will come but decides to go on the trail nevertheless. As the author puts it: "if she runs away from home, then the deal – this is how she thinks of it now – will be postponed a little, at least for a short while. The deal that the army and the war and the state may try to impose upon her very soon, maybe even tonight. The arbitrary deal that dictates that she, Ora, agrees to receive notification of her son's death, thereby helping them bring the complicated and burdensome process of his death to its orderly, normative conclusion."[13]

Although Grossman's protagonist calls her escape "a meagre and pathetic sort of protest,"[14] her journey may be seen as a search by the author for a different narrative for Israeli society, a search for a new story in which the protest by a mother who refuses to the above "deal" is considered a means of survival, while the existential state in which parents are waiting for the notification of their children's death in war becomes "meagre and pathetic." How successful is this search?

THE NOVEL AND REALITY

Before attempting to answer the above question on the basis of the literary text, a few words of caution are warranted in light of the tendency to read this novel as a reflection of reality. On 26 May 2008, Menachem Peri, the book's editor, posted a personal column on the publishing house's website in which he expressed his concern over the unprecedented response by tens of thousands of readers using superlatives to express their enthusiasm about the "book's intent," interpreted in accordance with their own narrow perspective. He rightly suggested that the novel be subjected to a variety of perspectives to enrich the reading experience.[15]

The superlatives, however, kept appearing in literary supplements, newspaper articles, and blogs. The novel was granted iconic stature and has been seen by many as the founding novel of Hebrew literature in the twenty-first century.[16] This is not necessarily expected for a 630-page novel which many readers found rather tedious.

The novel begins with long dialogues between three youngsters, two boys and a girl, hospitalized in the same darkened ward during the Six-Day War of 1967. The three – Ilan, Avram, and Ora – form a three-way bond of mythological proportions. Ora marries Ilan and gives birth to her older son, Adam, while her younger son, Ofer, is fathered by Avram who has never met him. Ilan and Avram's bond never unravels, even after Avram withdraws from the world as a result of his traumatic experience as a POW in Egypt during the 1973 war; the love between Ilan and Ora is also unaffected by their separation. Early in the plot, Ilan and Adam are travelling together in South America while Ofer is called to military service. He is summoned to take part in a major military offensive and Ora calls Sami, an Arab taxi owner and family friend, to drive her and her son to the army drop-off point. After sending Ofer off, she asks Sami to drive her to "where the country ends."[16a] She escapes to the INT, dragging Avram along, and as the two lovers walk the trail across hundreds of kilometres and hundreds of pages, the life story of one contemporary Israeli family unfolds.

The enthusiastic acceptance of the novel seems to have stemmed from the feeling that the author has seen deep into Israeli life. Robert Alter defined *To the End of the Land* as the definitive novel of the present Israeli condition. He writes:

> There are three major Hebrew novels that record the anguished way-stations of the Zionist experience: S.Y. Agnon's *Only Yesterday*, a masterpiece published in 1945, which deals with the early settlers in the first decade of the twentieth century, when he himself came to Palestine; S. Yizhar's vast stream-of-consciousness novel *The Days of Ziklag*, which appeared in 1958, and focuses on the Israeli War of Independence; and David Grossman's *To the End of the Land* (the original title in Hebrew was *A Woman Fleeing the News*), which . . . engages the condition of living in Israel in the era of terrorism and the occupation.[17]

To Alter, the novel is about a condition of terrorism and occupation. Others have interpreted it as an attempt to throw in the readers' faces the price of their silence about the wars dictated to them from above, or as a prophecy of destruction in the tradition of Jewish martyrdom. The various interpretations reflect a common tendency to blur the distinction between the novel's fictional tale and the author and to read it as a representation of Grossman's position as a spokesman for the Israeli Left. As noted in the former chapter, Grossman published *Sleeping on a Wire* and *The Yellow Wind*, two works of non-fiction composed of interviews, in which he forcefully reflected the agony of

Palestinian Arabs in Israel and in the occupied territories. Moreover, the tragic coincidence in which Grossman's son Uri was killed in an Israeli offensive in Lebanon in 2006, shortly before the completion of the novel, further blurred the distinction between the author and his fiction. As Jacqueline Rose notes, the novel "will never be read now without that knowledge, without that unspeakable pain, which is in danger of conferring on the book a mythical status." She adds, however, that "we do the novel, and Grossman, no favours if we turn it into a sacred object, beyond critical scrutiny and outside the reach of the history to which it so complexly and sometimes disturbingly relates."[18]

This valuable advice has largely been ignored. Michael Gluzman went as far as to suggest that, although Grossman began writing the novel five years before his personal tragedy occurred, it is inevitably read on the background of Uri's death in the controversial Lebanon war. This event, he wrote, endowed the text with historical and biographical validity; the fictional plot has been penetrated by reality. The conversation about the book, he contended, has now shifted from the literary supplements to the politics and current affairs sections of the newspapers. To him, the book has become a statement on the Israeli soul, its fears, loves, blindness, racist tendencies, and unsolved ethical conflicts.[19] Other reviewers concurred, writing that "David Grossman has mapped the genome of his beloved, tragic land"[20] and that he has "nationalized motherhood."[21]

By discussing the question posed previously, how successful Ora's escape is, we must remain within the realm of fiction; there is no reason to turn the author's protagonist into a representation of his own personal tragedy and his novel into a political manifesto. At the same time, it is the mark of great fiction that it enriches our thinking about the world we live in. Grossman's novel is clearly worth exploring for the light it sheds on contemporary Israel. Let me thus propose a reading of Ora's story in an attempt to derive from the fictional tale insights on the chances of an Israeli mother escaping to the end of the land to generate a new narrative for her and her country.

ESCAPISM ON THE INT

By placing his protagonist on the INT, Grossman brings us back to where the Israeli story began and where an alternative story might be sought. As geographer Yi-Fu Tuan has written, "In telling a human story, we may start at any point in time, but if we go back far enough we necessarily have nature, untouched nature, as stage: first the swamp, forest, bush, or desert, then . . . then what? Then humans enter and our story begins."[22] The story of modern Israel begins with the Zionist effort to dry swamps, plant forests, and make the desert bloom. As noted by Jonathan Klingler, "The early Zionists were in love with the land, literally the soil and the rocks of Israel. Connecting with the land was a central theme of Zionist ideology."[23] Zionist education in schools and youth movements put special emphasis on hiking and Israel's pre-state units, especially Palmach (a unit formed during the Second World War), were known for their long hikes on the land, which, to quote sociologist Oz Almog, "were a tool for creating drama and a sense of adventure, danger, suspense, and romanticism." Walking the land and sleeping in the open, writes Almog, "symbolized the unmediated contact with the soil of the Land of Israel and a direct connection with its landscape."[24] Today, thousands of hikers walk the INT, or parts of it, every year.

In Grossman's novel, escape can be found everywhere. All people walking the INT are in search of relief from a heavy burden: "They gave off a forlorn whiff of the persecuted, and disaster hovered over them."[25] Avram, for one, is the ultimate escapee. He runs away, we learn, "from the bad news that is life itself."[26] Throughout the journey he expresses hallucinatory visions for the State of Israel, such as the following:

> The museums will take their pictures and statues out of the galleries and warehouses. All the works of art . . . In the squares, in the tiniest alleys, on the beach, in the zoos,

everywhere you look there'll be some work of art, doesn't matter what, a kind of massive democracy of beauty."[27]

As the two lovers go on their journey, they meet a handful of characters, all of whom are in a mode of escape. The novel proposes many forms of escape, which may be classified by the degree to which they involve activity or inactivity and the degree to which they affect the personal or the public domain. A few examples follow.

1. Personal – Inactive

Escape into sleep: "His legs were already melting away. Soon another exhausting shift of awakeness would be over, and he'd be rid of himself for five or six hours."[28]

Escape into dreams: "An utterly white dream. Everything in it was white, the streets and the houses and the trees and the cats and dogs and the rock at the edge of the cliff."[29]

Escape into fictional literature: "Avram liked horribly long epics: about a world in which all human beings are children in the morning, adults at noon, elderly in the evening, and back again. And there was a serial play that described a world where humans only communicate honestly and openly in their sleep, through dreams, and know nothing about it when they awake."[30]

2. Personal – Active

Escape into play: "in the sketches he wrote and recorded at home on his reel-to-reel, in which he played all the parts – children and old men and women and ghosts and kings and wild geese and talking kettles and any number of other characters."[31]

Escape into the kitchen: "At seven-thirty that evening she stands cooking in the kitchen, wearing jeans and a T-shirt, and, for lyric effect, the floral apron of a real, hardworking, eager housewife; A chef. Piping-hot pots and pans dance on the stove top, stream curls up to the ceiling and thickens into aromatic clouds, and Ora suddenly knows that everything will work out."[32]

Escape into hyperactivity: "suddenly she lunged at the ground and started to dig with her hands, pulling out clods of earth and stones, uprooting plants."[33]

3. Public – Inactive

Escape into a new-age mode: "They roam in packs. The beaches of Sinai, Nitzanim, the Judean Desert, ashram in India, music festivals with drugs and free love in France, Spain, and the Negev."[34]

4. Public – Active

Escape into religious ecstasy: "At the head of the small procession walked a tall, skinny, bearded young man. Locks of black hair hung in his face, and a large colourful yarmulke covered his head. He danced and flung his limbs around in excitement as he sang and cheered, and ten or so men and women straggled behind him, hand in hand, zigzagging and daydreaming, mumbling his song or some feeble melody. Every so often they waved a tired foot, collapsed, bumped into each other."[35]

These categories are, of course, fluid. An escape into religious ecstasy may be seen as inactive as the escape into a new-age mode, but in Israel, as is well known, religious aspirations – commonly seen as a form of escapism – have turned into a force of substantial efficacy in the political arena. Also, escapist behaviours on the individual level, such as the tendency to focus on domestic affairs in lieu of public affairs, may have a substantial effect on voting behaviour. However that may be, the question is whether any of the escapist trends identified in Grossman's novel may lead to a new narrative for Israel that could be considered effective from an "evolutionary" perspective; that is, one that contributes to the state's security, peace, and quality of life.

THE FAILURE TO CONSTRUCT A NEW NARRATIVE

The author's answer is "No!" As his protagonists are taken to the starting point, to the heart and root of Israeli culture, they do not find the foundations on which a new story can be composed, for four main reasons.

1. The Culture of Bereavement

With over 20,000 Israeli soldiers having been killed since the establishment of the state in 1948, a whole culture of bereavement has evolved in the country. In the first few decades, that culture was created and guided by the state, which initiated commemoration ceremonies, erected monuments, legislated a Day of Remembrance Law, and insisted on standardized tombstones for fallen soldiers. In the 1980s, families stepped in and began to play a greater role in the commemoration of their loved ones, which resulted in what two scholars call "the politicization of bereavement;"[36] namely, the promotion of opposite political views by what they also call "practitioners of ideological bereavement."[37] Whether it was part of the state efforts or the initiative of families, the culture of bereavement uttered in political rhetoric, the mass media, and plaques of memory all over the country has become a dominant component of Israeli culture – so much so that the two protagonists cannot escape it, however hard they try to:

> Above the mountains, above the human tumult, a large eagle glides against the blue sky, floating on a warm, transparent air column that rises up from the valley. Avram and Ora take pleasure in its flight ... until Ora notices a plaque in memory of Sergeant Roi Dror, of blessed memory, who was killed below this cliff on June 18, 2002 ... Without a word, they get up and flee to the opposite end of the mountaintop, but there is another monument in their new place

of refuge, in memory of Staff Sergeant Zohar Mintz, killed in '96 in Southern Lebanon.[38]

Plaques such as the above are reminders of the ultimate sacrifice made by individuals for the national cause, and are often interpreted as signalling the nation's obligation to respect the heritage of the fallen by continuing the struggle they gave their lives for. In recent years, attempts were made to construct an alternative narrative as part of the culture of bereavement by the formation of Israeli and Palestinian bereaved mothers' associations for peace. Such a cultural shift, however, requires a long, active, continuous effort; bereavement cannot just be escaped, nor can the national bond it inspires, for, as Grossman shows, it is present everywhere.

2. The Failure of Coexistence

Contrary to the widespread argument that the early Jewish settlers in Palestine had no interest in the residents of the land, whether Arabs or Orthodox Jews, Israelis have always been concerned with indigenous life in the country. Early settlers in the late nineteenth and early twentieth centuries adopted many of the customs of rural Arabs, such as dress, food, and linguistic forms; Israel's pre-state youth movements attempted to imitate Arab ways of life; and Israeli writers such as S. Yizhar, A. B. Yehoshua, and others have been preoccupied with questions of coexistence between Jews and Arabs, both before and after the establishment of the state. The lasting wars in the Middle East, however, have taken their toll. One hundred years of bloodshed gave rise to hatred and intolerance, and the presence of peace movements in Israel has not prevented the development of militant attitudes in the country.

Grossman articulates in this novel his disenchantment over the two sides' failure to reach understanding in the Israeli–Palestinian conflict. Part of the novel is devoted to the relations between Ora and Sami, a taxi driver and long-time friend. Sami is a resident of Abu-Gosh, a peaceful, prosperous, Christian Arab village near Jerusalem, which is often seen as a symbol of coexistence between Jews and Arabs. Ora is aware of his delicate status as a Palestinian Arab in Israel and admires his gentleness in handling every situation in which this comes to bear, as when he drives Ora to the airport and is detained for half an hour by police at the checkpoint.

The relations between Ora and Sami represent coexistence between two reasonable people. Although Ora had completely cut herself off from the "situation" years ago, the two are drawn again and again into political conversations, keenly discussing the latest developments. These conversations, like the discourse in the country as a whole, produce nothing new, as nobody had, to use Grossman's words, "a single unused claim left in this eternal debate,"[39] but they leave Ora feeling optimistic about the Israeli-Palestinian future:

> When Sami used his Arabesque Hebrew to undermine the long winded, indignant, greedy pretenses of both Jews and Arabs, when he skewered the leaders of both peoples on a sharp Arab saying that often aroused from the depths of her memory the equivalent idiom in her father's Yiddish, she sometimes experienced a subtle latency, as if in the course of talking with him she suddenly discovered that the end, the end of the whole big story, must be good.[40]

But Ora and Sami's friendship falls prey to the Middle East conflicts. The two individuals, gentle and reasonable as they are, cannot ignore the fact that they belong to two camps fighting each other. This is vividly illustrated when Ora, absentminded on the day she sends her son off to war, becomes oblivious to Sami's sensitivities. When he hurries to open the taxi door for her he suddenly sees Ofer, whom he has known since he was born, coming down the steps from the house wearing his uniform and carrying his rifle on his way to fight the driver's brethren. The scene in which the three of them sit quietly in the car leaves no illusion about the prospects of coexistence between Jews and Arabs under the present circumstances.

When she escapes to the INT, Ora continues to seek coexistence. In the following paragraph, she affirms her conviction that the land belongs to two peoples, Israelis and Palestinians, but she also realizes how difficult it is to reach coexistence in view of a culture increasingly contaminated by militaristic language.

> 'Listen,' Ora says and holds his hand.
>
> 'To what?'
>
> 'To the path. I'm telling you, paths in Israel have a sound I haven't heard anywhere else' . . .
>
> 'Do you mean these paths speak Hebrew? Are you saying language springeth out of the earth?' . . .
>
> 'I wonder what it's like in Arabic,' she says, 'After all, it's their landscape too' . . .
>
> 'Do you still remember the Arabic words you learned for all those thistles and nettles, or didn't they teach you that in Intelligence?'
>
> Avram laughs. 'Mostly they taught us about tanks and planes and munitions, for some reason they didn't get around to nettles.'
>
> 'A grave mistake,' Ora decrees.[41]

3. The Geopolitical Setting

Grossman does not allow his readers to forget that whatever new story one tries to compose, the geopolitical environment in which the Israeli–Palestinian story unfolds is not conducive to a narrative of peace:

> A flock of partridges alights with beating wings from within the nearby thicket, and the bitch emerges, disappointed. 'And in those moments,' Ora says through her hat, 'I always think: This is my country, and I really don't have anywhere else to go. . . . But at the same time I also know that this country doesn't really have a chance. It just doesn't.' . . . What do you tell a six-year-old boy, a pip-squeak Ofer, who one morning, while you are taking him to school, holds you tight on the bike and asks in a cautious voice, 'Mommy, who's against us?' . . . . And of course you want to keep his world innocent and free of hatred, and you tell him that those who are against us don't always hate us, and that we just have a long argument with some of the countries around us about all sorts of things, just like children in school sometimes have arguments and even fights. But his little hands tighten around your stomach, and he demands the names of the countries that are against us.[42]

The list of those countries is endless: Syria, Jordan, Lebanon, Egypt, Saudi Arabia, Libya, Sudan, Kuwait, Yemen, Iran, Morocco, Tunisia, Algeria, Indonesia, Malaysia, Pakistan, Afghanistan, even Uzbekistan and Kazakhstan. No wonder that when the little boy is helped out of his bike seat, he feels heavier than ever.

4. The Curse of Occupation

The worst barrier to a new narrative is the occupation of millions of Palestinians living in the territories conquered by Israel in 1967. As claimed before, the debate over the occupation lasted over four decades and divided the country between those calling for immediate removal of the occupation as a way to avoid the destruction of the state and those suggesting the occupation is used as a pretext by an Arab world refusing to recognize Israel's existence within any borders, including those set by the United Nations in the Partition Resolution of November 1947, which divided the land between Jews and Arabs.

Wherever one stands on these issues and whatever the outcome of the endless debates may be, Grossman shows in *To the End of the Land* how deeply the occupation has already penetrated Israeli life. The discourse in Ora's home is so affected by the occupation that one wonders whether her escape to the end of the land can free her from its consequences. It is difficult for the reader to imagine the emergence of a new narrative beyond the tale of occupation, for Ora finds that her own son Ofer has internalized the role of a soldier in the occupied Palestinian territories. As the following paragraph demonstrates, this role has become an unavoidable mark on Ofer and the society he belongs to:

> A long time ago, at the beginning of Ofer's service in the Territories... she heard a strange sound from the steps that led from the back garden down to the path. She followed the sound to the edge of the garden and saw Ofer sitting there, wearing shorts and an army shirt – he was on leave – carving a beautiful stick with his penknife.... He smiles. 'It's a club. Club meet Mom. Mom, meet club.'[43]

CONCLUSION

"Escapism" is a conscious attempt to find relief from reality. In this chapter, I raised the possibility that the relief from reality may turn out to be effective from an evolutionary perspective. It is hard to determine a priori when an escape is effective and when it is not. Whether or not an act like Ora's journey to the end of the land in Grossman's novel is an escape or a form of escapism is open to interpretation. At the same time, the possibility that escapism may be functional under certain conditions is worth exploring. Although psychologists concerned with escape have largely focused on suicide, it must be remembered that suicide represents an extreme case of escape, while humans mostly adhere to the rules of evolution, not of death.

In my attempt to differentiate between escapism and escape on the cultural plane, I have suggested a measure of effectiveness based on the capacity to create an alternative narrative. I have also argued that Grossman's Ora failed to do so by escaping to the INT. This failure may be seen as a comment on political escapism in Israel; that is, on the failure of Israeli society as a whole to come up with an alternative story of its relations with the Palestinians.

Israel avoids the ideological choice between the option of abandoning the occupied territories and the option of annexing them, and the electorate continuously votes into power "centrist" parties characterized by indecision. The nineteen parliamentary seats given in the 2013 elections to Yair Lapid, a TV presenter with no clear political agenda, can largely be seen as stemming from disenchantment over the four-decade political deadlock in the country and a will to escape.

Following the elections, Ha'aretz columnist Levy made this point explicit:

> Israel made a decisive statement regarding what it wants: it wants nothing, only to be left alone. Voters want a quiet, good life, peaceful and bourgeois, and to hell with all those pesky nagging issues. Lapid epitomizes this attitude, being

the role model for the all-Israeli dream. He looks good and dresses well, he's well-spoken and well married, lives in the right neighborhood and drives the right kind of Jeep. With that, he doesn't say much. He's not an extremist, heaven forbid, that's not who we are, nor does he stick his hand in the fire, that's not us either. He stays away from any divisive issues, just as Israelis prefer. . . . Israel affirmed escapism.[44]

Grossman's novel provides an explanation of that phenomenon and points to its consequences. The four themes the author raises as his protagonists are trying to escape from their fate in contemporary Israel – the ever-present bereavement, the difficulty of achieving coexistence between the two claimants of the land, the geopolitical conditions, and the curse of occupation – hinder the formation of a new narrative. Contemporary Israel thus finds itself in a hopeless condition. That hopelessness stems not from the prospects of war, death, and destruction (which are often simply ignored) but from the little promise held even by an escape to the INT.

The INT represents everything Israelis hoping to escape the present political setting may be missing. It is where one can be immersed in nature, indulge in nostalgia over lost dreams, and engage in the reconstruction of new dreams about a peaceful, flourishing Israel. As one commentator puts it, the INT may be seen as a physical representation of ideological innocence.[45] But the memories of the past overshadow all visions for the future.

In the first two decades of Israel's existence, odes to peace were sung that envisioned peace in glowing terms of swords beaten into plowshares. Since the occupation of 1967, however, the vision of peace includes, at best, some pragmatic arrangements to be reached after long and agonizing negotiations between fierce enemies unable to overcome their mutual feelings of hatred and revenge. Grossman may be hinting at his own nostalgia for the twenty good old years, before the occupation destroyed all hope for a better future, when he makes Ora speak of twenty good years she and her family had which she is now not taking for granted. It is something the ancient Greeks would be punished for, she says. For twenty years the family lived "a small, unheroic life, one that deals as little as possible with the situation, God damn it ... Twenty good years. Until we got trapped."[46]

The feeling of entrapment is not eased by the escape to the end of the land. It is not that the escapees do not occasionally get distracted, as in a sweet fantasy. One such moment occurs when on the trail Ora meets a man in whose eyes she sees herself and her partner but who is more experienced in the practice of escape and makes them realize that the trail is not just a dark tunnel one escapes to but a location which has a name, "The Israel Trail," and where colours are changing, flowers blossoming, and so on. But this revelation provides no relief. Although the landscape is no longer seen in black and white, it does not turn into a scene that promises a bright future.

This feeling is consistent with recent findings by psychologists concerned with suicide who have shown that the appeal of suicide is less related to the forecasting of negative events than to the lack of affect people feel toward positive outcomes in the future. Studying how subjects feel about negative and positive futures presented to them (not only whether they expect them to be negative or positive), Brett Marroquín, Susan Nolen-Hoeksema, and Regina Miranda found that suicide attempters cannot be singled out by their attitude to negative events. Their main characteristic is that they envision less happiness even if positive events were to occur. If the future is therefore less valuable, the researchers conclude, forsaking it in the face of distress carries less of a cost and suicide becomes an option.[47]

Read from this perspective, Grossman's novel leaves little hope for Israelis. They may ignore war, death, and destruction, or push them to the back of their minds when they are at the ballot box, but the habitat they try to escape to bears little promise. Occasionally, the escapees feel a sense of satisfaction on the trail, as when Avram notes that there is something special about the walk in the wilderness and Ora concurs. "It's so different from my normal life," she says, "with the cars and the microwave and the computers, where you can defrost a whole chicken with the click of a button, or send a message to New York. . . . This heel-to-toe is much more suited to me. Maybe we can spend our whole lives just walking and walking without ever getting there."[48]

But this fantasy cannot last when one is reminded with every step of the culture of bereavement, the failure of coexistence, the geopolitical situation, and the curse of occupation, all of which make Israel's chances of survival gloomy. As Ora, speaking about her country, concludes: "if you think about it logically, if you just think numbers and facts and history, with no illusions, it doesn't have a chance."[49]

BODY AND MIND IN MARGARET ATWOOD'S *ORYX AND CRAKE*

The revolutionary developments in biotechnology and computing in the modern era have sparked the feeling that the human race has reached a crossroad. Once the deepest secrets of life are revealed, as when the genome is deciphered, people are given unprecedented power over their fate. As physicist Michio Kaku has claimed, "we are on the cusp of an epoch-making transition, from being *passive observers of Nature to being active choreographers of Nature.*"[1] Expecting the synergy between the revolutions in biology and computing to accelerate, Kaku notes the powers they grant us to extend life by growing new organs and bodies, by manipulating our genetic makeup, and by ultimately merging with our computerized creations. He expresses his hope, however, that when confronted with dizzying scientific and technological upheaval on such a scale, some voices would say "that we are going too far, too fast, that unforeseen social consequences will be unleashed by these scientific revolutions."[2]

These voices, however, have not become dominant in the public sphere. The public discourse about the social consequences of science and technology set in motion by atomic scientists and others after the Second World War has not ceased, but it has also not changed much in the last half-century and has not been adapted to the new scientific developments. This stems partly from the fact that the issues at stake have become too complex to be handled intelligently by non-scientists. Scholars in the humanities and social sciences occasionally refer to the benefits and dangers of science and technology and raise questions on how we may maintain our privacy in the digital age or who would be in charge of genetic engineering, but that discourse has been overshadowed by the fascination with the golden eggs laid by technology.

In the early twenty-first century, people all over the world are obsessively glued to their smartphones and other technological devices with the debate about their impact on the human mind and culture mostly silenced. Technology is taking over, but the consciousness about its effects is fading. And since much of the public discourse on the social impact of technology is held in cyberspace, it often takes on the characteristic qualities of Internet discourse – the pronouncement of uninformed and unsubstantiated statements and the resort to extreme arguments. Proponents of technology are promising a technological heaven while the opponents make doomsday prophecies.

Margaret Atwood's *Oryx and Crake* helps reset the boundaries of that discourse. The novel is an exemplar of "negative utopia," a literary genre consisting of the extrapolation into the future of developments in present societies as a way to highlight features that may lead to their destruction. But this novel goes one step further by placing the story of the modern technological society within the age-old philosophical dichotomy of body and mind, thus providing a rather coherent explanation of the forces endangering that society. In what follows, I discuss briefly the conversation about science and technology in recent decades and show how Atwood's fictional subordination of the mind to the body in the realms of genetic engineering and digital technology contributes to that conversation and enlightens us about the brave new world we live in.

THE CONVERSATION ABOUT SCIENCE AND TECHNOLOGY

In his 1956 essay "The Two Cultures," English scientist and author C. P. Snow noted the growing separation between two world views that fail to comprehend each other: the traditional literary culture, which behaves like "a state whose power is rapidly declining," and the growing scientific culture which is "expansive, not restrictive, confident at the roots, the more confident after its bout of Oppenheimerian self-criticism, certain that history is on its side, impatient, intolerant, creative rather than critical, good-natured and brash." The literary culture, wrote Snow, fears the scientific culture which, in turn, is irritated by the former. Observing the two cultures in Britain after the Second World War, Snow had no doubt which of them was more viable:

> The first thing, impossible to miss, is that scientists are on the up and up; they have the strength of a social force behind them. If they are English, they share the experience common to us all – of being in a country sliding economically downhill – but in addition (and to many of them it seems psychologically more important) they belong to something more than a profession, to something more like a directing class of a new society. In a sense oddly divorced from politics, they are the new men.[3]

To Snow, scientists are immune from the defeatism, self-indulgence, and moral vanity of traditional intellectuals. He saw them as "resilient," as having "frontier qualities," as being in "some kind of link with the world to come," and, of course, as "heterosexual." He was not sure how much of the traditional culture gets through to them but assumed that many scientists in Britain and elsewhere read as much as literary persons (even if they were less versed in literary gossip) and appreciated music. At the same time, the lack of scientific education among the literary classes, he felt, posed a major problem. "Not to have read

War and Peace and *La Cousine Bette* and *La Chartreuse de Parme* is not to be educated; but so is not to have a glimmer of the Second Law of Thermodynamics." In 1956, he realized that new scientific endeavours such as cybernetics might change the world, driving down into the problems of will and cause and motive. In other words, persons with scientific education might become more capable of considering the moral questions preoccupying humanity.

The importance of Snow's essay lay in highlighting the increasing role of scientists as a vanguard of social change in the 1950s. Snow not only showed that scientific developments were central to an understanding of the future but also that scientists had become a major force in determining the route society is taking and the moral constraints it ought to respect. Contrary to the view of the scientist as a zealot unconcerned with moral issues, represented in popular images like Mary Shelley's *Frankenstein*, Snow emphasized the importance of scientists in constraining irresponsible scientific and technological endeavours, a task attributed to them not because they read *War and Peace* or listen to music after working hours but because moral considerations in the modern world require an understanding of science. Snow heralded the rise of a new scientific elite replacing the traditional literary elite as a social compass, a role the latter had played since the Dreyfus Affair in the late nineteenth century, not only because members of the literary elite have betrayed humanity by their Leninist aspirations and their willingness to legitimize the evil forces of Communism and Fascism which brought about the Second World War but because they were not versed in science – the main moving force of society and the economy after the war.

Although scientists have never gotten rid of the Frankenstein image, partly as a result of its continuing advancement by a literary elite refusing to recognize its own removal from the social centre, the realization has set in that modern societies are as much guided by values derived from and related to the scientific enterprise as to ideological constructs designed in the minds of writers, philosophers and political activists. To use Snow's example, Norbert Weiner's *Cybernetics*, published in 1948, provided not only an innovative approach to natural and human systems as goal-seeking systems but also implied important social guidelines such as the importance of feedback in goal oriented action, an idea with far-reaching social and political consequences. Once feedback becomes a main functional devise in the maintenance of systems, governments are required not only to lead but also to listen to public demands. And in spite of warnings that science and technology may run amok, scholars concerned with knowledge and power have often expressed their belief in the capability of humans to maintain moral limits as they advance the scientific enterprise and make use of its technological fruits.

In the same year Snow came out with "The Two Cultures," English mathematician Jacob Bronowski published his lectures on *Science and Human Values*,[4] in which he suggested that the values accepted as permanent and self-evident in the post-war era have grown out of the scientific revolution. While realizing that individually, scientists have human weaknesses, he cherished the virtues they developed in order to maintain their enterprise, which, he reminds us, has lasted longer than any modern state. "They do not make wild claims, they do not cheat, they do not try to persuade at any cost, they appeal neither to prejudice not to authority, they are often frank about their ignorance, their disputes are fairly decorous, they do not confuse what is being argued with race, politics, sex or age, they listen patiently to the young and to the old who both know everything."[5]

Bronowski claimed that science is not a neutral activity but a mechanism of human progress and that the requirements of scientific inquiry such as the reliance on facts, the rejection of dogma, and the quest for truth reflect on modern societies since the Renaissance. "Men have asked for freedom, justice and respect precisely as the scientific spirit has spread among them."[6] He further claimed that the dilemma of today is not that science is uncontrolled by human values but that the machinery of government is not controlled by scientific values (as distinct from scientists, which he did not believe ought to rule). "We have not let either the tolerance or the empiricism of science," he wrote, "enter the parochial rules by which we still try to prescribe the behaviors of nations. Our conduct as states clings to a code of self-interest which science, like humanity, has long left behind."[7]

The idealized view of science as a source of social values promoted by Snow and Bronowski has not been shared by everybody. In the 1960s and 1970s, many studies were published on the excessive power of science and technology and the difficulty of controlling them. With science and technology having become major forces in shaping the world, it was unclear whether humans could maintain a degree of democratic control over them to avoid disastrous consequences like those witnessed in Hiroshima and Nagasaki. Social thinkers issued warnings of the "technological threat."[8] As Jacques Ellul wrote in 1964, "when technique enters into every area of life, including the human, it ceases to be external to man and becomes his very substance. It is no longer face to face with man but is integrated with him, and it progressively absorbs him."[9]

There was no question that science and technology must be adapted to human needs rather than be allowed to run out of control, but it was also realized that the control of science and technology requires skills that are hard to find in traditional political systems. It was feared that scientists would be put in charge of steering the polity, which would give the scientific elite greater power than is desirable in a democracy. In 1965, Ralph Lapp warned of a "new priesthood" taking over:

> To be sure, there is no danger of a coup or take-over for there is no conspiracy of scientists about to seize the reins of government.... But whether they aspire or not, scientists in key advisory positions wield enormous power.... The danger to our democracy is that national policy will be decided by a few acting without even attempting to enter into a public discourse on the issues.[10]

Lapp added that as modern society becomes more and more dependent on science and technology, it is inevitable that policy decisions become deeply snarled in the vocabulary and substance of technology. The fear prevailing in popular culture of the isolated scientist who develops dangerous technologies is here replaced by a fear of "technopolis," namely a society whose jargon, ways of thinking, and modes of communication and action are not derived from traditional moral and religious norms which evolved over centuries but from technology itself. When you see something that is technically sweet, Robert Oppenheimer warned, you go ahead and do it and you argue about what to do about it only after you have had your technical success.

Two scientific developments were considered most threatening to society: artificial intelligence and eugenics. Nigel Calder spelled out the social questions posed by both. Just as nuclear energy forces us to clarify our ideas about international relations forever, he wrote in *Technopolis*, so does the computer oblige us to adjust our attitudes toward the existence of machines that may become smarter than humans. Calder asks whether the future development of the super-intelligent computer transcending our intelligence means that individuals will accept the constraints it poses. "Shall we bow before it? Symptoms of computer worship are already visible, though the machines are, so far, not intelligent at all,"[11] he noted in 1969.

Calder also pointed to the enthusiasm about positive eugenics, which is concerned less with the prevention of bad genes than with the encouragement of good gene combinations, analogous to improvements of farm livestock by selective breeding. "Artificial insemination of egg implantation may be socially more acceptable than, say, the direct mating of young Nazis with favoured German women during the Hitler regime."[12] Eugenics is particularly favoured because of the promise of immortality it entails:

> If the individual's consciousness and identity are chiefly represented by his brain, one mode of immortality is not hard to identify. The culmination of a policy of replacing defective organs which threaten the survival of the brain will be the 'old' brain in a 'new' body – perhaps somebody else's,

who has no more use for it, because his brain is defective (or inferior?).[13]

In the four decades since these words were published, developments in genetic engineering and digital technology have burgeoned while the discourse has not caught up. Eugenics, mainly associated with the Nazi regime, has largely become a concern of the past, and the computer has become the way of the future. The effects of genetic engineering and of digital technology are enormous, and the dangers involved in projects running wild in these fields may be great but there is little public debate about them, if only because of the difficulty in grasping the issues.

This is where *Oryx and Crake's*[14] contribution comes in. Margaret Atwood uses the power of fiction to enlighten laypersons about genetic engineering and digital technology and the links between the two fields, the ways of thinking associated with them in their combined development, and their possible effect on humanity. As she leads us through the story, she provides an updated answer to some of the questions that ought to be raised in the discourse on science and technology: Who are the scientists involved in the great developments of the present age in terms of their upbringing and education? What are the different viewpoints prevailing in their communities? How is their enterprise structured, financed, and related to the overall culture within which it functions? How does the fascination with digital technologies affect their thinking? How far are scientists willing to experiment with "sweet" technologies? And what scenarios can be expected in light of the present synergy between computer science and biology?

BODY AND MIND

Like other negative-utopian novels, the book begins with a description of the world after its destruction. The ruins the reader is led through are filled with material artifacts found in present consumer societies: "a hubcap, a piano key, a chunk of pale green pop bottle smoothed by the ocean. A plastic BlyssPluss container, empty; a Chickienobs Bucket O'Nubbins, ditto. A computer mouse, or the busted remains of one, with a long wiry tail."[15] Once these artifacts are not flickering at us from show windows but appear in their crude state within a pile of garbage, their destructive effect on the environment is striking. The natural habitat is covered by tins of motor oil, caustic solvents, plastic bottles of bleach and other containers of scalding liquids, sickening fumes and poison dust contaminating the atmosphere. Atwood's protagonist Jimmy, known as Snowman, who is left alone on the beach with the "Crakers," lab-made creatures produced by his scientist friend Crake, is surrounded by such products of twenty-first-century consumer culture, which are now all but useless.

His watch, for example, is made of stainless steel and has a burnished aluminum band but does not work because even a shiny watch becomes non-functional in a world that has lost its sense of time and memory. In order for a human-made artifact to become functional, it must be related to a narrative, that is, have a role in the story of human development. When no such story is being told, then both nature and culture are overwhelmed by "technique" – the uncontrollable stream of material products. For example, to the Crakers who have no image of a baseball game, Snowman's baseball hat is just removable hair unless a fiction is invented that puts it in context and gives it meaning. This is why Snowman constructs the narrative of himself as a bird that has forgotten how to fly, the kind of myth humans have always invented in order to make sense of their existence.

Much of the book is concerned with the yielding of the narratives developed in the history of humanity to scientific thinking and technological production. The novel is set at a time in which nature has long been taken over by technology. Snowman laughs like a hyena and roars like a lion but these are just his ideas of a hyena and a lion because his only encounter with wild animals has been through electronic devices such as DVDs "featuring copulation and growling and innards, and mothers licking their young."[16] The electronic representation of nature is often seen as a way to bring nature to people in urban environments who would otherwise not be exposed to it at all, but over time the electronic representation destroys any memory of nature. As Atwood puts it, "Everything is so empty. Water, sand, sky, trees, fragments of past time."[17] Human-made products, such as furniture, which at one time were made to serve a human purpose were also reproduced to such an extent that the original artistic or utilitarian narrative that accompanied their creation has been lost and they became useless items. As Jimmy realizes, reproduction means that "for each reproduction item, there was supposed to be an original somewhere. Or there had been once. Or something."[18]

Atwood attributes the abandonment of the narratives that accompanied nature and culture to peoples' search for bodily perfection. As with many boys, one of the first lessons Jimmy learns from his mother when he grows up is about disease: "It could fly through the air or hide in the water, or on little boys' dirty fingers."[19] But the search for the perfect body free of disease must end in the yielding of all spiritual elements to it; in the ideal model of bodily perfection the body and mind merge. When we observe figures representing that ideal, such as the Aryan type in Nazi propaganda, soldiers in a formation in Red Square, or models in a fashion show, the contingencies of the mind and their expression in eye movements, hand waves and the like are tamed. Moreover, the emphasis on the body, its needs, and its pleasures requires that the restraints posed on it by culture and religion be dismissed. This is how this idea is expressed in the novel:

> When did the body first set out on its own adventures? Snowman thinks; after having ditched its old travelling companions, the mind and the soul, for whom it had once been considered a mere corrupt vessel or else a puppet acting out their dramas for them, or else bad company, leading the other two astray. It must have got tired of the soul's constant nagging and whining and the anxiety-driven intellectual web-spinning of the mind, distracting it whenever it was getting . . . into something good.[20]

The conflict between the desires of the body and the demands of the mind has always existed because humans have never agreed on the right balance between them. There were those who aspired to improve peoples' spiritual powers to perfection in lieu of the body's pleasures, and those who gave up on the spirit for the sake of those pleasures. In the modern scientific and technological era, Atwood claims, the body has won over the mind and the soul:

> It had dumped the other two back there somewhere, leaving them stranded in some damp sanctuary or stuffy lecture hall while it made a beeline for the topless bars, and it had dumped culture along with them: music and painting and poetry and plays. Sublimation, all of it; nothing but sublimation, according to the body. Why not cut to the chase?[21]

The demise of the cultural narratives that gave meaning to human life and had a sublimating effect on human behaviour is related by Atwood mainly to developments in genetic engineering and digital technology. Let me now show the modes of thought and action she associates with these fields.

GENETIC ENGINEERING

When he grows up, Jimmy lives with his parents in a compound where genetic engineers are engaged in the search for immortality. The team they are part of grows an assortment of foolproof human-tissue organs in transgenic knockout pig hosts which avoid rejection and fend off attacks by microbes and viruses. The project is led by scientists like Jimmy's father with little self-reflection, as it is natural for humans to look for cures to their diseases. Jimmy, for one, does not like to eat pigoons because he realizes they are creatures like him. "Neither he nor they had a lot of say in what was going on."[22] Atwood claims that the formation of such compounds is part of a deterministic process, for nobody would give up life in a compound with its "foolproof procedures" over life in the world as it is today with "the addicts, the muggers, the paupers, the crazies,"[23] or as it was in the past with the "endless labour, the digging, the hammering, the carving, the lifting, the drilling, day by day, year by year, century by century."[24]

It is not that the discourse on genetic engineering has been silenced, but it is presented in this novel as useless due to the extreme and repetitive positions voiced by the contenders. Jimmy's parents talk about their work but there is little chance they will reach understanding. The father, who is so busy at work that he forgets his son's birthdays (and when he remembers, sends him E-birthday cards) remains unimpressed by the mother's whining over the immorality of the project. In one scene, the father comes home in celebratory mood because of his lab's success in growing genuine human neocortex tissue in a pigoon, which could help stroke victims and others. The mother's reaction: "That's all we need . . . More people with the brains of pigs. Don't we have enough of those already?" The exchange that evolves resembles chats held in many families. The father asks: "Can't you be positive, just for once? All this negative staff, *this is no good, that is no good*, nothing's ever good enough, according to you?"[25] In response, the mother says she cannot respond positively to an achievement whose main result would be the ripping off of a bunch of desperate people due to the high cost involved. The father then repeats the cliché that once people are given hope they are not being ripped off, and mother reminds him that only people with money will get hope. She calls the whole process "sacrilegious" because of its interference with the building blocks of life, to which the father responds that there is nothing sacred about cells and tissues. The conversation between "Evil Dad" and "Righteous Mom" reflects the author's view of the contending forces discussing science and technology in today's public sphere:

> Evil Dad blustered and theorized and dished out pompous bullshit, Righteous Mom complained and accused. In Righteous Mom's cosmology, Evil Dad was the sole source

of hemorrhoids, kleptomania, global conflict, bad breath tectonic-plate fault lines, and clogged drains, as well as every migraine headache and menstrual cramp Righteous Mom had ever suffered.[26]

In light of the author's view of the spread of science and technology as a deterministic process, there is no question who wins the debate. Jimmy's mother falls into a depressive mood and vanishes forever. At this point Crake comes on stage and from now on we are introduced to the advance of science and technology after the debates are over, after the body has been freed of the righteous soul and skeptical mind constraining it on the road to perfection. The ideal type represented by Crake differs from the mad scientist in popular culture in his apparent solidity. Here, for example, is the description of Crake as a student in school:

> Not that he was popular, exactly, but people felt flattered by his regard. Not just the kids, the teachers too. He'd look at them as if he was listening, as if what they were talking about was worthy of his full attention though he would never say so exactly. He generated awe – not an overwhelming amount of it, but enough. He exuded potential, but potential for what?"[27]

The answer to the last question is given after the destruction of the world by Crake's irresponsible experiments with nature: "Crake took the chaos, and he poured it away,"[28] says Snowman to the Crakers who survived the destruction. The myth of Crake developing among them endows him with supreme powers because of his refusal to accept the imperfections of the world. This refusal made him engage in the "Great Rearrangement" leading to "Great Emptiness."[29] God is said to have set order over the chaos but that order was never perfect; human beings have not been created without faults and their expulsion from the Garden of Eden led to a life of pain and sorrow. Crake ventured to do away with the pain and sorrow, aiming at a return to paradise where humans, or rather their genetic replications, would be typified again by "their native optimism, their open friendliness, their calmness, and their limited vocabularies."[30] This project meant doing away with God, who for Crake was anyway just a cluster of neurons in the brain.

Once God is removed, and with him the norms and rules of conduct stemming from supreme authority, the scientist's road to perfection is paved. To Crake, humans are none but "hormone robots,"[31] although faulty ones in need of repair. Thus, he devotes his skills to getting rid of the ills nobody could deny need to be cured: "No more prostitution, no sexual abuse of children, no haggling over the price, no pimps, no sex slaves. No more rape."[32] The way to achieve it is to learn from animals that have adapted better than humans to their environment, that is, abandoning unrequited love, thwarted lust and any shadow between the desire and the sexual act. "Courtship begins at the first whiff, the first faint blush of azure, with the males presenting flowers to the females – just as male penguins present round stones . . . or as the male silverfish presents a sperm packet."[33] In case someone might miss the apparent joy of courtship in his perfect system of sexual behaviour, Crake makes assurances that there is courtship behaviour in his plan except that it would always succeed. In fact, he does not dismiss any human desires as long as they contribute to the perfect order rather than disrupt it. Even artistic expressions have a place in the world as long as their role in the order of things is clear. Singing, for example, is tolerated by the scientist who derives its function from observing the male frog in mating season. According to Crake, art is for the artist "an empty drainpipe. An amplifier. A stab at getting laid."[34] To the extent that such functionalism may seem wrong or immoral, Crake reminds us again and again of the ills it comes to cure. "There's no more jealousy, no more wife-butcherers, no more husband-poisoners."[35]

Genetic engineering is a major tool of this functionalism. Two examples of projects Crake is involved in during his college days should suffice. One is the growing of chicken parts rather than whole chicken. Chicken breasts or drumsticks are developed without eyes or beaks or anything, just a mouth opening at the top into which nutrients are dumped. All the brain functions that have nothing to do with digestion, assimilation and growth are removed. Atwood reminds the disgusted reader that this project is consistent not only with commercial interests – "Investors are lining up around the block"[36] – but with the demands of animal rights' activists. "No need for added growth hormones . . . the high growth rate's built in. You get chicken breasts in two weeks – that's a three-week improvement on the most efficient low-light, high density chicken farming operation so far devised. And the animal-welfare freaks won't be able to say a word, because this thing feels no pain."[37] The second project concerns the breeding of wolves looking like friendly dogs which take one's hand off when they are touched. The project is commissioned by corporations that put these engineered creatures in moats as defence systems. Clearly, they are more efficient than alarm systems because they cannot be disarmed. And to the extent they may escape and go on the rampage, this is a problem for which a technological fix would have to be found.

As Atwood describes these projects, it is hard to avoid thinking that while genetic engineering is brought here *ad absurdum*, the twenty-first century world already has come extremely close to the absurd reality described in the novel (e.g., in the mass production of meat) and that it has become very hard to raise arguments against the projects conducted by the scientific–commercial nexus today because it corresponds more than one dares to admit to popular sentiment. As in *The Handmaid's Tale*, Atwood contends that much of the evil we attribute to political leaders and corporations results not only from their quest for power and their greed but from the demand by righteous, politically correct social groups, such as the above-mentioned "animal-welfare freaks," for a clean, painless, perfect world. This is a major motive represented by the character of Crake in the novel. The beautiful creatures he forms as part of his vision of perfection are not unfamiliar to every consumer – they resemble the floor models found in furniture stores. In accordance with the emphasis placed in contemporary culture on eternal youth, they look like seven-year-olds and are programmed to drop dead at age thirty – suddenly, without getting sick of course. They come close to immortality not by avoiding death but by giving up the fear of it. The author makes Crake's chat about them seem like a regular chat of young parents wishing foolproof health for their babies. He creates in the laboratory populations with pre-selected characteristics that fit present wishes in the real world: "Beauty, of course; that would be in high demand. And docility: several world leaders had expressed interest in that . . . a UV-resistant skin, a built-in insect repellent . . . immunity from microbes." (304). As Crake concludes: "We've done our market research."[38]

DIGITAL TECHNOLOGY

The demise of all the narratives that restrained human behaviour in the past, whether or not they emerged from the belief in supreme powers, is attributed in this novel not to evil motives by Crake and his likes but to the unstoppable penetration of digital technology into all spheres of life. Digital technology is described as a major force that blurs the distinction between the body and the mind, thus allowing the body to take over without the sublimation forced by the mind. Once the distinction between the real and the virtual no longer exists, as the term "virtual reality" indicates, the body can develop, as Atwood writes, "its own cultural forms."[39] This point requires some explanation.

"Virtual reality" refers to something that exists in essence but not in fact. As Andrew Evans puts it, "What you see and what you do looks and feels real, but is only a computer simulation of the real situation."[40] Our engagement with virtual environments involves a sense of disembodiment as we are free to represent our corporeality in cyberspace in a variety of ways (we may, for example, hide a physical handicap on dating sites). Many have therefore defined the virtual experience as one in which the body is left behind while the mind is free to wander in cyberspace. Others have claimed that in spite of the new relations between the body and the mind in virtual environments, life is still lived through bodies. As Craig Murray and Judith Sixsmith write, in virtual reality the mind is not freed from the body; the experience of virtual reality brings its embodiment with it as bodies are bounded within the sensations they receive.[41]

The relations between the body and the mind in virtual reality have been theorized by Katherine Hayles as a new human condition, a "posthuman" one. Hayles defines the posthuman condition as the privileging of informational patterns over material instantiation so that "embodiment in a biological substrate is seen as an accident of history rather than an inevitability of life."[42] This theory blurs the distinction between human beings and intelligent machines and gives rise to the model of the individual as a cybernetic organism, or cyborg. "In the posthuman, there are no essential differences or absolute demarcations between bodily existence and computer simulation, cybernetic mechanism and biological organism, robot technology and human goals."[43]

Atwood raises the possibility that in the posthuman condition, the mind is not freed from the body but subordinated to it. When who I am becomes the product of my own self-presentation in cyberspace, there is no way to point to discrepancies between the real me and the imagined me and I will be less affected by moral rules and other products of the mind constraining my behaviour. There will also be no way to propose alternative narratives to the flow of historical events at any given time, because history becomes associated with its representation in virtual reality.

The blurring of the real and the imagined is demonstrated in the novel by a chess game. Crake has two computers in the room and suggests that he and Jimmy sit with their backs to each other, one at each computer. It seems to Jimmy weird to have the two of them in the same room, back to back, playing on computers and he asks why not use a real set, the old kind, with plastic men, which leads to the following dialogue:

"Why?" said Crake. "Anyway, this *is* a real set."

"No, it's not."

"Okay, granted, but neither is plastic men."

"What?"

"The real set is in your head."[44]

Once it is assumed that reality is the product of human imagination, the door is open to dismissal of any sublimation stemming from reality checks or from the attribution of moral ideas to corporal action. The novel describes, for example, computer games in which history and all the values that may be derived from its study are dismissed. One such game consists of the trading of human achievements and atrocities: "one *Mona Lisa* equalled Bergen-Belsen, one Armenian genocide equalled the *Ninth Symphony* plus three Great Pyramids."[45] Even more than older media have done, the Internet exposes young people to atrocious phenomena while blunting their meaning. For example, as young men, Crake and Jimmy watch live online shows of assisted suicides, public executions, and the amputation of hands of thieves and adulterers. The two are not too concerned about those sights because of the blurring of the boundaries between reality and its representation on the Internet. The possibility is even raised by Crake that the blood fests displayed online from locations in Asia and the Middle East may have taken place "on a back lot somewhere in California, with a bunch of extras rounded up off the streets,"[46] for it is hard to distinguish between true and false images in the age of digital technology.

Atwood, however, does not allow her readers to forget that behind the images they consume on the Internet there is still a reality, often a very grim one. This is where Oryx is introduced. She is a young girl from a village in some distant, foreign place. At a very young age, she is sold and resold to strangers, and her life story, spelled out in the novel at some length, provides a look into a horrifying reality that cannot be dismissed as "virtual." She comes into the story when Jimmy and Crake watch a global sex-trotting site showing "sex tourists filmed while doing things they'd put in jail for back in their home countries."[47] Oryx is a girl of about eight who appears on the site, coming from a country "where life was cheap and kids were plentiful"[48] and is described as "just another little girl on a porno site."[49] Atwood emphasizes the insensitivity toward such "digital clones"[50] who may not seem real but clearly are. By her detailed description of the circumstances which have led to this moment, the author reminds us of the existence of real situations in the Third World and elsewhere, and thus makes clear that the distinction between right and wrong should not be dismissed in the digital age.

CONCLUSION

In *Oryx and Crake*, Margaret Atwood touches on some of the important questions concerning the effect of science and technology on humanity. She provides an updated model of the scientist, not as an evil person secluded in the laboratory but as a person who follows popular demand and aims at perfection in light of the many imperfections in human and social life. We are exposed to the setting in which the work is done, the scientific and commercial interests involved, the questions raised within the community of scientists and technologists, the notions guiding the effort, and the dangers involved in the contemporary project.

As befits the "negative utopia" genre, the uncontrolled scientific experiments conducted by Crake, the protagonist-scientist in whose mind all the moral questions concerning the contemporary project have been settled, lead to a cataclysmic mass epidemic in the world. But there is one question the author admittedly fails to answer. Here is how she puts it toward the conclusion of the book: "Had he been a lunatic or an intellectually honourable man who'd thought things through to their logical conclusion?" The author's response to this unanswered question is particularly enlightening: "And was there any difference?"[51]

Here lies the main insight that can be derived from this novel about twenty-first-century life. Whether or not we follow the fictional literature of the past in attributing evil motives to those who conceive, develop, finance, and execute the scientific and technological projects of the day, the world is walking a dangerous path in which "technique" – the uncontrollable stream of material products – has overcome all intellectual and moral restraints traditionally standing in its way. Atwood places this issue within the body-mind dichotomy, with the mind being subordinated to the body as part of the search for corporeal perfection. She thus sheds light on our present condition, in which the combined power of genetic engineering and digital technology threatens the human mind and culture, a condition in which cybernetic mechanisms and biological organisms merge so as to turn individuals into cyborgs, that is, individuals whose behaviour is largely affected by their excessive presence in virtual environments. The march toward the posthuman is promising and exciting, as is argued whenever new digital devices are being marketed, but it also has its drawbacks, as Atwood demonstrates with the help of the Crakers.

As fictional characters, the Crakers are a very exaggerated version of the cyborg, as human behaviours, including the excessive use of computers, are not yet the product of genetic engineering. But having been programmed to live a perfect life, the Crakers allow us a glimpse at the world that can be expected once reality as we know it with all its faults is replaced by a virtual paradise. The means needed for the formation of such a paradise are already at hand as Evgeny Morozov reminds us. He mentions, for example, websites like LivesOn, which promises tweeters immortality by learning about their likes, tastes, and syntax in order to allow their tweets to be continued after their bodies die. Such services, he writes, highlight the dominant ideology of Silicon Valley today: "what could be disrupted should be disrupted – even death. Barriers and constraints – anything that imposes artificial limits on the human condition are being destroyed with particular gusto."[52] As noted before, some scholars point at the great promise of overcoming the barriers and constraints the mind has imposed on us in the course of history. "Operating in the economy of information," writes Katherine Hayles, "one can dream that social position and economic class will cease to matter, that one could even loosen the constraints of living in a single body located at a single position of space and time."[53] Margaret Atwood provides a different perspective, wherein the goal of corporeal perfection prevailing in many cultures today, and the power of science and technology to help fulfill it, lead to the demise of both the mind and the social fabric. Let me conclude this chapter with a quotation from the novel about the life of the Crakers which makes one wonder whether life among the perfect in paradise is the life we would like to live:

> They seemed happy enough, or at least contented. They grazed, they slept, they sat for long hours doing what appeared to be nothing. . . . Maybe I could do some social interaction, thought Jimmy. Help them invent the wheel. Leave a legacy of knowledge. Pass on all my words. No, he couldn't. No hope there.[54]

CHAPTER 11

A CANADIAN ALTERNATIVE TO THE CLASH OF CIVILIZATIONS: YANN MARTEL'S *LIFE OF PI*

In 1955, Lester Pearson, then Canadian secretary of state for external affairs who two years later won the Nobel Peace Prize, published *Democracy in World Politics*. In that book, Pearson wrote:

> The major issues of diplomacy for several centuries have, for the West, been reflections of the changing relations between the various states of Europe. Today the most far-reaching problems arise no longer between nations within a single civilization but between civilizations themselves.[1]

This observation, that civilizations are replacing nation-states as main actors in the international system, was accompanied by foreign policy conclusions that affected Canadian foreign policy for years to come. Pearson emphasized the renaissance of cultures in Asia. If in the nineteenth century the Orient gave the impression of stagnation, with its great periods of achievement behind it, a new vitality was now apparent. Pearson welcomed that vitality, writing that the new restlessness and vision among Islamic, Indian, and Southeast Asian civilizations "is something which all men of good-will should welcome."[2]

Pearson was aware of the fear created by rising new powers but claimed that the revival of ancient civilizations, however unfamiliar, may be "full of interest to those with the humility and awareness to learn."[3] He did not ignore the conflicts and wars between civilizations in the past but argued that they do not prevent an option of coexistence: "We are now emerging into an age when different civilizations will have to learn to live side by side in peaceful interchange, learning from each other, studying each other's history and ideas and art and culture, mutually enriching each other's lives. The alternative, in this overcrowded little world, is misunderstanding, tension, clash, and catastrophe."[4]

The need to coexist with other civilizations in order to avoid a clash has become a cornerstone of Canadian foreign policy. The devotion to peacekeeping, the operation of CIDA (Canadian International Development Agency), Canada's wheat sales to China and the Soviet Union during the Cold War, and its efforts to serve as honest broker in various international crises all grew out of a realization that Canada's national survival vis-à-vis friends and foes alike depends on its capacity to breach of worldwide political and cultural divides. Pearson's vision has become part of the Canadian saga, largely because that vision had deep roots. Canadian culture was always marked by an urge to distinguish itself from cultural allies like Great Britain and the United States while recognizing the rights of Aboriginal people and absorbing immigrants under the banner of multiculturalism, which has granted Canada the title of "first postmodern state."[5] It may thus not be incidental that one of the strongest objections to the "clash of civilizations" theory, so prevalent in world politics today, has been provided in a novel by a Canadian author.

The "clash of civilizations" theory was elaborated by Harvard professor Samuel Huntington in an article in *Foreign Affairs* in 1993 and three years later in a book titled *The Clash of Civilizations and the Remaking of World Order*. The book has been declared a work "touched by genius... a brilliant, riveting, and utterly original book, masterful in presentation and brimming with insight, its disturbing conclusions corroborated by an impressive array of data and well-chosen quotations."[6] Few books have sparked so much interest and discussion, especially after the terror attack on the United States on September 11, 2001, when Huntington's insights on international politics as dominated by cultural antagonisms seemed to many to have been confirmed by the events. Huntington argues that in the post–Cold War world, the most important distinctions between people are no longer ideological, political, or economic but cultural. Nations are preoccupied with their cultural identity and use politics not only to advance their interests but also to define that identity.

Huntington defines "civilization" as the highest level of identification to which a person belongs, emphasizing religion as a central defining feature of any civilization. The great religions prevailing in the world – Christianity, Islam, Hinduism, and Confucianism – are central in his design of international politics as dominated by seven civilizations: Sinic, Japanese, Hindu, Islamic, Orthodox, Western, and Latin American. Western civilization, for example, has its origins in "Western Christendom."[7] Western Christianity, Huntington writes, first Catholicism and then Catholicism and Protestantism, is historically the single most important characteristic of Western civilization, having provided its adherents with a sense of community that distinguished them from Islam, Eastern Orthodoxy, etc.

Considering the First Gulf War as the first conflict between civilizations in the modern era, Huntington predicts a sharpening of conflicts in the manner of tribal wars. "Civilizations are the ultimate human tribes," he writes, "and the clash of civilizations is tribal conflict on a global scale."[8] He points, in particular, to the clash between the West and Islam, claiming that its causes lie not in transitory phenomena such as twelfth-century Christian passion or twentieth-century Muslim fundamentalism but "flow from the nature of the two religions and the civilizations based on them."[9]

Critics have related to various aspects of the book. It has been argued that most Western states are now multi- or bi-cultural and becoming more so. They are thus potentially part of multiple civilizations, a situation Huntington glosses over by designating religion as the deciding factor.[10] If transnational efforts to impose one culture on another invite strife, it was asked, why should such efforts have harmonious results if attempted within a single nation-state, and is it not still possible for countries to have allies across the civilizational divide?[11] Some have called for public denunciation of the book, claiming that Huntington has made a pitch to the ears of the powerful – a worrisome pitch because of its xenophobic and self-fulfilling prophecy. Its thesis should not guide twenty-first century policy making.[12]

One of the strongest criticisms of the "clash of civilizations" theory can be found in Canadian author Yann Martel's novel *Life of Pi*, which provides a profound examination of the theory's philosophical foundations and proposes an alternative of coexistence between civilizations, consistent with Pearson's vision. I do not mean to imply that this novel, or for that matter any novel, can be read as a national emblem or that Martel's fiction is representative of Canadian literature. Martel has obviously not intended to provide a Canadian alternative to Huntington, but in many ways he did. For one, following his receipt of the prestigious Man Booker Prize for *Life of Pi* in 2002 he has been embraced by official Canada. His rejection of religious exclusionism, for instance, has been attributed by an official Foreign Affairs document to his being a child of the Quiet Revolution.[13] The "Quiet Revolution" refers to the social changes that took place in Quebec, Martel's province, under Liberal leader Jean Lesage in the 1960s.[14] Martel's extensive visits to mosques, churches, and temples, and his reading of the Bible, the Koran, and the Bhagavad Gita in preparation for *Life of Pi* have been attributed to that revolution, in which traditional religious boundaries were partly replaced by concerns with modernization, planning, and social change. In interviews he gave after publication of the novel, Martel himself emphasized his Canadian reference point: "I can't live for more than four years outside of Canada. . . . I'm Canadian, so ultimately that is my reference point."[15]

The Canadian origins of Martel's thought should not be stretched beyond their limits, especially since *Life of Pi* itself plays down any fixed identities, but it is hard not to see the roots of his message of coexistence between civilizations in legal documents such as the Constitution Act of 1982, recognizing the rights of Indian, Inuit, and Métis people; in the Canadian Multiculturalism Act, promoting "the understanding that multiculturalism is a fundamental characteristic of the Canadian heritage and identity and that it provides an invaluable resource in the shaping of Canada's future;"[16] in political organizations like the National Muslim-Christian Liaison Committee (NMCLC); in practices like the support given by the Canadian Jewish congress for Sikh army veterans who were prevented from entering the Royal Canadian Legions; or in cultural products like Leonard Cohen's "Sisters of Mercy," to mention only a few examples.

Let us now consider the alternative proposed in *Life of Pi* to the "clash of civilizations" theory. Martel presents the fictional tale of sixteen-year-old Pi Patel – an Indian boy who finds himself with a 450-pound Bengal tiger on a lifeboat in the Pacific Ocean – as a statement about reality: "That's what fiction is about, isn't it, the selective transforming of reality? The twisting of it to bring out its essence?"[17] The symbolic nature of *Life of Pi* allows us to consider it as a simplified model of the world, of the kind sought by Huntington, who admits that the picture of world politics he draws is highly simplified. Like Martel's tale of a boy and a tiger on a lifeboat, "it omits many things, distorts some things, and obscures others. Yet if we are to think seriously about the world, and act effectively in it, some sort of simplified map of reality, some theory, concept, model, paradigm, is necessary."[18] It thus seems useful to derive insights on world politics from a parable that, to a large extent, provides what Huntington calls "a map that both portrays reality and simplifies reality in a way that best serves our purposes."[19]

Both works are treated here as simplified models of the world order at the turn of the millennium and are examined for the prescriptions stemming from those models. In what follows, I analyze three foundations of Huntington's "clash of civilizations" theory: the consideration of religious revival in contradiction to scientific rationality, the tying of civilization to the negation of other civilizations, and the assumption that conflict between civilizations is immanent. Analyzing *Life of Pi* as a symbolic sea journey tale reminiscent of *Robinson Crusoe*, *Moby Dick*, or *The Old Man and the Sea*, and viewing the relations between the boy and the tiger as a metaphor, I show how each of these foundations is challenged.

1. RELIGION AND RATIONALITY

As a scholar of modernization, Huntington is concerned with processes of industrialization, urbanization, increasing levels of literacy, education and wealth, social mobilization, and diversifying occupational structures. Although he stresses that there is no one pattern of modernization, and clearly distinguishes modernization from Westernization, he draws a line between the scientific rationality underlying these processes of modernization and religion. While modernization is a product of the tremendous expansion of scientific and engineering knowledge beginning in the eighteenth century, religion is a twentieth-century response to it. "The most obvious, most salient, and most powerful cause of the global religious insurgence," he writes, "is precisely what was supposed to cause the death of religion: the processes of social, economic, and cultural modernization that swept across the world in the second half of the twentieth century."[20]

This view is shared by many who view the contemporary resurgence of religion as a reaction against the secularism, moral relativism, and self-indulgence of the modern industrial state as it makes use of the impressive achievements in science and engineering of the last two centuries to control and shape its environment. Its success in doing so creates vacuums filled by religious groups. As Huntington puts it, "In times of rapid social change, established identities dissolve, the self must be redefined, and new identities created. For people facing the need to determine Who am I? Where do I belong? religion provides compelling answers, and religious groups provide small social communities to replace those lost through urbanization."[21]

Martel, however, refuses to accept the distinction between a secular, scientific, rational culture associated with modernity, and religion. He portrays the distinction *ad absurdum* in the figure of Pi's biology teacher, Mr. Satish Kumar, who believes in science but not in God. Mr. Kumar's total adherence to science is apparent in the shape of his body: "His construction was geometric: he looked like two triangles, a small one and a larger one, balanced on two parallel lines."[22] He is a regular visitor in the zoo managed by Pi's father, where each animal represents the triumph of logic and mechanics. To him, nature is an exceptionally fine illustration of science: "When Mr. Kumar visited the zoo, it was to take the pulse of the universe, and his stethoscopic mind always confirmed to him that everything was in order, that everything *was* order. He left the zoo feeling scientifically refreshed."[23]

As a young man, Mr. Kumar was racked with polio, and it was not God who saved him but medicine, and this turned him into an atheist. Pi is influenced by him and begins to study zoology but also realizes that scientific knowledge without religious belief is meaningless. Once disaster strikes – the Japanese ship on which the Patels and their zoo animals are sailing to Canada sinks and his whole family dies – reason alone does not provide answers. "And what of my extended family – birds, beasts and reptiles?" asks the boy who has lost everything: "They too have drowned. Every single thing I value in life has been destroyed. And I am allowed no explanation? I am to suffer hell without any account from heaven? In that case, what is the purpose of reason. . . . Is it no more than to shine at practicalities – the getting of food, clothing and shelter? Why can't reason give greater answers?"[24]

Reason cannot give the answers and yet Pi does not give it up. The novel is in many ways a song of praise to reason that is not devoid of a belief in God, and to a belief in God that does not exclude reason. At no point, for instance, does Pi rely on external redemption: "I had to stop hoping so much that a ship would rescue me. I should not count on outside help. Survival had to start with me. In my experience, a castaway's worst mistake is to hope too much and do too little. Survival starts by paying attention to what is close at hand and immediate. To look out with idle hope is tantamount to dreaming one's life away."[25] Moreover, Pi's belief in God is not blind: "Faith in God is an opening up, a letting go, a deep trust, a free act of love – but sometimes it was so hard to love."[26] And most importantly, it does not promise survival: "God's hat was always unraveling. God's pants were falling apart. God's cat was a constant danger. God's ark was a jail. God's wide acres were slowly killing me. God's ear didn't seem to be listening."[27] But reason does also not assure survival unless accompanied by religious faith: "I was giving up. I would have given up – if a voice hadn't made itself heard in my heart. The voice said, 'I will not die. I refuse it. I will make it through this nightmare. I will beat the odds, as great as they are.'"[28] Once he hears the voice, Pi begins to accumulate every piece of scientific knowledge in the fields of zoology, physics, engineering, etc., in order to survive. For example, "You see, waves and steady winds are usually perpendicular to each other. So, if a boat is pushed by a wind but held back by a sea anchor, it will turn until it offers the least resistance to the wind – that is, until it is in line with it and at right angles to the waves, which makes for a front-to-back pitching that is much more comfortable than a side-to-side rolling. . . . What may seem like a detail to you was something which would save my life."[29]

Martel realizes the difficulty of accepting the combination he proposes between rational, knowledge-based action and religious belief. This difficulty is nicely demonstrated toward the end of the novel when the miraculous survival story is put to the test of reason. Two Japanese officials investigating the sinking of the ship listen to Pi's story in disbelief because they apply rational criteria to it, but Martel shows these criteria to be insufficient. Let me conclude this section by quoting from the exchange developing when the two rational officials say they do not believe that a sixteen-year-old boy could survive a journey on a lifeboat with a 450-pound Bengal tiger:

> "*In a lifeboat?* Come on, Mr. Patel, it's just too hard to believe!"
>
> "Hard to believe? What do you know about hard to believe?... Love is hard to believe, ask any lover. Life is hard to believe, ask any scientist. God is hard to believe, ask any believer. What is your problem with hard to believe?"
>
> "We're just being reasonable."
>
> "So am I! I applied my reason at every moment. Reason is excellent for getting food, clothing and shelter. Reason is the very best tool kit. Nothing beats reason for keeping tigers away. But be excessively reasonable and you risk throwing out the universe with the bathwater."[30]

2. CIVILIZATION AS NEGATION

Huntington's conception of civilization is strongly related to the negation of other civilizations, and much of the book is devoted to advancing the notion that civilizations are mutually exclusive. Considering the adherence to cultural heritage as a human need in the post–Cold War era, he writes that peoples and nations develop their identity by adhering to the things that mean most to them, which are determined in relation to others: "People use politics not just to advance their interests but also to define their identity. We know who we are only when we know who we are not and often only when we know whom we are against."[31]

Huntington believes that there can be no true friends without true enemies and that unless we hate what we are not, we cannot love what we are. "For peoples seeking identity and reinventing ethnicity," he writes, "enemies are essential and the potentially most dangerous enemies occur across the fault lines between the world's major civilizations."[32] The very definition of "civilization" in this book involves negation: "Civilizations are the biggest 'we' within which we feel culturally at home as distinguished from all the other 'them' out there."[33]

In support of the notion that civilizations are mutually exclusive and depend on each other's negation, Huntington makes use of social psychology theories such as "distinctiveness theory," claiming that people define themselves by what makes them different from others in a particular context. Citing findings in social psychology showing, for example, that a woman psychologist in the company of a dozen women who work at other occupations thinks of herself as a psychologist while in a company of a dozen male psychologists she thinks of herself as a woman, he concludes that "People define their identity by what they are not."[34] This conclusion is reinforced by a view of religion – a central component of any civilization – as "positing a basic distinction between believers and nonbelievers, between a superior in-group and a different and inferior out-group."[35]

The fictional character of sixteen-year-old Pi is used by Martel to challenge the notion of mutual exclusiveness of cultures. The author proposes an alternative notion of syncretism, that is, the adaptation and melding of different religious traditions. His starting point resembles Huntington's claim that there exists no universal religion or civilization and that it would be naïve to expect the coming together of humans throughout the world accepting common values, beliefs, orientations, practices, and institutions. As Huntington puts it, the sharing by people of a few fundamental values and institutions throughout history may explain some constants in human behaviour but does not illuminate or explain history.

Martel agrees that an exploration of contemporary culture cannot focus on what Huntington calls "the Davos culture,"[36] that is, the small percentage of people in the world who are fluent in English, travel a lot, control international institutions and business enterprises, and share values of individualism, market economy, and political democracy. *Life of Pi* is rooted in industrialized India and the Patel family is, to a large extent, part of the Davos culture. "We're a modern Indian family; we live in a modern way; India is on the cusp of becoming a truly modern and advanced nation."[37] Consider the description of Pi's father, the zoo manager: "Father saw himself as part of the New India – rich, modern and as secular as ice cream. He didn't have a religious bone in his body. He was a businessman, pronounced *busynessman* in this case, a hardworking, earthbound professional, more concerned with inbreeding among the lions than any overarching moral or existential scheme."[38]

Martel realizes that this form of existence often leads to a search for a more profound identity but does not presume mutual exclusiveness of religions. His protagonist constructs a religion based on incorporation rather than negation. When we first encounter Pi as an old man telling his story to the author, his house resembles a temple for all three religions: Hinduism, Christianity, and Islam. "Upstairs in his office there is a brass Ganesha sitting cross-legged next to the computer, a wooden Christ on the Cross from Brazil on a wall, and a green prayer rug in a corner."[39] As we follow Pi's encounter with the three religions, we are faced with the possibility that a cultural identity can be constructed that is based on incorporation of elements from all religions.

Pi was born a Hindu. "I owe to Hinduism the original landscape of my religious imagination, those towns and rivers, battlefields and forests, holy mountains and deep seas where gods, saints, villains and ordinary people rub shoulders, and, in doing so, define who and why we are."[40] The rubbing of shoulders, however, does not imply separation of one religious group from others but allows a confident look outward, toward other religions. By listening to Lord Krishna, Pi is led to meet Jesus Christ. This is not the meeting advocated by Christian evangelicals. Martel objects to evangelicals of all religions: "But we should not cling! A plague upon fundamentalists and literalists!"[41] Nor is it a simple revelation. To a young Hindu, Christian theology seems bizarre:

"What? Humanity sins but it's God's Son who pays the price?"[42] He can understand a god who puts up with adversity – after all, the gods of Hinduism also face their fair share of thieves, bullies, kidnappers, and usurpers, but the element of humiliation in Christianity is beyond his grasp. "I couldn't imagine Lord Krishna consenting to be stripped naked, whipped, mocked, dragged through the streets and, to top it off, crucified – and at the hands of mere humans, to boot."[43]

Christianity is too hurried for the Hindu boy: "If Hinduism flows placidly like the Ganges, then Christianity bustles like Toronto at rush hour."[44] And yet it appeals to him because of its temporality: "Christianity stretches back through the ages, but in essence it exists only at one time: right now."[45] Since Pi lives "right now" he becomes a Christian, as well as a Muslim. Islam, he says, has a reputation even worse than other religions: "fewer gods, greater violence,"[46] but it provides him with an element lacking in other religions: the immediacy of the contact with God: "It felt good to bring my forehead to the ground. Immediately it felt like a deeply religious contact."[47]

Martel is aware of the tendency of organized religions to consider their ceremonies and rituals as mutually exclusive, but to him this is neither a necessary nor a deterministic trend. The dialogue he constructs between Pi's father and three wise men belonging to the three organized religions – Hinduism, Christianity, and Islam – may be read as an ironic statement on the assumption that the clash of civilizations is inevitable: "'What is your son doing going to temple?' asked the priest. 'Your son was seen in church crossing himself,' said the imam. 'Your son has gone Muslim,' said the pandit."[48] This kind of talk seems anachronistic in comparison to Pi's new identity (shared, it seems, by many early twenty-first-century individuals) that cuts across organized religions and cultures. As only Pi's mother seems to understand by nature of her being mum, bored and neutral on the subject of religion and hence a sharp observer of the contemporary world, the boy is "marching to a different drumbeat of progress."[49] He is certainly marching to a different drumbeat than the three wise men marching toward a clash of civilizations.

Martel makes explicit what he understands Pi's consciousness to consist of: "moral exaltation; lasting feelings of elevation, elation, joy; a quickening of the moral sense, which strikes one as more important than an intellectual understanding of things; an alignment of the universe along moral lines, not intellectual ones."[50] The author realizes that in a world believing either in scientific rationality or in fundamentalism and literalism, both of which lack a vision for life, it may be hard to develop such a moral attitude, but he believes that human consciousness marked by "a trusting sense of presence and of ultimate purpose"[51] may be developing because, as in the case of Pi, neither science nor organized religion provides us with answers in the face of disaster.

3. THE IMMANENCE OF CONFLICT

Huntington leaves little doubt that the mapping of world politics along the lines of civilizations implies an immanent conflict, which can be expected to be bloodier than the conflict between states. Wars between clans, tribes, ethnic groups, religious communities, and nations, he writes, have been prevalent in every era because they are rooted in the identities of people. They tend to be vicious and bloody, since fundamental issues of identity are at stake. Conflicts of identity can be expected to involve massacres, terrorism, rape, and torture and are particularly hard to resolve through negotiations and compromise.

Although he realizes the existence of many forms of conflict: cold peace, cold war, trade war, quasi-war, uneasy peace, troubled relations, intense rivalry, competitive coexistence, arms races, and the like, Huntington sees little chance to avoid gigantic wars between states of different civilizations, and he even coins a special term – "fault line wars" – to describe them. "Fault line wars go through processes of intensification, expansion, containment, interruption, and, rarely, resolution. These processes usually begin sequentially, but they also often overlap and may be repeated. Once started, fault line wars, like other communal conflicts, tend to take a life of their own and to develop in an action-reaction pattern."[52]

Huntington sees the emergence of a "hate dynamics"[53] in which mutual fears, distrust, and hatred feed on each other. "Each side dramatizes and magnifies the distinction between the forces of virtue and the forces of evil and eventually attempts to transform this distinction into the ultimate distinction between the quick and the dead."[54] In his description of the dynamics of these wars, religion is given a central role. "In the course of the war, multiple identities fade and the identity most meaningful in relation to the conflict comes to dominate. That identity almost always is defined by religion. Psychologically, religion provides the most reassuring and supportive justification for struggle against 'godless' forces which are seen as threatening."[55]

"As the fault line war intensifies," Huntington adds, "each side demonizes its opponents, often portraying them as subhuman, and thereby legitimates killing them."[56] These words sound so accurate that it is hard to imagine an intellectual construct contradicting them, and yet, such a construct is worth considering, if only to avoid the turning of Huntington's assumptions, widely accepted by policy makers and large parts of the public, into a self-fulfilling prophecy. Martel raises the option of coexistence between the fiercest enemies nature has produced but – most interestingly – presents it not as a form of idealism but as a realistic strategic option and policy program.

At no point in Martel's novel is there a shred of delusion that Bengal tigers are not dangerous enemies and would not remain so under all circumstances. As a child, Pi learnt about the wild nature of animals: "I quite deliberately dressed wild animals in the tame costumes of my imagination. But I never deluded myself as to the real nature of my playmates."[57] When the boy finds himself on a lifeboat with the tiger named Richard Parker, the fear of the animal's wild nature is not lessened just because the two share the same fate. "He was a fierce, 450-pound carnivore. Each of his claws was as sharp as a knife.... Any second I expected to see Richard Parker rising up and coming for me."[58]

Martel does not expect harmony on the lifeboat, and any illusions the reader may have for a Disney-like tale are shattered by a gruesome description of the way various animals that are present in the beginning on the lifeboat are killed one by one. "A massive paw landed on its shoulders. Richard Parker's jaws closed on the side of the hyena's neck. Its glazed eye widened. There was a noise of organic crunching as windpipe and spinal cord were crushed. The hyena shook. Its eyes were dull. It was over."[59] Slowly and gradually, Martel leads us to the point where the harsh reality cannot be overlooked. "Now we were two. In five days the populations of orang-utans, zebras, hyenas, rats, flies and cockroaches had been wiped out. Except for the bacteria and worms that might still be alone in the remains of the animals, there was no other life on the lifeboat but Richard Parker and me."[60]

Not only is the existential state of affairs clear, so is the lack of good options to cope with it. As with a state – or civilization – finding itself face to face with a fierce and dangerous enemy, all the options predicted by Huntington to be taken under these conditions – massacres, terrorism, rape, torture – are considered but are also found lacking. The parable may be seen as a demonstration of the futility of a whole range of options floating in the international sphere today. Here is Pi calculating his options:

> *Plan Number one: Push Him off the Lifeboat.* What good would that do? Even if I manage to shove 450 pounds of living, fierce animal off the lifeboat, tigers are accomplished swimmers. . . . *Plan Number Two: Kill Him with the Six Morphine Syringes.* But I had no idea what effect they would have on him. Would they be enough to kill him? . . . *Plan Number Three: Attack Him with All Available Weaponry.* Ludicrous. I wasn't Tarzan. . . . *Plan Number Four: Choke Him.* . . . A clever, suicidal plan. *Plan Number Five: Poison Him, Set Him on Fire, Electrocute Him.* How? With What? *Plan Number Six: Wage a War of Attrition. . .*[61]

This list of strategies aimed at overcoming the tiger by force exposes a common fallacy that military plans are more "realistic" than a search for coexistence. Pushing, killing, and attacking one's enemy with all available weaponry is often mistaken for *realpolitik*, but not by Martel, who considers all the above options, including the option of attrition, to be an outgrowth of fear, life's only true opponent. Fear leads one to make rash decisions. "You dismiss your last allies, hope and trust. There, you've defeated yourself. Fear, which is but an impression, has triumphed over you."[62]

Once the sixteen-year-old boy gives up the futile military plans (whose futility seems to grow proportionately to the degree of fear), he begins to make practical use of the unique combination of reason and faith he is endowed with. He decides that in order to survive, a training program must be devised for the tiger that would delimit the territory between them and make Pi's territory utterly forbidden for Richard Parker. The interesting point about this training program, described at length in the novel, is its reliance on the continuing presence of the tiger in the boat. "It was not a question of him or me, but of him *and* me. We were, literally and figuratively, in the same boat. We would live – or we would die – together."[63] Pi gets inspiration, strength, and will to live from Richard Parker. It is the irony of the story, writes Martel, that the tiger's presence brought peace, purpose, and even wholeness to the boy.

This point should be stressed. The immanence of war between civilizations implies that any civilization would feel more comfortable were it left alone in the universe. Martel reminds us, however, that multiculturalism, a concept Huntington dismisses, may not merely be a comfortable political solution (or slogan) when incumbents of different cultures are forced to live side by side but also has intrinsic value. "I will tell you a secret: a part of me was glad about Richard Parker. A part of me did not want Richard Parker to die at all, because if he died I would be left alone with despair, a foe even more formidable than a tiger. If I still had the will to live, it was thanks to Richard Parker. He kept me from thinking too much about my family and my tragic circumstances. He pushed me to go on living. I hated him for it, yet at the same time I was grateful."[64]

Martel's belief in coexistence between civilizations stems from his insight that war is nobody's desirable alternative if it can be avoided. This is sometimes hard to believe in light of the swiftness in which minor incidents spark major wars between nations, but it may be at least partly true in the human sphere as it is in the animal kingdom: "If I survived my apprenticeship as a high seas animal trainer, it was because Richard Parker did not really want to attack me. Tigers, indeed all animals, do not favor violence as a means of settling scores."[65] At the same time, Martel understands that the line between coexistence and being killed is very thin. As he advises any animal trainer, "you must be careful. You want to provoke your animal, but only so much. You don't want it to attack you outright. If it does, God be with you. You will be torn to pieces, trampled flat, disembowelled, very likely eaten."[66]

CONCLUSION

As hard as it is to derive insights on world politics from fictional tales whose interpretation is always uncertain, the symbolism we found in *Life of Pi* sparks fresh ideas that challenge the "clash of civilization" theory and provide a different set of policy prescriptions than the theory implies. Huntington is not explicit on what the world ought to do in light of the transformation it undergoes from economic, political, and ideological wars to fault line wars, but from the examples he uses it becomes clear that the mapping of the world along cultural lines means that people of similar cultures ought to stick together and not develop illusions about long-lasting coalitions crossing the cultural divide.

In his discussion of the relations between Russia and Ukraine, for instance, he claims that since the cultural divide crosses not between these two states but between Orthodox Eastern Ukraine and Uniate Western Ukraine, the state-oriented approach that predicts conflict between the two states, and therefore urges Ukraine to develop nuclear capability if it is to stand up to Russia, should be replaced by a different policy: "A civilizational approach would encourage cooperation between Russia and Ukraine, urge Ukraine to give up its nuclear weapons, promote substantial economic assistance and other measures to help maintain Ukrainian unity and independence, and sponsor contingency planning for the possible breakup of Ukraine."[67]

In other words, peoples and nations ought to define their allies in cultural terms. Europe and America in particular, being the backbone of Western civilization, ought to align. This prescription adheres to the common sense of many, but Martel's challenge is worth considering. The analysis of *Life of Pi* as a symbolic tale, and of the relations between the boy and the tiger as a metaphor, makes one conclude that much more effort ought to be devoted to coexistence across the cultural divide. By constructing a metaphor of coexistence, Martel does not exclude the possibility of a clash. He also does not promise us that in conditions of coexistence, utopia will prevail. To the contrary, he draws a rather gloomy picture of human existence: "Life on a lifeboat isn't much of a life. It is like an end game in chess, a game with few pieces. The elements couldn't be more simple, nor the stakes higher. Physically it is extraordinarily arduous, and morally it is killing. You must make adjustments if you want to survive."[68]

One of the adjustments, however, is giving up the fascination with the "clash of civilizations" theory. Unlike Huntington, Martel does not allow us to rub shoulders and indulge in the justice of the Western cause. He rather makes us realize that in order to cope with the harsh political realities we face, we need to reach out to other cultures and religions, for the knowledge, love, hope and a sense of purpose required to survive the hard journey into the twenty-first century may be found outside our own civilization.

This is advocated as a realistic approach to human affairs, which brings up once again Lester Pearson's claim that coexistence is a realistic policy. As Pearson writes in *Democracy in World Politics*, "The true realist is the man who sees things both as they are and as they can be. In every situation there is the possibility of improvement, in every life the hidden capacity for something better. True realism involves a dual vision, sight and insight. To see only half the situation, either the actual or the possible, is to be not a realist but in blinkers."[69]

NOTES

1 • POLITICS AND LITERATURE

1. Henry J. Aaron, *Politics and the Professors: The Great Society in Perspective* (Washington, DC: Brookings Institution, 1978).

2. Daniel Bell, *The End of Ideology: On the Exhaustion of Political Ideas in the Fifties* (New York: Free Press, 1962), 404.

3. Ibid., 405.

4. John Kenneth Galbraith, *The New Industrial State* (Boston: Houghton Mifflin, 1967), 60.

5. Ibid., 291.

6. Amitai Etzioni, *The Active Society: A Theory of Societal and Political Processes* (New York: Collier-Macmillan, 1968), 15.

7. Ibid., 16.

8. Wilson Carey McWilliams, "Introduction," in *The Active Society Revisited*, ed. Wilson Carey McWilliams (Lanham MD: Rowman & Littlefield, 2006).

9. Etzioni, *The Active Society*, 184.

10. Karl Deutsch, *The Nerves of Government: Models of Political Communication and Control* (New York: Free Press, 1963), 164.

11. Ibid., 124.

12. Ibid., 256.

13. Michael Keren, "Ideological Implications of the Use of Open Systems Theory in Political Science," *Behavioral Science* 24 (September 1979): 311–24.

14. See Fátima Vieira and Marinela Freitas eds., *Utopia Matters: Theory, Politics, Literature and the Arts* (Porto, Portugal: University of Porto Press, 2005).

15. Yann Martel, *Life of Pi* (Orlando, FLA: Harcourt, 2001), vii.

16. Martha C. Nussbaum, *Poetic Justice: The Literary Imagination and Public Life* (Boston: Beacon 1995), 3.

17. Paul J. Dolan, *Of War and War's Alarms: Fiction and Politics in the Modern World* (New York: Free Press, 1976), 3.

18. Milan Kundera, *The Art of the Novel*, translated from the French by Linda Asher (New York: Grove Press, 1988), 78.

19. Robert Boyers, *The Dictator's Dictation – The Politics of Novel and Novelists* (New York: Columbia University Press, 2005), 3–4.

20. Steven Smith, "International Relations Theory and September 11," *International Studies Quarterly* 48 (2004): 499–515.

21. See, for example, Moira Fradinger, *Binding Violence: Literary Visions of Political Origins* (Palo Alto, CA: Stanford University Press, 2010); Cerwyn Moore, "Reading the Hermeneutics of Violence: The Literary Turn and Chechnya," *Global Society* 20, no. 2 (2006): 179–98; Cerwyn Moore, "On Cruelty: Literature, Aesthetics and Global Politics." *Global Society* 24 (July 2010): 311–29.

22. Catherine Zuckert, "Why Political Scientists Want to Study Literature," *PS: Political Science & Politics* 29 (1995): 189.

23. John Horton, "Life, Literature and Ethical Theory: Marta Nussbaum on the Role of the Literary Imagination in Ethical Thought." In *Literature and the Political Imagination*, ed. John Horton and Andrea T. Baumeister (London: Routledge, 1996), 76.

24. John Horton and Andrea T. Baumeister, "Literature, Philosophy and Political Theory," in *Literature and the Political Imagination*, 13.

25. Roland Bleiker, "The Aesthetic Turn in International Political Theory," *Millennium: Journal of International Studies* 30 (2001): 520.

26. Roland Bleiker, *Aesthetics and World Politics* (Houndmills, UK: Palgrave Macmillan, 2009), 23.

27. Ibid., 28.

28. Robert A. Dahl, "The Behavioral Approach in Political Science: Epitaph for a Monument to a Successful Protest," *American Political Science Review* 55 (December 1961): 763.

29. Ibid., 763–72.

30. Ibid., 769.

31. Ibid., 769.

32. Michael Mack, *How Literature Changes the Way We Think* (London: Continuum, 2012), 1.

33. Ibid., 2.

34. Ibid., 10.

35. Lindsay Waters, "Literary Aesthetics: The Very Idea," *Chronicle of Higher Education*, 52, no. 17 (2005): B6–B9.

36. Ibid.

37. Raymond Taras, "Why We Need the Novel: Understanding World Politics through Literature," *Fletcher Forum of World Affairs* 37, no. 2 (Summer 2013): 189.

38. Marcia Eaton, "The Truth Value of Literary Statements," *British Journal of Aesthetics* 12, no. 2 (1972): 164–65.

39. Lola Frost, "Aesthetics and Politics," *Global Society* 24, no. 3 (2010): 436.

40. Ibid., 437.

41. Moore, "Reading the Hermeneutics of Violence," 198.

42. Michael S. Kochin, "Postmetaphysical Literature: Reflections on J. M. Coetzee's *Disgrace*," *Perspectives on Political Science* 33, no. 1 (Winter 2004): 4.

43. Ibid.

44. Ibid.

45. Richard Devetak, "After the Event: Don DeLillo's *White Noise* and September 11 Narratives," *Review of International Studies* 35, no. 4 (2009): 814.

46. Erich Auerbach, *Mimesis: The Representation of Reality in Western Literature* (Garden City, NY: Doubleday, 1953), 19.

47. Leroy Searle, "Literature Departments and the Practice of Theory," *MLN* 121, no. 5 (2006): 1237–61.

48. Ibid.

49. All quotations from the novels are taken from their translations into English.

2 • THE "ORIGINAL POSITION" IN JOSÉ SARAMAGO'S *BLINDNESS*

1. John Rawls, *A Theory of Justice*, rev. ed. (Cambridge, MA: Harvard University Press, 1999), 118.
2. Ibid., 119.
3. Brian Barry, *Justice as Impartiality* (Oxford: Clarendon, 1995); Robert Nozick, *Anarchy, State and Utopia* (New York: Basic Books, 1974); David Lewis Schaefer, *Justice or Tyranny? A Critique of John Rawls's A Theory of Justice* (Port Washington, NY: Kennikat, 1979); Michael J. Sandel, *Liberalism and the Limits of Justice* (Cambridge: Cambridge University Press, 1982).
4. Benjamin Barber, "Justifying Justice: Problems of Psychology, Politics and Measurement in Rawls," in *Reading Rawls: Critical Studies on Rawls' A Theory of Justice*, ed. Norman Daniels (New York: Basic Books, 1975), 292–318.
5. See Robert Paul Wolff, *Understanding Rawls* (Princeton, NJ: Princeton University Press, 1977).
6. Rawls, *A Theory of Justice*, 16.
7. Harold Bloom, ed., *José Saramago* (Philadelphia: Chelsea House 2005); Adriana Alves de Paula Martins, "José Saramago's Historical Fiction," *Portuguese Literary & Cultural Studies* 6 (Spring 2001): 49–72.
8. José N. Ornelas, "Convergences and Divergences in Saramago's Ensaio sobre a Cegueira and Camus's The Plague," in *Dialogue with Saramago: Essays in Comparative Literature*, ed. Adriana Alves De Paula Martins and Mark Sabine (Manchester: Manchester Spanish & Portuguese Studies, 2006), 125.
9. Quoted in Ornelas, "Convergences and Divergences," 123.
10. Rawls, *A Theory of Justice*, 119.
11. José Saramago, *Blindness*, trans. Giovanni Pontiero (Orlando: Harcourt, 1997), 57.
12. *Blindness*, 10.
13. *Blindness*, 29.
14. *Blindness*, 67.
15. *Blindness*, 97
16. *Blindness*, 98.
17. *Blindness*, 99.
18. *A Theory of Justice*, 155.
19. *A Theory of Justice*, 309.
20. *A Theory of Justice*, 323.
21. *Blindness*, 85.
22. *A Theory of Justice*, 384.
23. *A Theory of Justice*. 385–86.
24. *A Theory of Justice*, 386.
25. *A Theory of Justice*, 386.
26. David Frier, "Righting Wrongs, Re-Writing Meaning and Reclaiming the City in Saramago's Blindness and All the Names," *Portuguese Literary & Cultural Studies* 6 (Spring 2001): 103.
27. *Blindness*, 91.
28. *Blindness*, 139.
29. *Blindness*, 140.
30. *Blindness*, 143.
31. *A Theory of Justice*, 133.
32. *Blindness*, 151.
33. George Klosko, *Political Obligations* (Oxford: Oxford University Press, 2005), 75.
34. Ronald Dworkin, "The Original Position," in *Reading Rawls*, 19.
35. *Blindness*, 217.
36. *Blindness*, 78.
37. *Blindness*, 219.
38. *Blindness*, 252.
39. *Blindness*, 17.
40. *Blindness*, 276.

41 Anna Klobucka, A Writer's Progress: An Interview with Nobel-Prize Winning Portuguese Novelist José Saramago, Massachusetts Foundation for the Humanities, 2002, http://masshumanities.org/about/news/s02-wp/.

42 *A Theory of Justice*, 17.

43 *A Theory of Justice*, 297.

44 Tim Parks, "Sightgeist," *New York Review of Books*, 18 February 1999, http://www.nybooks.com/articles/588.

45 Ornelas, "Convergences and Divergences," 135.

46 Parks, "Sightgeist."

47 *Blindness*, 278.

48 *Blindness*, 276.

3 • ABSURDITY AND REVOLT IN CORMAC MCCARTHY'S *THE ROAD*

1 Cormac McCarthy, *The Road* (New York: Vintage, 2006), 191–92.

2 Albert Camus, *The Myth of Sisyphus, and Other Essays*, trans. Justin O'Brien (New York: Vintage 1955), 6.

3 *The Road*, 130.

4 *The Myth of Sisyphus*, 51.

5 *The Myth of Sisyphus*, 121.

6 *The Myth of Sisyphus*, 121.

7 *The Myth of Sisyphus*, 123.

8 *The Myth of Sisyphus*, 55.

9 Albert Camus, *The Plague*, trans. Stuart Gilbert (London: Penguin, 2010), 124.

10 *The Plague*, 126.

11 *The Plague*, 13.

12 *The Plague*, 68.

13 *The Plague*, 158.

14 *The Plague*, 262.

15 *The Plague*, 259.

16 Albert Camus, *The Rebel: An Essay on Man in Revolt*, trans. Anthony Bower (New York: Vintage, 1956), 22.

17 See Jane Duran. "The Philosophical Camus." *Philosophical Forum* 38, no. 4 (2007): 365–71.

18 *The Rebel*, 295.

19 See Christine Margerrison, Mark Orme, and Lissa Lincoln, eds., *Albert Camus in the Twenty-First Century: A Renaissance of His Thinking at the Dawn of the New Millennium* (Amsterdam: Rodopi, 2008).

20 *The Plague*, 268.

21 Neil Postman, *Amusing Ourselves to Death: Public Discourse in the Age of Show Business* (New York: Penguin, 1985).

22 See Elana Shefrin. "Lord of the Rings, Star Wars, and Participatory Fandom: Mapping New Congruencies between the Internet and Media Entertainment Culture," *Critical Studies in Media Communication* 21 (2004): 261–81.

23 Bill McKibben, *The Age of Missing Information* (New York: Penguin, 1993).

24 Ibid., 149.

25 Wade Rowland, *Spirit of the Web: The Age of Information from Telegraph to Internet* (Toronto: Key Porter, 1999), 372.

26 See Benjamin R. Barber, "Which Technology and Which Democracy?" in *Democracy and New Media*, ed. David Thorburn and Henry Jenkins (Cambridge, MA: MIT Press, 2003), 33–47.

27 See Michael Keren, *Blogosphere: The New Political Arena* (Lanham MD: Lexington, 2006).

28 *The Road*, 3.

29 *The Road*, 10.

30 *The Road*, 18.

31 See Havi Carel, *Life and Death in Freud and Heidegger* (Amsterdam: Rodopi, 2006).
32 *The Road*, 3, 28.
33 *The Road*, 189.
34 See William Barrett, *Irrational Man: A Study in Existential Philosophy* (Garden City, NY: Doubleday, 1958); Walter Kaufmann, *Existentialism from Dostoevsky to Sartre* (New York: Meridian, 1956); Rudi Visker, "Was Existentialism Truly a Humanism?" *Sartre Studies International* 13 (2007): 3–15.
35 Jean-Paul Sartre, "Existentialism Is a Humanism" (1946), http://www.marxists.org/reference/archive/sartre/works/exist/sartre.htm.
36 John Duncan, "Sartre's Pure Critical Theory," *PhaenEx* 4 (2009): 165.
37 *The Road*, 27.
38 *The Road*, 88–89.
39 *The Road*, 162.
40 *The Road*, 168–69.
41 *The Road*, 87–88.
42 *The Road*, 32.
43 *The Road*, 54.
44 *The Road*, 154.
45 *The Road*, 268.
46 Roy Peachey, "*The Road* by Cormac McCarthy," *Catholic Fiction*, 18 June 2011, http://catholicfiction.net/book-review/the-road.php/.
47 *The Road*, 32.
48 See Jeffrey Gordon, "The Triumph of Sisyphus," *Philosophy and Literature* 32 (April 2008): 183–91.
49 *The Road*, 170.
50 *The Road*, 172.
51 *The Road*, 32–33.
52 *The Road*, 56.
53 *The Road*, 58.
54 *The Rebel*, 22.
55 See Avi Sagi, *Albert Camus and the Philosophy of the Absurd*, trans. Balya Stein (Amsterdam: Rodopi, 2002).
56 *The Road*, 3.
57 *The Road*, 116.
58 *The Road*, 4.
59 *The Road*, 5.
60 *The Road*, 77.
61 *The Road*, 247–48.
62 *The Road*, 273.
63 *The Road*, 279.
64 *The Road*, 279.
65 *The Road*, 286.
66 *The Road*, 286.
67 *The Plague*, 183.
68 *The Road*, 29.
69 *The Road*, 208.
70 See Sharon Krishek, *Kierkegaard on Faith and Love* (New York: Cambridge University Press, 2009); Philip N. Lawton, Jr., "Love and Justice: Levinas' Reading of Buber," *Philosophy Today* 20 (Spring 1976): 77–83.

4 • THE BYSTANDER'S TALE: GIL COURTEMANCHE'S *A SUNDAY AT THE POOL IN KIGALI*

1 Gil Courtemanche, *A Sunday at the Pool in Kigali*, trans. Patricia Claxton (Toronto: Vintage 2004).
2 Linda Melvern, *Conspiracy to Murder: The Rwandan Genocide* (London: Verso, 2006).
3 Philip Gourevitch, *We Wish to Inform You that Tomorrow We Will Be Killed with Our Families: Stories from Rwanda* (New York: Farrar Straus & Giroux, 1998).
4 Immaculee Ilibagiza, *Left to Tell: Discovering God Amidst the Rwandan Holocaust* (Carlsbad: Hay House, 2006).

5   *Rwanda: The Preventable Genocide*, 2000, http://www.refworld.org/docid/4d1da8752.html.

6   *International Criminal Tribunal for Rwanda*, http://www.unictr.org/.

7   Jane Sullivan, "When Truth is Plainer in Fiction," *The Age*, 9 August 2003, http://www.theage.com.au/articles/2003/08/06/1060145719381.html.

8   Roméo Dallaire, *Shake Hands with the Devil: The Failure of Humanity in Rwanda* (Toronto: Random House, 2003), 5.

9   See Noah Richler, "And Now We Are Warriors," *Maclean's*, 26 May 2008.

10 Sherene Razack, *Dark Threats and White Knights: The Somalia Affair, Peacekeeping and the New Imperialism* (Toronto: University of Toronto Press, 2004), 10.

11 Dallaire, *Shake Hands with the Devil*, 7.

12 Joseph Conrad, *Heart of Darkness* (Harmondsworth, UK: Penguin, 1973), 57.

13 *Heart of Darkness*, 99.

14 Chinua Achebe, "An Image of Africa: Racism in Conrad's Heart of Darkness," in *Postcolonial Discourses: An Anthology*, ed. Gregory Castle (Oxford: Blackwell, 2001), 214.

15 Ibid., 215.

16 Patrick Brantlinger, "Victorians and Africans: The Genealogy of the Myth of the Dark Continent," in *Joseph Conrad's Heart of Darkness*, ed. Gene M. Moore (New York: Oxford University Press, 2004), 43–88.

17 *We Wish to Inform You*, 7.

18 *We Wish to Inform You*, 19.

19 *A Sunday*, 254.

20 *A Sunday*, 234.

21 *A Sunday*, 60.

22 Tim Fulford and Peter J. Kitson, eds., *Romanticism and Colonialism: Writing and Empire, 1780–1830* (Cambridge: Cambridge University Press, 1998).

23 *Heart of Darkness*, 89.

24 *Heart of Darkness*, 94.

25 *Heart of Darkness*, 100.

26 See John Clement Ball, *Satire and The Postcolonial Novel: V. S. Naipaul, Chinua Achebe, and Salman Rushdie* (London: Routledge, 2003); Ania Loomba, *Colonialism/Postcolonialism* (London: Routledge, 2005).

27 *A Sunday*, 1.

28 *A Sunday*, 2.

29 *A Sunday*, 17.

30 *A Sunday*, 87.

31 *A Sunday*, 14.

32 *A Sunday*, 44.

33 *A Sunday*, 162.

34 *A Sunday*, 62.

35 See, for example, Ka Tzetnik (Yehiel Dinur), *House of Dolls* (New York: Simon and Schuster, 1955).

36 *A Sunday*, 78.

37 *A Sunday*, 78.

38 *A Sunday*, 81.

39 *A Sunday*, 83.

40 *A Sunday*, 62.

41 *A Sunday*, 37.

42 *A Sunday*, 94.

43 *A Sunday*, 97.

44 *A Sunday*, 104.

45 *A Sunday*, 73.

46 *A Sunday*, 74.

47 *A Sunday*, 77.

48 *A Sunday*, 77.

49 *A Sunday*, 252.

50 *A Sunday*, 253.

51 A Sunday, 224.
52 A Sunday, 95.
53 Gil Courtemanche, "The Nightmare Diaries." *The Guardian*, 23 April 2005, http://www.theguardian.com/books/2005/apr/23/highereducation.news3.
54 A Sunday, 12.
55 A Sunday, 222.
56 A Sunday, 226–27.
57 A Sunday, 63.
58 A Sunday, 111–12.
59 A Sunday, 111.
60 See Phil Clark, "Hero, Failure or Casualty? A Peacemaker's Experience of Genocide." *Dissent* (Spring 2005): 115–21.
61 See Levon Boyajian and Haigaz Grigorian, "Psychological Sequelae of the Armenian Genocide," in *The Armenian Genocide in Perspective*, ed. Richard G. Hovannisian (Piscataway, NJ: Transaction, 1987), 177–86.
62 Simone Gigliotti, "Genocide Yet Again: Scenes of Rwanda and Ethical Witness in the Human Rights Memoir," *Australian Journal of Politics and History* 53 (2007): 85.
63 Tony Kushner, "'Pissing in the Wind'? The Search for Nuance in the Study of Holocaust 'Bystanders'," in *Bystanders to the Holocaust: A Reevaluation*, ed. David Cesarani and Paul A Levine (Oxford: Taylor & Francis 2002), 60–61.
64 Ibid., 60.
65 Arne Johan Vetlesen, "Genocide: A Case for the Responsibility of the Bystander," *Journal of Peace Research* 37 (2000): 521.
66 Melvern, *Conspiracy to Murder*, 268.
67 A Sunday, 116.
68 A Sunday, 117.

5 • FICTION AND THE STUDY OF SLUMS: ANOSH IRANI'S *THE CRIPPLE AND HIS TALISMANS*

1 UN Habitat (2006–7), *State of the World Cities*, http://www.unhabitat.org/pmss/getPage.asp?page=bookView&book=2101.
2 UN Habitat (2001), *Cities in a Globalizing World: Global Report on Human Settlements*, http://ww2.unhabitat.org/Istanbul+5/globalreport.htm.
2a UN Habitat, *The State of African Cities* (2014), http://unhabitat.org/the-state-of-african-cities-2014/.
3 Mike Davis, *Planet of Slums* (London: Verso, 2006).
4 Suketu Mehta, *Maximum City: Bombay Lost and Found* (New York: Knopf, 2004), 73.
5 Maggie Ann Bowers, *Magic(al) Realism* (London: Routledge, 2004); Lois Parkinson Zamora and Wendy B. Faris, eds., *Magical Realism: Theory, History, Community* (Durham, NC: Duke University Press, 1995).
6 Anosh Irani, *The Cripple and his Talismans* (Vancouver, BC: Raincoast, 2005), 241.
7 *The Cripple*, 246.
8 *The Cripple*, 252.
9 *The Cripple*, 131.
10 *The Cripple*, 223.
11 *The Cripple*, 223.
12 *The Cripple*, 141.
13 *The Cripple*, 232.
14 *The Cripple*, 112.
15 *The Cripple*, 58.
16 *The Cripple*, 60.
17 *The Cripple*, 108.
18 *The Cripple*, 123.
19 *The Cripple*, 15.
20 *The Cripple*, 157.
21 *The Cripple*, 36.

22 *The Cripple*, 222.
23 *The Cripple*, 130.
24 *The Cripple*, 57.
25 *The Cripple*, 161–62.
26 *The Cripple*, 136.
27 *The Cripple*, 146.
28 *The Cripple*, 147.
29 *The Cripple*, 148.
30 *The Cripple*, 149.
31 *The Cripple*, 148.
32 *The Cripple*, 159.
33 *The Cripple*, 201.
34 *The Cripple*, 198.
35 *The Cripple*, 198.
36 *The Cripple*, 198.
37 *The Cripple*, 25.
38 *The Cripple*, 234.
39 *The Cripple*, 11.
40 Davis, *Planet of Slums*, 23.

6 • NARRATIVE AND MEMORY IN HARUKI MURAKAMI'S *KAFKA ON THE SHORE*, GÜNTER GRASS'S *CRABWALK*, AND ANDRÉ BRINK'S *THE RIGHTS OF DESIRE*

1 Jerome Bruner, "Life as Narrative." *Social Research* 71 (Fall 2004): 708.

2 Molly Patterson and Kristen Renwick Monroe, "Narrative in Political Science," *Annual Review of Political Science* 1 (1998): 321.

3 Antonina Harbus, "Exposure to Life-Writing as an Impact on Autobiographical Memory," *Memory Studies* 4 (2011): 213.

4 Christopher Kelly, *Rousseau's Exemplary Life: The Confessions as Political Philosophy* (Ithaca: Cornell University Press, 1987).

5 Jacob L. Talmon, *The Origins of Totalitarian Democracy* (New York: Norton, 1970).

6 Cro Stelio, *Noble Savage: Allegory of Freedom* (Waterloo, ON: Wilfrid Laurier University Press, 1990).

7 Charles Taylor, *Sources of the Self: The Making of the Modern Identity* (Cambridge, MA: Harvard University Press, 1989).

8 Joel S. Kahn, *Modernity and Exclusion* (London: Sage, 2001), 130.

9 Sidonie Smith, *Subjectivity, Identity and the Body: Women's Autobiographical Practices in the Twentieth Century* (Bloomington: Indiana University Press, 1993), 8–9.

10 Edward W. Said, *Representations of the Intellectual* (New York: Pantheon, 2004), 44.

11 Ibid., 32–33.

12 Dominick LaCapra, *History and Memory after Auschwitz* (Ithaca, NY: Cornell University Press, 1998), 9.

13 Robert I. Rotberg, ed., *Israeli and Palestinian Narratives of Conflict: History's Double Helix* (Bloomington: Indiana University Press, 2006), vii.

14 Robert Meister, "Human Rights and the Politics of Victimhood," *Ethics & International Affairs* 16 (September 2002): 93.

15 Ibid., 96.

16 Dan Bar-On, *Tell Your Life Story: Creating Dialogue Among Jews and Germans, Israelis and Palestinians* (New York: Central European University Press, 2006).

17 Sigmund Freud, "Remembering, Repeating and Working-Through," *Standard Edition of the Complete Psychological Works of Sigmund Freud*, vol. 12 (London: Hogarth, 1914), 145–56.

18 Haruki Murakami, *Kafka on the Shore*, trans. Phillip Gabriel (London: Harvill, 2004).

19 Günter Grass, *Crabwalk* (New York: Harcourt, 2002).

20 André Brink, *The Rights of Desire* (London: Secker & Warburg, 2000).

21 Madhu Dubey, "Speculative Fictions of Slavery," *American Literature* 82 (December 2010): 780.

22 Ibid., 785.

23 Avery F. Gordon, *Ghostly Matters: Haunting and the Sociological Imagination* (Minneapolis: University of Minnesota Press, 1997), 8.

24 Ibid., 18.

25 Anatoly M. Khazanov and Stanley G. Payne, "How to Deal with the Past?," *Totalitarian Movements and Political Religions* 9 (June–September 2008): 415.

26 Dan Diner, "The Historians' Controversy – Limits to the Historization of National Socialism," *Tikkun* 2, no. 1 (1987): 74.

27 *Kafka on the Shore*, 32.

28 *Kafka on the Shore*, 41.

29 *Kafka on the Shore*, 89.

30 *Kafka on the Shore*, 91.

31 *Kafka on the Shore*, 15.

32 *Kafka on the Shore*, 59.

33 *Kafka on the Shore*, 364.

34 *Kafka on the Shore*, 207.

35 *Kafka on the Shore*, 387.

36 *Kafka on the Shore*, 359.

37 *Kafka on the Shore*, 360.

38 *Crabwalk*, 80.

39 *Crabwalk*, 43.

40 *Crabwalk*, 5.

41 *Crabwalk*, 45.

42 *Crabwalk*,, 160.

43 *Crabwalk*, 210.

44 J. M. Coetzee, *Disgrace* (London: Secker & Warburg, 1999).

45 *The Rights of Desire*, 154.

46 *The Rights of Desire*, 206.

47 *The Rights of Desire*, 261.

48 *The Rights of Desire*, 3.

49 *The Rights of Desire*, 98.

50 *The Rights of Desire*, 47-48.

51 Alec Marsh, "To Haunt or Not to Haunt: The Role of Ghosts in Literature," *Muhlenberg Weekly*, 27 Oct. 2005, http://www.muhlenbergweekly.com/news/view.php/384498/To-haunt-or-not-to-haunt-The-Role-of-Ghosts-in-Literature.

52 Ibid.

53 *The Rights of Desire*, 275.

54 *The Rights of Desire*, 142.

55 *The Rights of Desire*, 214.

56 *The Rights of Desire*, 134.

57 *The Rights of Desire*, ???

58 *The Rights of Desire*, 250.

59 *The Rights of Desire*, 306.

60 *The Rights of Desire*, 84.

61 See Isidoe Diala, "Nadine Gordimer, J. M. Coezee, and André Brink: Guilt, Expiation, and the Reconciliation Process in Post-Apartheid South Africa," *Journal of Modern Literature* 25 (2001–2): 50–68.

62 *The Rights of Desire*, 154.

7 • THE POLITICS OF VICTIMHOOD IN JOHN LE CARRÉ'S *ABSOLUTE FRIENDS*

1 See Michael Keren, "Intellectuals without borders," in *Dilemmas of International Intervention: Sovereignty vs. Responsibility*," ed. Michael Keren and Don Sylvan (London: Frank Cass, 2002), 27–39.

2 Edward Shils, "The Intellectuals and the Powers: Some Perspectives for Comparative Analysis," in *On Intellectuals*, ed. Philip Rieff (Garden City, NY: Anchor, 1970), 27–51.

3 Karl Mannheim, *Ideology and Utopia: An Introduction to the Sociology of Knowledge* (London: Routledge and Kegan Paul), 1936.

4 Talcott Parsons, "'The Intellectual': A Social Role Category," in *On Intellectuals*, 3–26.

5 Julien Benda, *The Treason of the Intellectuals*, trans. Richard Aldington (New York: William Morrow & Co.), 1928. Excerpt online at http://www.swans.com/library/art9/jbenda01.html.

6 Ibid.

7 George Steiner, "Our Homeland: the Text," *Salmagundi* 66 (Winter–Spring 1985): 25.

8 Michael Walzer, *The Company of Critics: Social Criticism and Political Commitment in the Twentieth Century* (New York: Basic Books, 1988), 38.

9 Ibid., 41.

10 Edward W. Said, *Representations of the Intellectual* (New York: Pantheon, 2004), 27–28.

11 Ibid., 29.

12 Ibid., 32.

13 Ibid., 32–33.

14 Ibid., 33.

15 Ibid., 35.

16 Ibid., 44.

17 Edward W. Said, "Introduction," in *Blaming the Victims: Spurious Scholarship and the Palestinian Question*, ed. Edward W. Said and Christopher Hitchens (London: Verso, 1988), 2.

18 Edward W. Said, "The Essential Terrorist," in *Blaming the Victims*, 157.

19 Ibid., 153.

20 Ibid., 149.

21 Ibid., 158.

22 John Le Carré, *Absolute Friends* (London: Hodder & Stoughton, 2004), 54.

23 *Absolute Friends*, 53.

24 *Absolute Friends*, 53.

25 *Absolute Friends*, 64–65.

26 *Absolute Friends*, 64.

27 *Absolute Friends*, 91.

28 *Absolute Friends*, 256.

29 *Absolute Friends*, 80.

30 *Absolute Friends*, 80.

31 *Absolute Friends*, 277.

32 *Absolute Friends*, 259.

33 *Absolute Friends*, 277.

34 *Absolute Friends*, 278.

35 *Absolute Friends*, 278.

36 *Absolute Friends*, 362.

8 • THE QUEST FOR IDENTITY IN SAYED KASHUA'S *LET IT BE MORNING*

1 Mohammed Saif-Alden Wattad, "I Believe: Israeli Arabs – Lost in a Sea of Identities," *Beijing Law Review* 2, no. 1 (2011): 1–7.

2 Yitzhak Reiter, *National Minority, Regional Majority: Palestinian Arabs versus Jews in Israel* (Syracuse, NY: Syracuse University Press, 2009), 26.

3 Sammy Smooha, *Index of Arab-Jewish Relations 2004* (Haifa: University of Haifa, 2005).

4 In Ra'anan Cohen, *Strangers in their Homeland: A Critical Study of Israel's Arab Citizens* (Brighton, UK: Sussex Academic Press, 2008).

5 Ibid., xiv.

6 Ibid., 2.

7 Reiter, *National Minority*, 5–6.

8 Lawrence Louër, *To Be an Arab in Israel* (New York: Columbia University Press, 2007), 203.

9 Hillel Frisch, *Israel's Security and its Arab Citizens* (New York: Cambridge University Press, 2011), 3.

10 Dan Rabinowitz and Khawla Abu-Baker, *Coffins on Our Shoulders: The Experience of the Palestinian Citizens*

of Israel (Berkeley: University of California Press, 2005), 6.
11 Ibid., 8.
12 Ibid., 184.
13 As'ad Ghanem, *Ethnic Politics in Israel: The Margins and the Ashkenazi Center* (London: Routledge, 2010).
14 Amal Jamal, "Strategies of Minority Struggle for Equality in Ethnic States: Arab Politics in Israel," *Citizenship Studies* 11, no. 3 (2007): 277.
15 Ibid., 278.
16 David Grossman, *Sleeping on a Wire: Conversations with Palestinians in Israel* (New York: Farrar, Straus and Giroux, 1993), 20.
17 *Sleeping on a Wire*, 111.
18 *Sleeping on a Wire*, 17.
19 *Sleeping on a Wire*, 204–5.
20 *Sleeping on a Wire*, 205.
21 Quoted in *Sleeping on a Wire*, 250.
22 *Sleeping on a Wire*, 254.
23 *Sleeping on a Wire*, 256.
24 *Sleeping on a Wire*, 262.
25 *Sleeping on a Wire*, 267.
26 Shlomi Eldar, "Sayed Kashua: I'm a Writer, Not a Traitor," Interview, *Al-Monitor*, 8 February 2013, http://www.al-monitor.com/pulse/originals/2013/02/author-sayed-kashua-hides-pain-within-his-humor.html#ixzz2PPyvbh22
27 Karen Grumberg, *Place and Ideology in Contemporary Hebrew Literature* (Syracuse, NY: Syracuse University Press, 2011), 125.
28 Ibid., 153.
29 Ibid., 155.
30 Adia Mendelson-Maoz and Liat Steir-Livny, "The Jewish Works of Sayed Kashua: Subversive or Subordinate?" *Israel Studies Review* 26, no. 1 (2011): 110–11.
31 Ibid., 117.
32 Batya Shimoni, "Shaping Israeli-Arab Identity in Hebrew Words: The Case of Sayed Kashua," *Israel Studies* 18, no. 1 (2013): 148.
33 Sayed Kashua, *Let It Be Morning*, trans. Miriam Shlesinger (New York: Black Cat, 2006).
34 *Let It Be Morning*, 16.
35 *Let It Be Morning*, 11.
36 *Let It Be Morning*, 19
37 *Let It Be Morning*, 20–21.
38 *Let It Be Morning*, 21.
39 *Let It Be Morning*, 31–32.
40 *Let It Be Morning*, 39.
41 *Let It Be Morning*, 53.
42 *Let It Be Morning*, 94–95.
43 *Let It Be Morning*, 121–22.
44 *Let It Be Morning*, 203.
45 *Let It Be Morning*, 158.
46 *Let It Be Morning*, 55.
47 *Let It Be Morning*, 73.
48 *Let It Be Morning*, 82.
49 *Let It Be Morning*, 83.
50 *Let It Be Morning*, 264.

9 • POLITICAL ESCAPISM IN CONTEMPORARY ISRAEL: DAVID GROSSMAN'S *TO THE END OF THE LAND*

1 Jos J. Schall and Eric R. Pianka, "Evolution of Escape Behavior Diversity," *American Naturalist* 115, no. 4 (April 1980): 551.
2 Andrew Evans, *The Visual Life: Escapism and Simulation in Our Media World* (London: Fusion 2001).
3 Churchill Centre and Museum Website, http://www.winstonchurchill.org/learn/speeches/speeches-of-winston-churchill/128-we-shall-fight-on-the-beaches.

4   Jerome Bruner, "Life as Narrative," *Social Research* 71 (Fall 2004): 708.

5   David Grossman, *To the End of the Land* (Toronto: McClelland & Stewart, 2010).

6   Roy E. Baumeister, "Suicide as Escape from Self," *Psychological Review* 97, no. 1 (1990): 90–113.

7   Yael Yishai, "Escape from Politics: The Case of Israel," in *For the People, By the People, Without the People*, ed. Tamar Hermann (Jerusalem: Israel Democracy Institute, 2012), 288–313.

8   Bernard Susser and Giora Goldberg, "Escapist Parties in Israeli Politics," *Israel Affairs* 11, no. 4 (2005): 636.

9   Ibid., 637.

10 Ibid.

11 Mark Leonard, "Netanyahu's Triple Escapism," *New Statesman*, 22 November 2012, http://www.newstatesman.com/politics/politics/2012/11/netanyahu%E2%80%99s-triple-escapism.

12 Khaled Diab, "Palestinian Liberation Through the Israeli Ballot Box," *The Chronikler*, 31 January 2013, http://chronikler.com/middle-east/israel-palestine/israeli-elections-palestinians/.

13 *To the End of the Land*, 105.

14 *To the End of the Land*, 105.

15 Menachem Peri, "Bikoret Bora'hat Misefer," 26 May 2008, http://www.newlibrary.co.il/article?c0=14221 (Hebrew).

16 Ariana Melamed, "Me'hir Hashtika," YNET, 3 April 2008 (Hebrew), http://www.ynet.co.il/articles/0,7340,L-3527203,00.html.

16a *To the End of the Land*, 149.

17 Robert Alter, "In the Name of the Mother," *New Republic*, 9 October 2010, 37.

18 Jacqueline Rose, "To the End of the Land by David Grossman," *The Guardian*, 18 September 2010, http://www.theguardian.com/books/2010/sep/18/david-grossman-end-of-the-land.

19 Michael Gluzman, "Im Lo Tihiye Yerushalayim," *Ha'aretz*, 5 May 2008 (Hebrew).

20 Rick Archbold, "If They Can't Find Me, He Isn't Dead," *Globe and Mail*, 8 October 2010, http://www.theglobeandmail.com/arts/books-and-media/book-review-to-theend-of-the-land-by-david-grossman/article4190511/.

21 Avraham Balaban, "Ima Lo Yekhola Lishmor al Ben Bemilim," *Ha'aretz*, 24 October 2008, http://www.haaretz.co.il/literature/1.1355952 (Hebrew).

22 Yi-Fu Tuan, *Escapism* (Baltimore: Johns Hopkins University Press, 1998), 9–10.

23 Rabbi Jonathan Levshalem's blog, http://www.wjcshul.org/blog---hiking-the-israel-trail.

24 Oz Almog, *The Sabra: The Creation of the New Jew* (Berkeley: University of California Press, 2000), 177.

25 *To the End of the Land*, 315.

26 *To the End of the Land*, 319.

27 *To the End of the Land*, 569.

28 *To the End of the Land*, 138.

29 *To the End of the Land*, 4.

30 *To the End of the Land*, 276.

31 *To the End of the Land*, 11.

32 *To the End of the Land*, 75–76.

33 *To the End of the Land*, 177.

34 *To the End of the Land*, 474.

35 *To the End of the Land*, 184.

36 Gideon Doron and Udi Lebel, "Penetrating the Shields of Institutional Immunity: The Political Dynamic of Bereavement in Israel," *Mediterranean Politics* 9, no. 2 (Summer 2004): 201.

37 Ibid., 202.
38 *To the End of the Land*, 480.
39 *To the End of the Land*, 59.
40 *To the End of the Land*, 59–60.
41 *To the End of the Land*, 492.
42 *To the End of the Land*, 420–21.
43 *To the End of the Land*, 502.
44 Gideon Levy, "What Israelis Really Want: To Be Left in Peace." *Ha'aretz*, 23 January 2013.
45 Edna Shemesh, "Kum Ve'hithalekh Ba'aretz," *Iton 77*, no. 330 (May–June 2008), http://www.iton77.com/330/shemesh330.html (Hebrew).
46 *To the End of the Land*, 299.
47 Brett Marroquín, Susan Nolen-Hoeksema, and Regina Miranda, "Escaping the Future: Affective Forecasting in Escapist Fantasy and Attempted Suicide," *Journal of Social and Clinical Psychology* 32, no. 4 (2013): 446–63.
48 *To the End of the Land*, 418–19.
49 *To the End of the Land*, 420.

10 • BODY AND MIND IN MARGARET ATWOOD'S *ORYX AND CRAKE*

1 Michio Kaku, *Visions: How Science Will Revolutionize the 21st Century* (New York: Anchor, 1997).
2 Ibid.
3 C. P Snow, "The Two Cultures," *New Statesman*, 6 October 1956, http://www.newstatesman.com/cultural-capital/2013/01/c-p-snow-two-cultures.
4 Jacob Bronowski, *Science and Human Values* (New York: Harper & Row, 1956).
5 Ibid., 59.
6 Ibid., 70.
7 Ibid.
8 See Jack D. Douglas, ed., *The Technological Threat* (Englewood Cliffs, NJ: Prentice Hall, 1971).
9 Jacques Ellul, *The Technological Society* (New York: Vintage, 1964), 6.
10 Ralph Lapp, *The New Priesthood: The Scientific Elite and its Uses of Power* (New York: Harper & Row, 1965), 2.
11 Nigel Calder, *Technopolis: Social Control of the Uses of Science* (New York: Clarion, 1969), 225.
12 Ibid., 233.
13 Ibid., 237.
14 Margaret Atwood, *Oryx and Crake* (Toronto: McClelland & Stewart, 2003).
15 *Oryx and Crake*, 7.
16 *Oryx and Crake*, 10.
17 *Oryx and Crake*, 11.
18 *Oryx and Crake*, 26.
19 *Oryx and Crake*, 20.
20 *Oryx and Crake*, 85.
21 *Oryx and Crake*, 85.
22 *Oryx and Crake*, 24.
23 *Oryx and Crake*, 27.
24 *Oryx and Crake*, 45.
25 *Oryx and Crake*, 56.
26 *Oryx and Crake*, 60.
27 *Oryx and Crake*, 75.
28 *Oryx and Crake*, 103.
29 *Oryx and Crake*, 103.
30 *Oryx and Crake*, 153.
31 *Oryx and Crake*, 100.
32 *Oryx and Crake*, 165.
33 *Oryx and Crake*, 165.
34 *Oryx and Crake*, 168.
35 *Oryx and Crake*, 168.
36 *Oryx and Crake*, 203.
37 *Oryx and Crake*, 203.
38 *Oryx and Crake*, 306.

39 *Oryx and Crake*, 85.

40 Andrew Evans, *This Virtual World: Escapism and Simulation in Our Media World* (London: Fusion, 2001), 193.

41 Craig D. Murray and Judith Sixsmith, "The Corporeal Body in Virtual Reality," *Ethos* 27, no. 3 (September 1999): 315–43.

42 N. Katherine Hayles, *How We Became Posthuman: Virtual Bodies in Cybernetics, Literature and Informatics* (Chicago: University of Chicago Press, 1999), 2.

43 Ibid., 3.

44 *Oryx and Crake*, 77.

45 *Oryx and Crake*, 79.

46 *Oryx and Crake*, 82.

47 *Oryx and Crake*, 89.

48 *Oryx and Crake*, 89–90.

49 *Oryx and Crake*, 90.

50 *Oryx and Crake*, 90.

51 *Oryx and Crake*, 343.

52 Evgeny Morzov, "The Perils of Perfection," *New York Times*, 2 March 2013.

53 N. Katherine Hayles, "Escape and Constraint: Three Fictions Dream of Moving from Energy to Information," in *From Energy to Information: Representation in Science and Technology, Art, and Literature*, ed. Bruce Clarke and Linda Dalrymple Henderson (Stanford, CA: Stanford University Press, 2002), 235.

54 *Oryx and Crake*, 339.

11 • A CANADIAN ALTERNATIVE TO THE CLASH OF CIVILIZATIONS: YANN MARTEL'S *LIFE OF PI*

1 Lester Pearson, *Democracy in World Politics* (Toronto: S. J. Reginald Saunders, 1955), 82.

2 Ibid., 83.

3 Ibid., 83.

4 Ibid., 83–84.

5 Jack Bumsted, "Visions of Canada: A Brief History of Writing on the Canadian Character and the Canadian Identity," in *A Passion for Identity: Canadian Studies for the 21st century*, ed. David Taras and Beverly Rasporich (Scarborough, ON: Nelson Thomson Learning, 2001).

6 A. J. Bacevich, "Who Are You? The Clash of Civilizations and the Remaking of World Order," *First Things* 73 (May 1997): 40.

7 Samuel Huntington, *The Clash of Civilizations and the Remaking of World Order* (New York: Simon & Schuster, 2003), 70.

8 *The Clash of Civilizations*, 207.

9 *The Clash of Civilizations*, 210.

10 James Graham, "Samuel Huntington's Clash of Civilizations," May 2004, http://www.historyorb.com/world/clashofcivilizations.php.

11 Michael Elliott, "When Cultures Collide," *Washington Post*, 1 December 1996, http://www.washingtonpost.com/wp-srv/style/longterm/books/reviews/clashofcivilizations.htm.

12 Robin O'Brien, "The Clash of Civilizations and the Remaking of World Order," *SAIS Review* 17 (1997): 208–10.

13 "Yann Martel's Success," Foreign Affairs and International Trade Canada, 2003, http://www.dfait-maeci.gc.ca/arts/ss_yann-en.asp.

14 Claude Bélanger, "The Quiet Revolution," in *Quebec History* (2000). http://faculty.marianopolis.edu/c.belanger/quebechistory/events/quiet.htm.

15 "Third Time Lucky: Portrait," *The Guardian*, 23 October 2002, http://www.theguardian.com/books/2002/oct/23/bookerprize2002.thebookerprize.

16 Canadian Multiculturalism Act, Department of Justice Canada, 1985, s. 3(1) (b), http://laws.justice.gc.ca/en/c-18.7.
17 Yann Martel, *Life of Pi* (Orlando, FLA: Harcourt, 2001), viii.
18 *Life of Pi*, 29.
19 *The Clash of Civilizations*, 31.
20 *The Clash of Civilizations*, 97.
21 *The Clash of Civilizations*, 97.
22 *Life of Pi*, 25.
23 *Life of Pi*, 26.
24 *Life of Pi*, 98.
25 *Life of Pi*, 169.
26 *Life of Pi*, 208.
27 *Life of Pi*, 209.
28 *Life of Pi*, 148.
29 *Life of Pi*, 170.
30 *Life of Pi*. 297–98.
31 *The Clash of Civilizations*, 21.
32 *The Clash of Civilizations*, 20.
33 *The Clash of Civilizations*, 43.
34 *The Clash of Civilizations*, 67.
35 *The Clash of Civilizations*, 97.
36 *The Clash of Civilizations*, 57.
37 *Life of Pi*, 74.
38 *Life of Pi*, 65.
39 *Life of Pi*, 46.
40 *Life of Pi*, 50.
41 *Life of Pi*, 49.
42 *Life of Pi*, 53.
43 *Life of Pi*, 54.
44 *Life of Pi*, 57.
45 *Life of Pi*, 57.
46 *Life of Pi*, 58.
47 *Life of Pi*, 61.
48 *Life of Pi*, 64.
49 *Life of Pi*, 75.
50 *Life of Pi*, 63.
51 *Life of Pi*, 63.
52 *The Clash of Civilizations*, 266.
53 *The Clash of Civilizations*, 266.
54 *The Clash of Civilizations*, 266.
55 *The Clash of Civilizations*, 267.
56 *The Clash of Civilizations*, 271.
57 *Life of Pi*, 34.
58 *Life of Pi*, 108.
59 *Life of Pi*, 151.
60 *Life of Pi*, 171.
61 *Life of Pi*. 157–58.
62 *Life of Pi*, 162.
63 *Life of Pi*, 164.
64 *Life of Pi*, 164.
65 *Life of Pi*, 206.
66 *Life of Pi*, 203.
67 *The Clash of Civilizations*, 37.
68 *Life of Pi*, 217.
69 Pearson, *Democracy in World Politics*, 121.

BIBLIOGRAPHY

Aronoff, Myron J. *The Spy Novels of John Le Carré: Balancing Ethics and Politics*. New York: St. Martin's Press, 1999.

Atwood, Margaret. *Oryx and Crake*. Toronto: McClelland & Stewart, 2003.

Auerbach, Erich. *Mimesis: The Representation of Reality in Western Literature*. Garden City, NY: Doubleday, 1953.

Ball, John Clement. *Satire and the Postcolonial Novel: V. S. Naipaul, Chinua Achebe, and Salman Rushdie*. London: Routledge, 2003.

Bleiker, Roland. "The Aesthetic Turn in International Political Theory." *Millennium – Journal of International Studies* 30, no. 3 (2001): 509–33.

———. *Rethinking Peace and Conflict Studies*. Houndmills, UK: Palgrave Macmillan, 2009.

Bloom, Harold. *José Saramago*. Philadelphia: Chelsea House, 2005.

Bowers, Maggie Ann. *Magic(al) Realism*. London: Routledge, 2004.

Boyers, Robert. *The Dictator's Dictation – The Politics of Novel and Novelists*. New York: Columbia University Press, 2005.

Brink, André. *The Rights of Desire*. London: Secker & Warburg, 2000.

Bruner, Jerome. "Life as Narrative." *Social Research* 71, no. 3 (2004): 691–710.

Castle, Gregory, ed. *Postcolonial Discourses: An Anthology*. Oxford: Blackwell, 2001.

Courtemanche, Gil. *A Sunday at the Pool in Kigali*. Translated by Patricia Claxton. Toronto: Vintage, 2004.

Diala, Isidoe. "Nadine Gordimer, J. M. Coezee, and André Brink: Guilt, Expiation, and the Reconciliation Process in Post-Apartheid South Africa." *Journal of Modern Literature* 25, no. 2 (2001–2): 50–68.

Dolan, Paul J. *Of War and War's Alarms: Fiction and Politics in the Modern World*. New York: Free Press, 1976.

Dubey, Madhu. "Speculative Fictions of Slavery." *American Literature* 82, no. 4 (2010): 779–805.

Eaton, Marcia. "The Truth Value of Literary Statements." *British Journal of Aesthetics* 12, no. 2 (1972): 164–65.

Fátima, Vieira, and Freitas, Marinela, eds. *Utopia Matters: Theory, Politics, Literature and the Arts*. Porto, Portugal: University of Porto Press, 2005.

Fradinger, Moira. *Binding Violence: Literary Visions of Political Origins*. Palo Alto, CA: Stanford University Press, 2010.

Frier, David. "Righting Wrongs, Re-Writing Meaning and Reclaiming the City in Saramago's Blindness and All the Names." *Portuguese Literary & Cultural Studies* 6 (2001): 97–122.

Frost, Lola. "Aesthetics and Politics." *Global Society* 24, no. 3 (2010): 433–43.

Fulford, Tim, and Peter J. Kitson, eds. *Romanticism and Colonialism: Writing and Empire, 1780–1830*. New York: Cambridge University Press, 1998.

Gigliotti, Simone. "Genocide Yet Again: Scenes of Rwanda and Ethical Witness in the Human Rights Memoir." *Australian Journal of Politics and History* 53 (2007): 84–95.

Gordon, Avery F. *Ghostly Matters: Haunting and the Sociological Imagination*. Minneapolis: University of Minnesota Press, 1997.

Gordon, Jeffrey. "The Triumph of Sisyphus." *Philosophy and Literature* 32 (2008): 183–191.

Grass, Günter. *Crabwalk*. New York: Harcourt, 2002.

Grossman, David. *Sleeping on a Wire: Conversations with Palestinians in Israel*. New York: Farrar, Straus, and Giroux, 1993.

———. *To the End of the Land*. Toronto: McClelland & Stewart, 2010.

Grumberg, Karen. *Place and Ideology in Contemporary Hebrew Literature*. New York: Syracuse University Press, 2011.

Harbus, Antonina. "Exposure to Life-Writing as an Impact on Autobiographical Memory." *Memory Studies* 4, no. 2 (2011): 206–20.

Howe, Irving. *Politics and the Novel*. New York: Horizon Press, 1957.

Hayles, N. Katherine. "Escape and Constraint: Three Fictions Dream of Moving from Energy to Information." In *From Energy to Information: Representation in Science and Technology, Art, and Literature*, edited by Bruce Clarke and Linda Dalrymple Henderson. Palo Alto, CA: Stanford University Press, 2002.

Horton, John, and Andrea T. Baumeister eds. *Literature and the Political Imagination*. London: Routledge, 1996.

Huntington, Samuel. *The Clash of Civilizations and the Remaking of World Order*. New York: Simon & Schuster, 2003.

Irani, Anosh. *The Cripple and His Talismans*. Vancouver, BC: Raincoast, 2005.

Kashua, Sayed. *Let It Be Morning*. Translated by Miriam Shlesinger. New York: Grove Press, 2006.

Kelly, Christopher. *Rousseau's Exemplary Life: The Confessions as Political Philosophy*. Ithaca, NY: Cornell University Press, 1987.

Keren, Michael. *The Citizen's Voice: Politics and Literature in the Twentieth Century*. Calgary: University of Calgary Press, 2003.

Khazanov, Anatoly M., and Stanley G. Paine. "How to Deal with the Past?" *Totalitarian Movements and Political Religions* 9, nos. 2–3 (2008): 411–31.

Klosko, George. *Political Obligations*. Oxford: Oxford University Press, 2005.

Kochin, Michael S. "Postmetaphysical Literature: Reflections on J. M. Coetzee's *Disgrace*." *Perspectives on Political Science* 33, no. 1 (2004): 4–9.

Kompridis, Nikolas, ed. *The Aesthetic Turn in Political Thought*. New York: Continuum, 2012.

Kundera, Milan. *The Art of the Novel*. Translated by Linda Asher. New York: Grove Press, 1988.

Le Carré, John. *Absolute Friends*. London: Hodder & Stoughton, 2004.

Mack, Michael. *How Literature Changes the Way We Think*. London: Continuum, 2012.

Margerrison, Christine, Mark Orme and Lissa Lincoln, eds. *Albert Camus in the 21st Century: A Renaissance of his Thinking at the Dawn of the New Millennium*. Amsterdam: Rodopi, 2008.

Martel, Yann. *Life of Pi*. Orlando, FLA: Harcourt, 2001.

Martins, Adriana Alves de Paula. "José Saramago's Historical Fiction." *Portuguese Literary & Cultural Studies* 6 (2001): 49–72.

Martins, Adriana Alves De Paula, and Mark Sabine, eds. *In Dialogue with Saramago: Essays in Comparative Literature*. Manchester: Manchester Spanish & Portuguese Studies, 2006.

McCarthy, Cormac. *The Road*. New York: Vintage, 2006.

Mehta, Suketu. *Maximum City: Bombay Lost and Found*. New York: Knopf, 2004.

Meister, Robert. "Human Rights and the Politics of Victimhood." *Ethics & International Affairs* 16, no. 2 (2002): 91–108.

Mendelson-Maoz, Adia, and Liat Steir-Livny. "The Jewish Works of Sayed Kashua: Subversive or Subordinate?" *Israel Studies Review* 26, no. 1 (2011): 107–29.

Moore, Cerwyn. "Reading the Hermeneutics of Violence: The Literary Turn and Chechnya." *Global Society* 20, no. 2 (2006): 179–98.

———. "On Cruelty: Literature, Aesthetics and Global Politics." *Global Society* 24, no. 3 (2010): 311–29.

Murakami, Haruki. *Kafka on the Shore*. Translated by Phillip Gabriel. London: Harvill, 2004.

Nussbaum, Martha C. *Poetic Justice: The Literary Imagination and Public Life*. Boston: Beacon, 1995.

Patterson, Molly, and Kristen Renwick Monroe. "Narrative in Political Science." *Annual Review of Political Science* 1 (1998): 315–31.

Rawls, John. *A Theory of Justice*. Revised ed. Cambridge: Harvard University Press, 1999.

Rotberg, Robert I., ed. *Israeli and Palestinian Narratives of Conflict: History's Double Helix*. Bloomington IN: Indiana University Press, 2006.

Sagi, Avi. *Albert Camus and the Philosophy of the Absurd*. Translated by Balya Stein. Amsterdam: Rodopi, 2002.

Said, Edward W. *Representations of the Intellectual*. New York: Pantheon, 2004.

———, and Christopher Hitchens, eds. *Blaming the Victims: Spurious Scholarship and the Palestinian Question*. London: Verso, 1988.

Saramago, José. *Blindness*. Translated by Giovanni Pontiero. Orlando, FLA: Harcourt, 1997.

Sartre, Jean-Paul. *What Is Literature?* Translated by Bernard Frechtman. New York: Philosophical Library, 1949.

Searle, Leroy. "Literature Departments and the Practice of Theory." *MLN* 121, no. 5 (2006): 1237–61.

Shimoni, Batya. "Shaping Israeli-Arab Identity in Hebrew Words: The Case of Sayed Kashua," *Israel Studies* 18, no. 1 (2013): 146–69.

Smith, Steven. "International Relations Theory and September 11." *International Studies Quarterly* 48 (2004): 499–515.

Steiner, George. "Our Homeland: The Text." *Salmagundi* 66 (1985): 4–25.

Stelio, Cro. *Noble Savage: Allegory of Freedom*. Waterloo, ON: Wilfrid Laurier University Press, 1990.

Stow, Simon. *Republic of Readers?: The Literary Turn in Political Thought and Analysis*. Albany: SUNY Press, 2007.

Taras, David, and Beverly Rasporich, eds. *A Passion for Identity: Canadian Studies for the 21st Century*. Scarborough, ON: Nelson Thomson Learning, 2001.

Taras, Raymond. "Why We Need the Novel: Understanding World Politics through Literature." *Fletcher Forum of World Affairs* 37, no. 2 (2013): 185–95.

Vetlesen, Arne Johan. "Genocide: A Case for the Responsibility of the Bystander." *Journal of Peace Research* 37, no. 4 (2000): 519–32.

Walzer, Michael. *The Company of Critics: Social Criticism and Political Commitment in the Twentieth Century*. New York: Basic Books, 1988.

Waters, Lindsay. "Literary Aesthetics: The Very Idea." *Chronicle of Higher Education* 52, no. 17 (2005): B6–B9.

Zamora, Lois Parkinson, and Wendy B. Farris, eds. *Magical Realism: Theory, History, Community*. Durham, NC: Duke University Press, 1995.

Zuckert, Catherine. *Natural Right and the American Imagination: Political Philosophy in Novel Form*. Savage MD: Rowman & Littlefield, 1990.

———. "Why Political Scientists Want to Study Literature." *PS: Political Science & Politics* 29 (1995): 189–90.

INDEX

A

Absolute Friends (Le Carré), 22, 125, 133, 139
absurd, absurdity, 20, 47–48, 52, 54–55, 59, 63, 66–67
Abu-Baker, Khawla, 144–45
Achebe, Chinua, 72, 78
Adenauer, Conrad, 105
aesthetic, aesthetics, 9, 12, 14–19, 106
   approach, turn, 10–13
   representations, 7, 15
Agnon, Shmuel Yosef, 170
Al Jazeera, 154
Almog, Oz, 172
Almond, Gabriel, 2
Alter, Robert, 170
anti-globalization movement, 22, 135. See also globalization
Apartheid, 103, 108–9, 118–19, 122. See also post-Apartheid
artificial intelligence, 191
Atwood, Margaret, 23, 185–86, 192–95, 199, 201–5
Auerbach, Erich, 18

B

Bakunin, Mikhail, 133
Barber, Benjamin, 26
Baumeister, Andrea, 11
Baumeister, Roy, 165
BBC, 83
behaviouralism, 11, 13
Bell, Daniel, 2
Ben-Ami, Shlomo, 143
Benda, Julien, 126–29, 132
Bingham, George Caleb, 14
Bishara, Azmi, 147
Bleiker, Roland, 12–13
Blindness (Saramago), 8, 20, 25, 27–28, 30–31, 35, 39, 42–45
body and mind, body-mind dichotomy, 185–86, 192, 200–201, 204
Boulding, Kenneth, 2
Brandt, Willy, 108
Brink, André, 22, 101, 105, 109, 117, 119, 121
Bronowski, Jacob, 189–90
Bruner, Jerome, 101, 164
Bush, George W., 18
bystander(s), 38, 45, 69–71, 73, 76–79, 85–86

249

C

Calder, Nigel, 191
Camus, Albert, Camusian, 8, 20, 28, 47–51, 55, 63, 66, 155
Canadian International Development Agency, 208
Canadian Jewish Congress, 211
Canadian Multiculturalism Act, 211
Chomsky, Noam, 130, 135
Churchill, Winston, 164
Civil Rights Movement, 11, 106
clash of civilizations, 23, 207–12, 218, 223–24
Clash of Civilizations and the Remaking of World Order, The (Huntington), 208
Clinton, Bill, 87
CNN, 83–84
Coetzee, J. M., 117
coexistence, 8, 23, 122, 147, 176–78, 182, 184, 208, 210–11, 219–24
Cohen, Leonard, 211
Cohen, Ra'anan, 143
Cold War, 5–7, 104, 108, 208–9, 215
colonial, colonialism, colonialist, 72–77, 82, 91, 102–4, 107, 118, 122, 133, 137, 142
Conrad, Joseph, 72
Constitution Act (Canada), 211
Courtemanche, Gil, 21, 69–70, 73, 75, 77, 79, 81–83, 85, 88
Crabwalk (Grass), 22, 101, 105, 113, 116
Cripple and his Talismans, The (Irani), 21, 89, 91, 100
Curtis, Mark, 135
cybernetic, cybernetics, 4–5, 16, 188, 201, 204
cybernetic organism, cyborg, 201, 204
Cybernetics (Wiener), 188

D

Dahl, Robert, 2, 13
Dallaire, Roméo, 71, 82, 85
Davis, Mike, 90
De Gaulle, Charles, 83
DeLillo, Don, 18
Deutsch, Karl, 2, 4
Devetak, Richard, 18
digital age, digital revolution, 67, 186, 203
digital clones, 203
digital technology, digital technologies, 156, 186, 191–92, 195, 200, 202, 204. *See also* digital media, new media
Distinctiveness Theory, 216
District Six, 119
Dolan, Paul, 9
Downs, Anthony, 2
Dreyfus, Alfred, Dreyfus Affair, 127, 138, 188
Dubey, Madhu, 106
Duncan, John, 58
Dworkin, Ronald, 38

E

Easton, David, 2
Eaton, Marcia, 17
Einstein, Albert, 128
Ellul, Jacques, 190
Engels, Friedrich, 41
Erasmus, Desiderius, 126
escapism, 163–168, 172, 174, 181
    defined, 163
Etzioni, Amitai, 2–4
eugenics, 191–192
Evans, Andrew 200
existentialism, existentialist, 47, 57, 62, 66, 68

F

Fanon, Frantz, 137
fiction, 8, 11, 18–20, 70, 89, 91, 94, 99–100, 105–6, 171, 192–93, 210–11. *See also* fictional, literature, novels
    and the past, 106
    as escape, 8, 173
    contribution of, 20, 22, 99, 122, 133, 171, 192
    Martel's definition of, 211
fictional, 16, 94, 99–100, 105–6, 109, 114, 170–71, 173, 186, 204, 211, 216, 223. *See also* fiction

First Gulf War, 209
First World War, 115
Frankfurter, David, 115
Friedrich, Karl, 7
Frier, David, 36
Frisch, Hillel, 144
Frost, Lola, 17
Fukuyama, Francis, 6

G

Galbraith, John Kenneth, 2–4
genetic engineering, 23, 186, 192, 195, 200, 204
genocide(s), 19, 21, 69–73, 77–79, 81–82, 84–87, 103, 107, 122–23, 134
    Rwandan, 5, 21, 69–74, 77–78, 81, 85
    Armenian, 202
George, Susan, 135
Ghanem, As'ad, 145
ghost(s), ghostly, 106–7, 109, 117, 119–21, 122
Ginat, Joseph, 143
globalization, 75, 80, 82, 89, 100. *See also* anti-globalization movement
Gluzman, Michael, 171
Goldberg, Giora, 166
Golding, William, 8
Gordon, Avery, 106
Gourevitch, Philip, 72
Gramsci, Antonio, 130
Grass, Günter, 22, 101, 105, 109, 113–16, 121
Great Society, 1
Grossman, David, 22, 147–49, 163–64, 168, 170–72, 174, 176, 179–83
Grumberg, Karen, 150
Gustloff, Wilhelm, 115

H

Ha'aretz, 149, 152, 181
Hammerstein, Oscar, 112
Harbus, Antonina, 102
Hayles, Katherine, 201, 205
Historians' Controversy, 108

Hitler, Adolf, 191
Hobbes, Thomas, 33
Horton, John, 11
humanitarian intervention, 69, 83
human rights, 44, 70, 85, 104
    Universal Declaration of, 70
    UN Commission on, 87
Huntington, Samuel, 23, 208–13, 216, 219–24
Huxley, Aldous, 48

I

identity, identities, 29, 75, 79, 129, 132, 156, 159, 191, 217
    and Arab citizens of Israel, 141–42, 145–52
    Canadian, 211
    ethnic, 22, 128
    fixed, established, 211, 213
    indigenous, 147, 152, 160
    multifaceted, multiple, 122, 158–61, 218, 220
    and negation, conflict, 215–16, 219–20
Ilibagiza, Immaculee, 72
imaginary, 18, 91, 115
    political order, political context, 9, 20
    tales(s), 9, 14
intellectual(s), public intellectuals, 4, 22, 67, 103, 125–33, 135–39, 145, 148, 165, 187
    defined, 125
International Monetary Fund, 75, 76
Irani, Anosh, 21, 89, 91–92, 98–99,
Iraq War, 134–35, 137
Israeli Arabs, Arab citizens, Arab minority, 141–49, 151–53, 157, 159–61

J

Jamal, Amal, 146
Johnson, Lindon, 1
Jordan, Michael, 79

K

Kafka, Franz, 7
Kafka on the Shore (Murakami), 22, 101, 105, 109–10
Kahn, Herman, 2
Kahn, Joel, 102
Kaku, Michio, 185
Kant, Immanuel, Kantian, 17, 26
Kashua, Sayed, 22, 141–42, 149–52, 154, 157–58, 160
Kennedy John F., 1
Khazanov, Anatoly, 107–8
King Leopold (Leopold II of Belgium), 72
Klein, Naomi, 135
Klingler, Jonathan, 172
Klobucka, Anna, 41
Klosko, George, 38
Kochin, Michael, 17–18
Kosinsky, Jerzy, 8
Kundera, Milan, 7, 10
Kushner, Tony, 85–86

L

LaCapra, Dominick, 103–4
Lapid, Yair, 181
Lapp, Ralph, 190
Lasswell, Harold, 2
Lazarsfeld, Paul, 2
Le Carré, John, 22, 125, 133, 137, 139
Lenin, Vladimir, 8
Leonard, Mark, 167
Lesage, Jean, 210
Let It Be Morning (Kashua), 22, 141, 150, 152, 160
Levi, Primo, 29, 70
Levy, Gideon, 181
Life of Pi (Martel), 8, 23, 207, 210–12, 217, 223–24
life writing, 101–2
literature, 9, 37, 119, 125, 169, 204, 210. *See also* fiction, novels
  and escape, 173
  and politics, political inquiry, 1, 7, 16, 18–19, 27, 45
  and social change, 15–16
  and truth, 17
Louër, Laurence, 144
Luther, Martin, 126

M

Machiavelli, Niccolo, 4
Mack, Michael, 15
Magritte, René, 10
MacArthur, Douglas, 112
magical realism, 91–92, 100
Major, John, 87
Mandela, Nelson, 118
Mannheim, Karl, 125
Marinesko, Alexander, 113
Marroquín, Brett, 183
Marsh, Alec, 119
Martel, Yann, 8–9, 23, 207, 210–11, 213–14, 216, 218–24
Marx, Karl, Marxist, 41, 134
McCarthy, Cormac, 20–21, 47, 55, 57–58, 62, 65–67
McKibben, Bill, 53
media, 8, 52–53, 55, 70, 81, 83–86, 131–33, 154, 175, 202
  digital media, new media, 52, 54–55, 66–68, 117, 133. *See also* digital technology, digital technologies
Mehta, Suketo, 91
Meister, Robert, 104
Melvern, Linda, 69, 87
memory, 2, 29, 39, 41, 50, 58, 73, 103, 110–11, 121–22, 130, 175, 177, 193–94
  and the Historians' Controversy, 108
  collective, 145
  cultural, 17, 102
  historical, 107–8, 142
  narrative and, 101
  politics of, 102, 108
Mendelson-Maoz, Adia, 150–51
Michael, Sammy, 147
Miranda, Regina, 183
Mock, Richard, 14
Monbiot, George, 135
Monroe, Kristen Renwick, 102

Moore, Cerwyn, 17
moral conscience, 41, 43
Morozov, Evgeny, 204
Murakami, Haruki, 22, 101, 105, 109, 112, 121
Murray, Craig, 201
Myth of Sisyphus, The (Camus), 48–49

N

Nakba, 142, 152
narrative of reconciliation, 22, 105, 109
National Muslim-Christian Liaison Committee, 211
Netanyahu, Benjamin, 167
Nietzsche, Friedrich, 57
Nolen-Hoeksema, Susan, 183
Nolte, Ernst, 108
novels, 19, 22–23, 28, 70, 100, 105, 107, 114, 121–22, 125, 149. *See also* fiction, literature
    and a narrative of reconciliation, 109, 112, 122
    and political inquiry, 7–9, 11–12, 16, 20
    Hebrew, 170
    negative-utopian, 192
    political, 19
    speculative, 106
Nussbaum, Martha, 9

O

Oppenheimer, Robert, 191
Organization of African Unity, 70
Ornelas, José, 28, 42
Orwell, George, 7
Oryx and Crake (Atwood), 23, 185–86, 192

P

Palestinian(s), 22, 131, 137, 146–48, 150–52, 157–60, 164–65, 167–68, 171, 176–81
Parks, Tim, 42–43
Parsons, Talcott, 2, 125
Patterson, Molly, 101
Payne, Stanley, 107–108

Pearson, Lester, 207–8, 210, 224
Peri, Menachem, 169
Picasso, Pablo, 13
Pilger, John, 135
Plague, The (Camus), 28, 49–50, 52, 65, 155
Plato, 8
political science, 7, 11, 13–14, 18–19, 75
political scientist(s), 2, 7–11, 13, 16, 18
politics, 1, 4–5, 19, 51, 54, 77, 131, 138, 271, 187, 189
    and identity, 215
    and literature, aesthetics, 1, 9, 12–13, 15–18
    and evil, 45, 123
    democratic, 15
    escape from, 118, 165–66
    of memory, 102
    of solitude, 54
    of slums, 21, 92, 97
    of victimhood, 22, 104, 122, 125, 132–33, 137–39, 160–61
    scientific, behavioural study of, 11, 13
    world, 10, 12, 123, 207–9, 211, 219, 223–24
post-Apartheid, 18, 104, 117, 120. *See also* Apartheid
postcolonial, 74–75, 77, 79, 83, 150–51. *See also* postcolonialism
    doctrine, 138
    public intellectual, 22
    soul, 80
    world, 87, 133, 138
postcolonialism, 74, 137. *See also* postcolonial
    defined, 74
posthuman, 201, 204
Postman, Neil, 52
poverty, 1, 6, 11–12, 19, 21, 75, 90–91, 93–94, 99–100, 120, 135

Q

Quiet Revolution 210

R

Rabinowitz, Dan, 144–45
Radio-France Internationale, 83
Rapoport, Anatol, 2
Rawls, John, 20, 25–31, 33–38, 40–41, 43–45

Razack, Sherene, 71
Rebel, The (Camus), 51, 63
Reiter, Yitzhak, 142, 144
Representations of the Intellectual (Said), 103, 129
Riesman, David, 2
Rights of Desire, The (Brink), 22, 101, 105, 117
Rilke, Rainer Maria, 121
Road, The (McCarthy), 20, 47–48, 55–58, 60, 62–68
Rodgers, Richard, 112
Rogers, J. T., 70
Rose, Jacqueline, 171
Rotberg, Robert, 104
Rousseau, Rousseauian, 33, 51, 102, 152
Roy, Arundhati, 135
"Rwanda: The Preventable Genocide" (OAU), 70
Rwandan Genocide. *See* genocide: Rwandan

S

Said, Edward, 22, 103, 128–33, 137, 160
Saramago, José, 8, 14, 20, 25, 27–29, 32–45
Sartre, Jean Paul, 57
Second World War, 20, 47, 49–50, 108, 110–14, 116, 134, 172, 185, 187–88
Seeing (Saramago), 14, 43
Shake Hands With The Devil (Dallaire), 71, 82
Shammas, Anton, 148
Shelley, Mary, 188
Shils, Edward, 2, 125
Shimoni, Batya, 151
Simon, Herbert, 2
Sisyphus, Sisyphean, Sisyphusian, 20–21, 48–52, 54, 58
Six-Day War, 165, 169
Sixsmith, Judith, 201
Skinner, B. F., 2
Sleeping on a Wire (Grossman), 14, 170
Smith, Sidonie, 102–3
Smith, Steven, 10
Smooha, Sammy, 143

Snow, C. P., 187–88, 190
social contract, 7, 25, 28, 33–34, 38, 43
Springer, Axel, 114
Stand Tall Generation, 145, 156, 161
Steiner, George, 127
Steir-Livny, Liat, 150–51
Stiglitz, Joseph, 135
Stranger, The (Camus) 8
Sunday at the Pool in Kigali, A (Courtemanche), 21, 69, 71, 73, 84, 86
Susser, Bernard, 166

T

Taras, Raymond, 17
terror, terrorism, 9, 11, 18–19, 22, 64, 122, 131, 170, 209, 219, 221. *See also* terrorist(s), terrorize
terrorist(s), terrorize, 22, 131, 137–38. *See also* terror, terrorism
Theory of Justice, A (Rawls), 25, 28, 33, 35, 37–38, 45
Treason of the Intellectuals, The (Benda), 126, 128
To the End of the Land (Grossman), 22, 163–64, 168, 170, 180
Truth and Reconciliation Commission, TRC 81, 104, 108–9, 118
Tuan, Yi-Fu, 172
Tutu, Desmond, 109

U

UN, United Nations, 21, 36, 70, 71, 81, 82, 83, 91, 99, 180
UN Commission on Human Rights, 87
UN-Habitat, 89
UNAMIR (United Nations Assistance Mission in Rwanda), 71, 82, 87
United Nations' International Criminal Tribunal for Rwanda, 70
Universal Declaration of Human Rights, 70
utopia, utopian, 2, 9, 224
negative, 23, 186, 192, 203

V

Vetlesen, Arne Johan, 86
Vidal, Gore, 130
virtual reality, virtual, 54, 66, 200–201, 203–4
Vietnam War, 134

W

War of Independence (Israel), 143, 170
Walzer, Michael, 127, 132
Waters, Lindsay, 16
Wattad, Mohammed Saif-Alden, 141
Weber, Max, 7–8
Weiner, Norbert, 188
Werfel, Franz, 70

Wiener, Norbert, 4
Wiesel, Eli, 70
Wilhelm Gustloff (ship), 113–14, 116
World Bank, 76

Y

Yehoshua, A. B., 148–50, 176
Yishai, Yael, 166
Yizhar, S., 170, 176
Yom Kippur War, 1973 War, 165, 169

Z

Zionism, Zionist, 142, 145, 151, 153, 158–59, 172
Zola, Emile, 138–39
Zuckert, Catherine, 11

www.ingramcontent.com/pod-product-compliance
Lightning Source LLC
Chambersburg PA
CBHW070757230426
43665CB00017B/2399